INHERITING THE LAND

INTERNATIONAL THEOLOGICAL COMMENTARY

George A.F. Knight and Fredrick Carlson Holmgren,
General Editors

INHERITING THE LAND

A Commentary on the Book of

Joshua

E. JOHN HAMLIN

WM. B. EERDMANS PUBL. CO., GRAND RAPIDS
THE HANDSEL PRESS LTD, EDINBURGH

In memory of
Earle I. Hamlin
and
Anna Marjorie Howes Hamlin
my beloved father and mother

First published 1983 by William B. Eerdmans Publishing Company,
255 Jefferson Ave. S.E., Grand Rapids, Michigan 49503
and
The Handsel Press Limited
33 Montgomery Street, Edinburgh EH7 5JX

Eerdmans edition 0-8028-1041-1
Handsel edition 0 905312 29 5

Library of Congress Cataloging in Publication Data
Hamlin, E. John.
Inheriting the land.
Bibliography: p. 205
1. Bible. O.T. Joshua — Commentaries. I. Title
BS1295.3.H35   1983   222'.207   83-16314
ISBN 0-8028-1041-1

CONTENTS

EDITORS' PREFACE

The Old Testament alive in the Church: this is the goal of the *International Theological Commentary*. Arising out of changing, unsettled times, this Scripture speaks with an authentic voice to our own troubled world. It witnesses to God's ongoing purpose and to his caring presence in the universe without ignoring those experiences of life that cause one to question his existence and love. This commentary series is written by front rank scholars who treasure the life of faith.

Addressed to ministers and Christian educators, the *International Theological Commentary* moves beyond the usual critical-historical approach to the Bible and offers a *theological* interpretation of the Hebrew text. The authors of these volumes, therefore, engaging larger textual units of the biblical writings, assist the reader in the appreciation of the theology underlying the text as well as its place in the thought of the Hebrew Scriptures. But more, since the Bible is the book of the believing community, its text in consequence has acquired ever more meaning through an ongoing interpretation. This growth of interpretation may be found both within the Bible itself and in the continuing scholarship of the Church.

Contributors to the *International Theological Commentary* are Christians — persons who affirm the witness of the New Testament concerning Jesus Christ. For Christians, the Bible is *one* scripture containing the Old and New Testaments. For this reason, a commentary on the Old Testament may not ignore the second part of the canon, namely, the New Testament.

Since its beginning, the Church has recognized a special relationship between the two Testaments. But the precise character of this bond has been difficult to define. Thousands of books and articles have discussed the issue. The diversity of views represented in these publications make us aware that the Church is not of one mind in expressing the "how" of this relationship. The authors of this commentary share a developing consensus that any serious explanation of the Old Testament's relationship to the New will uphold the integrity of the Old Testament. Even though Christianity is rooted in the soil of the Hebrew Scriptures, the biblical interpreter must take care lest he "christianize" these Scriptures.

Authors writing in this commentary will, no doubt, hold varied views concerning *how* the Old Testament relates to the New. No attempt has been made to dictate one viewpoint in this matter. With the whole Church, we are convinced that the relationship between the two Testaments is real and substantial. But we recognize also the diversity of opinions among Christian scholars when they attempt to articulate fully the nature of this relationship.

In addition to the Christian Church, there exists another people for whom the Old Testament is important, namely, the Jewish community. Both Jews and Christians claim the Hebrew Bible as Scripture. Jews believe that the basic teachings of this Scripture point toward, and are developed by, the Talmud, which assumed its present form about A.D. 500. Christians, on the other hand, hold that the Old Testament finds its fulfillment in the New Testament. The Hebrew Bible, therefore, "belongs" to both the Church and the Synagogue.

Recent studies have demonstrated how profoundly early Christianity reflects a Jewish character. This fact is not surprising because the Christian movement arose out of the context of first-century Judaism. Further, Jesus himself was Jewish, as were the first Christians. It is to be expected, therefore, that Jewish and Christian interpretations of the Hebrew Bible will reveal similarities *and* disparities. Such is the case. The authors of the *International Theological Commentary* will refer to the various Jewish traditions that they consider important for an appreciation of the Old Testament text. Such references will enrich our understanding of certain biblical passages and, as an extra gift, offer us insight into the relationship of Judaism to early Christianity.

An important second aspect of the present series is its *international* character. In the past, Western church leaders were considered to be *the* leaders of the Church — at least by those living in the West! The theology and biblical exegesis done by these scholars dominated the thinking of the Church. Most commentaries were produced in the Western world and reflected the life-style, needs, and thoughts of its civilization. But the Christian Church is a worldwide community. People who belong to this universal Church reflect differing thoughts, needs, and lifestyles.

Today the fastest growing churches in the world are to be found, not in the West, but in Africa, Indonesia, South America, Korea, Taiwan, and elsewhere. By the end of this century, Christians in these areas will outnumber those who live in the West. In our age, especially, a commentary on the Bible must transcend the parochialism of Western civilization and be sensitive to issues that are the special problems of persons who live outside of the "Christian" West, issues such as race relations, personal survival and fulfillment, liberation, revolution, famine, tyranny, disease, war, the poor, religion and state. Inspired of God, the authors of the Old Testament knew what life is like on the edge of existence. They addressed themselves to everyday people who often faced more than everyday problems. Refusing to limit God to the "spiritual," they portrayed him as one who heard and knew the cries of people in pain (see Exod. 3:7-8). The contributors to the *International Theological Commentary* are persons who prize the writings of these biblical authors as a word of life to our world today. They read the Hebrew Scriptures in the twin contexts of ancient Israel and our modern day.

The scholars selected as contributors underscore the international aspect of the Commentary. Representing very different geographical, ideological, and ecclesiastical backgrounds, they come from over seventeen countries. Besides scholars from such traditional countries as England, Scotland, France, Italy, Switzerland, Canada, New Zealand, Australia, South Africa, and the United States, contributors from the following places are included: Israel, Indonesia, India, Thailand, Singapore, Taiwan, and countries of Eastern Europe. Such diversity makes for richness of thought. Christian scholars living in Buddhist, Muslim, or Socialist lands may be able to offer the World Church insights into the biblical message — insights to which the scholarship of the West could be blind.

The proclamation of the biblical message is the focal concern of the *International Theological Commentary*. Generally speaking, the authors of these commentaries value the historical-critical studies of past scholars, but they are convinced that these studies by themselves are not enough. The Bible is more than an object of critical study; it is the revelation of God. In the written Word, God has disclosed himself and his will to humankind. Our authors see themselves as servants of the Word which, when rightly received, brings *shalom* to both the individual and the community.

John Hamlin's volume *Joshua: Inheriting the Land* is an unusually good commentary for ministers and church educators. Departing from approaches that often leave the reader remembering Joshua as a problem book, Dr. Hamlin sets this inspired writing at the center of the biblical tradition. It continues the story of the Exodus, and witnesses of God's faithfulness in fulfilling promises made to Abraham. The teaching of Sinai and the concerns of the later prophets are prominent in the Joshua narrative, and a number of its themes are developed in the New Testament writings. The author's thorough knowledge of the Bible is reflected in his commentary; frequently he refers to biblical passages which relate to Joshua. He draws the reader into a dialogue with the biblical tradition, and in so doing encourages "biblical preaching."

Professor Hamlin, however, does not overlook the difficult passages in the book of Joshua. Confronting them, he often hands the reader information that enables him to arrive at a better understanding of these texts. His work is an axe blow to the root of the long-held, caricatured understanding of the Joshua narrative.

The book of Joshua is an ancient book; but because it speaks of a conflict known to people of every age, the years have drained it of little power. Joshua, says the author, witnesses of the God who stands with his oppressed people in the overthrow of an unjust society in order to establish a new community structured by his righteousness. "The Joshua story is a paradigm and a sign for every generation. It is a *paradigm* of the kingdom struggle which goes on in every age. It is a *sign* pointing to God's ultimate victory over the powers that distort, subvert, and destroy life" (p. 3). Joshua is not a problem book, nor is it merely an ancient writing; it is a word that sits at the edge of our ear waiting to be heard.

—GEORGE A. F. KNIGHT
—FREDRICK CARLSON HOLMGREN

AUTHOR'S PREFACE

This book has come to reality only with the help of many people who contributed in a variety of ways. Dr. James Muilenburg taught me to see the biblical text whole. My discussions with students from China, Thailand, Burma, and Singapore helped to clarify my thinking on the meaning of the OT, and especially the book of Joshua. I hope that some of them will benefit from reading this volume. Studying at the Ecumenical Institute for Theological Research at Tantur, Jerusalem, enabled me to see and walk on the land Joshua saw and trod. The library at the Institute was a good place to begin my work. San Francisco Theological Seminary provided excellent facilities for me to continue my efforts. I also want to thank the many friends who offered valuable suggestions after reading parts of the manuscript. I will mention only Robert Boling, Marvin Chaney, and Robert Coote. George Knight and Fredrick Holmgren, series editors, gave me constant encouragement, as well as careful attention to the manuscript. Finally, I must express my deep appreciation to Frances Jane Cade Hamlin, a true partner in the task of writing and the joy of living.

E. JOHN HAMLIN

INTRODUCTION

INTERPRETING THE BOOK OF JOSHUA

Problems

The book of Joshua presents a number of problems which prevent our seeing in it a clear message from God. The most commonly quoted words in the book are God's command and promise to Joshua (1:9) and Joshua's courageous witness to the people (24:15). Apart from these two verses, this part of the Bible is often ignored or spiritualized.

A further reason for contemporary neglect of Joshua may be a misuse of it in recent years. Past generations of colonists from Christianized lands have found in the Joshua story encouragement to invade, conquer, and settle lands already occupied by peoples considered inferior. Missionaries have used triumphalist language reminiscent of the Joshua story in speaking about "occupying" and "possessing" mission lands for Christ. Some Israeli Jews today find in Joshua a mandate for repossessing Palestine without regard for Palestinians on the land, while others are deeply troubled by this interpretation.

Many readers, moreover, whether Christian, Jewish, or of other persuasions, are repelled by the Joshua accounts of divinely sanctioned mass killings. They find the apparent hatred of foreigners offensive and the long lists of cities and boundary lines boring. For some, a superficial reading of the Joshua story is enough to turn them away from the whole OT, if not the entire body of Christian Scripture. A Burmese teacher in a theological seminary in Insein, Burma, reports that the OT was formerly kept away from new Christians precisely because of its portrayal of a God who not only approves but commands the kind of violence recorded in the book of Joshua.

A Fresh Look

Despite these problems, the fact remains that the book of Joshua
is part of the canon, handed down from ancient Israel, early
Judaism, and the early Church across the centuries to our own
day. It has been a partner in dialogue with believing communities
in past ages "out of their ever-changing contexts, asking two
questions: who are we, and what must we do?" (J. A. Sanders,
"Hermeneutics," *IDBS*, 403). We who live in a different age
should continue this dialogue with other questions. Only in this
way can we make our way through the problems to the message.

Joshua and Abraham

Joshua occupies a key position in the Bible because of its relation
to God's promises to Abraham. The first promise was that God
would give to Abraham's descendants the land of Canaan (Gen.
12:1; 15:7). The Joshua story tells how the people received the
gift of the land. The fulfillment of the promise in the Joshua story
took on new meaning when the land was lost in the 6th cent.
B.C. In NT times, Christians would ponder the meaning of the
Promised Land for a Church on a mission to the nations.

The establishment of a new society on the land (Josh. 13 – 22)
is related to the second promise to Abraham, that God would
make of his descendants "a great nation" (Gen. 12:2). The covenanted society which appears at the end of the Joshua story
looks forward to the Davidic monarchy (2 Sam. 5:3), and to its
hoped-for renewal during the reign of Josiah (2 Kgs. 23:3). Christians may see in it the dim outlines of the establishment of the
kingdom of God under Jesus (Luke 22:15-16), whose name is a
Greek form of Joshua.

The canonical setting of Joshua prompts us to look for some
relationship to the third promise to Abraham, that "in you all
the families of the earth shall be blessed" (Gen. 12:3 RSV mg).
The only hints of this in the Joshua story itself are in the figures
of Rahab and the Gibeonites. A comparison of the texts of Joshua
and Isaiah 40 – 55, however, will show the outlines of a new
interpretation of the Joshua story for the Jewish exiles in Babylon. This, in turn, prepared the way for the NT application of
the Joshua story to Jesus.

The Joshua story takes on new meaning when it is seen in

relation to the wider context of the divine promises to the patriarchs and the whole sweep of biblical history.

Joshua and Exodus

The Joshua story is the continuation and conclusion of the events of the Exodus. At the same time we find a recurrence of the Exodus themes in a new setting. In Egypt there was a successful liberation movement against the power of the pharaoh. In Canaan there was a similar movement of the disinherited against the tyrannous rule of the Canaanite kings. The sea crossing out of a land of slavery is balanced by the river crossing into a land of freedom. The newly formed covenant people at Sinai is similar to the new covenant people at Shechem. Guidelines for living are given both at Mt. Sinai and at Mt. Ebal. And the new allies in the wilderness (Exod. 18) are parallel to the new allies in Canaan (Josh. 2, 9).

We should try to understand the Joshua story as a recurrence of the Exodus pattern of salvation in the Promised Land: liberation, covenant bonding, and training.

The Exodus themes found in Joshua reappear in the New Testament. There the struggle against tyrannical powers is raised to a cosmic level. In place of the pharaoh and the Canaanite kings we find "principalities, . . . powers, . . . world rulers of this present darkness, . . . spiritual hosts of wickedness in high places" (Eph. 6:12). By setting these words alongside the Exodus and Joshua narratives, we are reminded that such powers are not only discarnate, but also incarnate in our societies today. When we read of "the immeasurable greatness of his power in us who believe" (Eph. 1:19), or the "divine power to destroy strongholds" (2 Cor. 10:4), the Joshua story reminds us that such strength is to be used in the struggle against the very powers that destroy life in our contemporary world. When we read of God's final victory over the power of evil (e.g., Rev. 12:7-11; 17:14; 19:11-15), the Joshua story reminds us that there are small victories to be won while we wait for the final victory song.

THE JOSHUA STORY

The book of Joshua is an interpretation of past events for the benefit of present readers. It is more than a mere report by eye-witnesses. The Joshua story is remembered, condensed, and structured history.

Remembered

The story was remembered, told, and retold over several hundred years before being written down in the present form. Some of the events were related to visible objects in the land. There were the stones at Gilgal and the Jordan (4:9), the heaps of stones in the Valley of Achor (7:26) and at the ruins of Ai (8:29), and the stones blocking the mouth of the cave at Makkedah (10:27). Further, a stone monument witnessed the sealing of the covenant at Shechem (24:26-27). There were altars at Mt. Ebal (8:30) and beside the Jordan (22:34), the ruins of Jericho (6:26) and Ai (8:28), and the place names recalling important events — the "Hill of Foreskins" (5:3 RSV mg), Gilgal (5:9), and the Valley of Achor (7:26). The memories of these great events of the past were incorporated in the story.

Another way of remembering the past was through religious ceremonies in which the events were acted out. Christian liturgy does something like this when it reenacts the Last Supper. It is probable that there was at Gilgal, in the period before the monarchy, an annual reenactment of the crossing of the Jordan, the rite of circumcision, the observance of Passover and Unleavened Bread, followed by the ritualized "battle of Jericho." These ceremonies may well have been among the sources of remembered history which were to form part of the Joshua story.

Condensed

The Joshua story is condensed history. We are not told how much time elapsed between the crossing of the Jordan and the covenant at Shechem. The note about Joshua's advanced age after the making of the covenant (24:29) would suggest a period of many decades. Yet the events in the story seem to follow each other rapidly. The conclusion follows that many events and details must have been left out because of lack of space, or for other reasons.

One example of omission is found in the statement about the conquest in 11:16-18: "So Joshua took all that land. . . ." It is clear from the book of Joshua itself (13:1, 13; 15:63; 16:10; 17:12) that this is a condensation of a very long and complicated process, with many details omitted and some perhaps rearranged.

Another example of this kind of condensed history is found in the detailed boundary lists (e.g., 16:1-9) and city lists (e.g., 15:21-62) included in the account of the distribution of the land in chs. 13 – 19. Many scholars believe that these details were in fact taken from lists after the time of Joshua — either in the time before the monarchy, or from the period of the monarchy as early as the time of David, or as late as the time of Josiah. A later retelling of the Joshua story included these lists from the early monarchy, which would be meaningful for listeners who lived long after the time of Joshua.

Structured

The Joshua story is carefully structured by the writer to carry his message to his readers. A glance at the table of contents of this commentary will show an orderly progression of events from preparation to climactic ending. This structure does not necessarily reflect the actual course of events, which were doubtless much more complex, extended in time, and without the simple order found in the story as we have it.

The structure is not always clear (see, e.g., p. 178 below). At times we find problems in discerning the relationship between sections. Too great an emphasis on these problems, however, will cause us to overlook the structural unity of the work. A patient study of the text will enable the reader to get some idea of the writer's design. Here are a few clues:

1. The similarities between chs. 1 and 23 are quite obvious. Joshua's words to the people at the end of the study reflect God's words to him at the beginning.

2. Various stages of the narrative are marked by summarizing statements (see below, p. 141). The final such summary (21:43-45) is clearly related to ch. 1 and ties the whole story together up to that point.

3. The reading of the Covenant Teaching at Mt. Ebal (8:30-35) appears to be the centerpiece of the entire narrative. It looks *back* to the first mention of the Teaching (1:7-8), then to the celebration of Passover and Unleavened Bread (5:11) which were a part of the Teaching, and finally to the sin of Achan, which was a violation of the Teaching (7:11). From Ebal, the narrative looks

forward to the establishment of "Torah Centers" on the land (ch. 21; see below, pp. 140-56), the final summaries of the Teaching (23:6-11; 24:14, 23), and the restatement of the Teaching at the covenant ceremony at Shechem (24:25).

4. A hint of an intended structure may be seen in the three festivals which mark the beginning, midpoint, and end of the story: Passover-Unleavened Bread (5:11), the ceremonial reading of the Teaching (8:30-35), and the renewal of the covenant (24:1-18; see below, p. 73).

The final form of the Joshua story, which we now have in the book of Joshua, is probably the work of a nameless author whom we shall call the Teacher. He was a member of a reform group which worked many decades from the time of King Hezekiah to the time of King Josiah, and on into the exilic period. It was this group which inspired the great reform led by Josiah in 622 B.C., called the Deuteronomic Reform. The Teacher used already existing materials, including an earlier version of Joshua 2 – 12 contributed by a northern writer in the 9th cent. B.C. whom we shall call the Narrator.

Thus, we must keep many different periods of history in mind when we read the book of Joshua. Perhaps the most important of these are the period of Joshua himself and the reign of Josiah (640-609 B.C.).

The Joshua Story Today

The telling of the Joshua story by the ancient Israelites stirred each successive generation to remember what had happened and to believe that in some way it could happen again. Likewise today, we who are "newcomers" from the nations may appropriate the Joshua story as part of our past and receive encouragement for the present. It tells us of

the faithfulness of God to his oppressed people;
the struggle for a place to live (land);
a successful movement of the disinherited against oppression, injustice, and tyranny;
the beginning of a new society based on justice, freedom, and loyalty.

THE PEOPLE OF CANAAN

The Joshua story was a lesson in history for the Israelites of later generations about their responsibilities on the land Yahweh had given them. When the story was written down many years after the events, many details about the people of Canaan and their society had been forgotten. Some things like the following were remembered:

As They Were Remembered

The people living in Canaan were remembered as Canaanites or Amorites (5:1). They were symbolically grouped into six (9:1; 11:3; 12:8) or seven (3:10; 24:11) "nations." They were organized into city-states ruled by kings (12:7-24). These kings could make alliances with each other (9:17; 10:3-5; 11:1-5). Some of them, like Rahab or the Gibeonites, became part of Israel, while others lived alongside the Israelites in the days before the monarchy (13:13; 15:63; 16:10; 17:12). These inhabitants of Canaan were remembered as very wicked (Deut. 9:4-5).

Modern readers will want to fill in some of the gaps left by the writers, so that they can better understand and interpret the Joshua story for today. For this background we must turn to archeology and sociology.

Oppressors and Oppressed

The discovery of letters from Canaanite kings to the Egyptian pharaoh, written in the 14th cent. B.C. and found in Amarna about 320 km. (200 mi.) S of Cairo on the Nile River in Egypt, has increased our knowledge of Canaanite society. The use of sociological tools to interpret this information has given us a profile of a typical city-state in Canaan, as shown in diagram on p. xviii.

From the diagram it can be seen that the Egyptian overlord, the local king, and the aristocratic class of nobles lived from the work of the villagers. We learn from the Amarna Letters that the power of Egypt was declining in the 14th cent. B.C. and continued to grow weaker throughout the 13th cent. B.C. This meant increasing opportunity for the kings and nobles to expand their power at the expense of other kings. The result was greater oppression of the villagers. Free farmers would become debt slaves

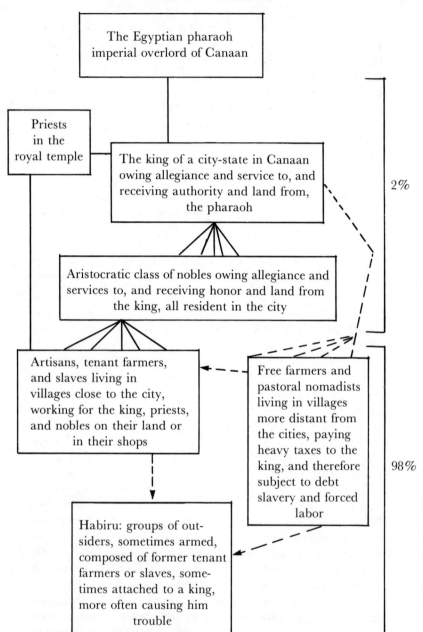

THE STRUCTURE OF CANAANITE SOCIETY
(see also below, pp. 115-116)

or tenant farmers. Many of the oppressed people were leaving the domain of the city-states to become armed "outlaws" something like those gathered around David (1 Sam. 22:2). These bands of outlaws were called Habiru. Sometimes they would hire themselves out to a king. But at other times they would remain on the fringes of society and cause trouble for the king.

Thus we find that Canaan at the time of the coming of the Joshua group was in a state of social turmoil, with many of the villagers attempting to find a way out of the social system. There was need for liberation.

Religion and Society

Although Canaanite religion taught that the high God (named El) cared for widows and orphans, and commanded the king to do the same, the oppressive social order did not live up to that ideal. The priests were close to the king and dependent on him for their support. The king would grant them land, which was worked by slaves. The gods were the deified powers of nature. Although El was called "father of the gods," the most important deities for the daily life of the people were Baal the storm-god who brought rain, and Anath his wife who brought fertility to crops, herds, flocks, and people.

The orgies of men and women at festivals were believed to be imitations of and encouragements to the divine world to bring about fertility. Temple priestesses and priests, sometimes called cult prostitutes, were part of this religious system.

Human sacrifice was also part of the practice of Canaanite religion, as we know from the OT (see Lev. 18:21; Deut. 12:31; 2 Kgs. 23:10; Jer. 7:31).

In addition to religious rites related to fertility, the Canaanites also had a cult of the dead. We know from the OT laws that there were special mediums who were supposed to contact the dead in order to get power or special information from them (Lev. 19:26, 31; Deut. 18:9-11). This cult gave special authority to the dead and made it more difficult for society to change in any way that would reduce the oppression of the people.

The "abominable practices" of the people who lived in Canaan (Deut. 18:9) included cultic activities related to sex and the dead. Both supported the Canaanite social order. Concentration of power in the royal urban elite led to injustice for the poor.

Canaanites in the Time of King Josiah

When the Narrator was retelling the Joshua story in the 9th cent.
B.C., the Canaanites had already ceased to be a separate social
identity. They had been absorbed into the social reality of Israel
at the time of Solomon. In King Josiah's time, the "Canaanites"
were symbols of the corrupt religious and social practices in Judah which, in the view of the Teacher, were the root cause of the
national crisis. The only way to national salvation was by an
unconditional break with these Canaanite ways and a return to
the Covenant Teaching.

THE ISRAELITES

Israel as It Came to be

The readers of the book of Joshua did not have to ask who the
Israelites were (as we do), because they were themselves Israelites. When they read the expression "all Israel" (3:7), or "the
people of Israel" (8:33), or "the tribes of Israel" (3:12), they
naturally thought of the Israel of their own time—during the
reign of Solomon, of Jeroboam II, or of Josiah, during the Exile,
or in restored Jerusalem after the Exile. In other words, they
thought of Israel as it had come to be, and might become in the
future.

Israel as It was at the Beginning

As modern readers, we wish to know more about Israel as it was
in the time of Joshua. Scholars of our day have focused much
attention on this. Certain points stand out:

The Joshua group. The group of Israelites referred to in the
book of Joshua—we call them the Joshua group—was itself a
"mixed multitude" (Exod. 12:38) composed of pastoral nomads
with their cattle and herds and flocks, fisherfolk, farmers, artisans, former soldiers, and prisoners of war. These became a powerful and dynamic society through three events related in the
Exodus story: (a) liberation from oppression, (b) covenant bonding with Yahweh and with each other in an ordered society, and
(c) discipline and training during the years in the wilderness.

A new social reality. The Joshua group entered Canaan not as a distinct ethnic group, but as a new social reality that had revolutionary effects on the disintegrating and oppressive city-state system of Canaan. The revolutionary elements were: (a) a strong loyalty to one free and sovereign Lord, named Yahweh, instead of the many gods of Canaan who were themselves part of the oppressive social system, (b) a conviction of being one people in place of the many competing city-states in Canaan, (c) a society based on justice and freedom, instead of a hierarchical society based on special privilege and oppression, (d) a religion without the cult of sex, the cult of the dead, or the cult of the king, and without a powerful, entrenched priesthood.

Proto-Israelites. The Joshua group attracted discontented farmers, slaves, Habiru outlaws, and others in Canaan to join them and assist in the overthrow of the kings and their nobles. We may call these proto-Israelites (Israelites-to-be). They were already in the regions of Galilee and central Canaan before the Joshua group arrived in Canaan.

The Joshua group which had experienced the great liberation entered Canaan as liberators. Bound in a covenant to Yahweh and to each other, they also accepted others in Canaan into the covenant society. They were liberated and liberating, covenanted and covenanting.

Israelites in the time of King Josiah. When the Teacher wrote the book of Joshua, Israel was again reduced to a fragment of what it had been in the days of David and Solomon. "All Israel" was a memory of the past and a hope of the future. Only the tribe of Judah remained on the land. The Israelites of Samaria, Galilee, and the Transjordan had been taken into exile a century before.

With the rapid decline of Assyrian power after 630 B.C., the time seemed right for a movement of national renewal that would cast off Canaanite ways, return to Covenant Teaching, and recover lost territories as a home for returning exiles. It was at that time that the Teacher retold the Joshua story as a call for a new movement of liberation, openness to newcomers, and a covenant bonding to form a new people.

The death of King Josiah in 609 B.C. and the disastrous events that followed showed that the hopes of revival were false. Yet the message of renewal has a universal appeal.

THE JOSHUA STORY AND ISRAELITE HISTORY: A PROPOSED RECONSTRUCTION

About 1200 B.C.

The Joshua group crosses Jordan and begins to "inherit the land."

A liberation movement among the oppressed majority of Canaanites is stimulated by the arrival of the Joshua group. These Canaanites assist in the overthrow of Canaanite ruling power.

A new egalitarian society is set up in Canaan.

1150-1000 B.C.

The events which took place on the arrival of the Joshua group are remembered by dramatic reenactment at annual shrine festivals at Gilgal.

1000-922 B.C.

David and Solomon incorporate the territory of Canaan with its people into the Israelite kingdom. "Canaanites" become "Israelites."

Tribal boundaries and town lists, cities of refuge and levitical cities from this period are later used to describe the organization of society under Joshua (Josh. 13 – 21).

About 900 B.C.

The northern Narrator gathers traditions associated with Gilgal, Jericho, Ai, and Gibeon into a continuous narrative in order to make clear that Joshua the Ephraimite, successor to Moses (and not David), was the one who led Israel to possess the whole land given by God.

800-700 B.C.

Israelite society in both the northern and southern kingdoms reflects the pre-Joshua Canaanite society. The prophets Amos, Hosea, Micah, and Isaiah try to call the people back to God and to the righteousness and justice of the past.

Assyria seizes the whole of the northern kingdom as well as the Transjordan territory which was once part of Israel under David and Solomon. Many of the Israelite residents are deported.

Hezekiah leads a reform movement and gives royal support to a reform party which includes levitical priests from the north.

The reform party begins work on a new presentation of Mosaic teachings. This later becomes our book of Deuteronomy.

700-587 B.C.

Manasseh's corrupt and repressive reign brings a return to "Canaanite" as well as Assyrian religious and social ways. Despite persecution, the reform group continues its work in secret.

Josiah ascends the throne at the age of eight. He is nurtured and guided by the reform group. He institutes a thorough-going purge of religion from its Canaanite and Assyrian practices and attempts to recover lost territory from a powerless Assyria.

The Teacher, a member of the reform group, writes a new version of the Joshua story, using materials from the Narrator, from the records of the monarchy, and from other traditions. His purpose is to present Joshua as a role-model for the youthful monarch.

Other members of the reform group prepare a history of Israel from Moses to Josiah, of which the Joshua story is a part. This history is known to scholars as the Deuteronomic history. Following the untimely death of Josiah in 609 B.C., a later edition of this history contains materials dealing with the death of Josiah and the fall of Jerusalem.

587-538 B.C.

The Joshua story is an inspiration to many Israelites who dream of a return to their land from exile.

A radical new interpretation of the Joshua story is made by the prophetic author of Isaiah 40 – 55.

PART I

ENTERING THE LAND
Joshua 1– 5

CHAPTER 1

PREPARATION
Joshua 1:1-18

Who among you will give ear to this,
will attend and listen for the time to come?   — Isaiah 42:23

. . . to make ready for the Lord a people prepared.   — Luke 1:17

The Joshua story is a paradigm and a sign for every generation. It is a *paradigm* of the kingdom struggle which goes on in every age. It is a *sign* pointing to God's ultimate victory over the powers that distort, subvert, and destroy life.

The story itself is set in the period of social breakdown at the end of the Bronze Age and the beginning of the Iron Age, when the Joshua group was forming the nucleus of a liberated and liberating people. Its strength as paradigm and sign is demonstrated by the fact that the story was rewritten with new meanings in the 9th and 7th cents. B.C.

The first chapter is an introduction to the entire story by the Teacher. He also lived and taught in a time of breakdown and chaos, and saw the Joshua story as an illustration of hope in the power of God. According to the tradition preserved in 2 Chr. 34:3, sixteen-year-old King Josiah "began to seek the God of David his father" in the eighth year of his reign, 632 B.C. Perhaps this introductory chapter was written about that time to instruct, inspire, and strengthen the youthful king.

If in those days there had been the custom of writing a dedication for a book, the Teacher might have put these words at the beginning:

> *Dedicated to the young King Josiah,*
> *and the renewal of the Kingdom*

SECTION I. GOD PREPARES JOSHUA (1:1-9)

The first section, in the form of a message from God to Joshua, sets forth the Teacher's guiding ideas for Josiah's role in the renewal of God's people on the land.

Continuity with the Mosaic Tradition

The Teacher strongly affirms that the establishment or renewal of God's kingdom society must be a continuation of the work of Moses. The name Moses appears eleven times in the first chapter alone, and forty-eight times in the other chapters. God's promises to, presence with, and instructions to Moses are all inherited by Joshua. The allotment of the land to the tribes will be according to Moses' commands (vv. 13-15). The people's allegiance to Moses is now transferred to Joshua (v. 17).

The message for Josiah is the same. His work of reform and renewal must be a continuation and fulfillment of the work and teaching of Moses. We should note that Jesus, the NT "Joshua," likewise affirmed that he had come to fulfill "the law and the prophets" (Matt. 5:17). The same principle is seen in the words of Eph. 2:20, where the Church is said to be a continuation of the work of the apostles and prophets.

God's "Now" (1:2)

The Joshua story begins with a turning point in history. The old age has passed with the death of Moses. The new is about to begin, and with it comes a call to present action on which the future depends. The entire development of Israel's history in the land, the coming of Jesus, and the formation of the Christian Church all hinged on Joshua's response to God's imperative: "Now therefore arise" (v. 2).

Perhaps the Teacher was also thinking of the turning point in the 7th cent. B.C. The old age of Assyrian dominance had passed with the death of Ashurbanipal, the last great Assyrian monarch. It was in 628 B.C. that the twenty-year-old king of Judah responded to a similar call to decisive action. "He began to purge Judah and Jerusalem of . . . the Asherim and the graven and the molten images," and carried the reform northward into Assyrian-controlled Manasseh, Ephraim, and Naphtali, and probably into Gilead in Transjordan as well (2 Chr. 34:3-7; J. Bright, *A History of Israel*, 3rd ed., 317).

4

Causing the People to Inherit the Land (1:6)

Joshua's lifework after his commissioning by Moses (Deut. 31:23) was to make something happen: he was to enable the people to inherit the land promised by God (v. 6, repeating what had been said five times in Deuteronomy; see 1:38; 3:28; 31:3, 7, 23). The picture being used by the Teacher is this: God is the owner of the land (Lev. 25:23; Ps. 24:1), and he has granted it to his people as tenants to use for his purposes. This is the meaning of the words in v. 3, "I have given. . . ." Certain conditions must be fulfilled by the tenants, however, before they can have full use of the land. It is also the meaning of the different wording in v. 2, "I am giving. . . ." Joshua's role was to enable the people to fulfill the conditions.

The conditions as we find them in the Joshua story are as follows: (1) They must cross the Jordan River. See vv. 2, 11, which look forward to chs. 3 – 4. (2) They must enter the land, for they cannot inherit it without actual presence there. See v. 11; cf. Deut. 11:24. (3) They must engage in a long, hard struggle against the forces of oppression in the land. See v. 5, which looks forward to chs. 6 – 12. (4) They must do away with internal corruption. See v. 18, which looks forward to ch. 7. (5) They must agree to a fair distribution of the land among the tribes. See v. 6, which looks forward to chs. 13 – 19. (6) They must organize their society according to God's Covenant Teaching. See v. 7, which looks forward to 8:30-35. To summarize, God's purpose in choosing Joshua was that the people should inherit the land.

The Teacher must have seen in Joshua a model for Josiah, who by his reform would renew his people's inheritance. Josiah's death at Megiddo in 609 B.C. (2 Kgs. 23:28-30), however, brought the 7th-cent. B.C. "Joshua" to a tragic end. The exilic prophet Deutero-Isaiah may well have reinterpreted the victorious Joshua and the tragic Josiah as the Servant of Yahweh, who would fulfill God's purpose by his death. In so doing he would make "many to be accounted righteous" (Isa. 53:10-11) and enable them to receive a new inheritance (Isa. 54:17).

The NT writers pictured Jesus in the role of Joshua/Josiah who realized God's eternal purpose, and by his death caused his people to come into their inheritance (see Eph. 1:11-14; 3:11).

God's Covenant Teaching: The Key to Success (1:7-8)

In these two verses, the Teacher tells Joshua/Josiah that this risky enterprise can succeed only by scrupulous observance of God's Teaching.

The Hebrew word *torah* (RSV "law") has the basic meaning of guidance, instruction, teaching. In the days after the Exile the Jews came to apply the word to the first five books of the Hebrew Scriptures.

When the Hebrew word *torah* was translated into Septuagint Greek, the word *nomos,* meaning "law," was used, and from there it came into other ancient and modern translations. The effect of this translation was an overemphasis on the regulations or laws which form a large part of the Pentateuch. Narrative, which also makes up much of the first five books of the OT, did not fit the meaning of the Greek word *nomos* or the English word "law."

Although the Teacher was not thinking of the Pentateuch when he referred to the *torah,* we know from both Deuteronomy and Joshua that he understood it to include both law and story. For this reason we do not use "law" to translate it, but rather "God's Covenant Teaching" or simply "God's Teaching."

According to Josh. 1:7-8, God's Teaching not only is to be performed (v. 7), but also is to be taken into the heart and mind, or "your mouth" (v. 8; cf. Jer. 31:33; Isa. 51:7). The meaning of God's Teaching in Joshua's mouth is twofold. (1) The mouth is for eating. God's Teaching is to be "chewed," "swallowed," and "digested" so that it becomes part of the person's very self in thought and action. (2) The mouth is also for speaking. The one who has received God's Teaching in his mouth must also teach, warn, and encourage others (Josh. 8:34-35; cf. Jer. 1:9; 15:6; Ezek. 2:8– 3:3).

When the exilic prophet Deutero-Isaiah reflected on the disaster of 587 B.C., he said that it was caused by a failure to live by God's Teaching (Isa. 42:24-25). But he went on to say that this divine Teaching was applicable to all nations (42:21; 51:4), and that it was the mission of God's servant people to carry it to the most distant places (Isa. 42:4). Although this perspective from the exilic period is broader than that of the Teacher, there is no contradiction between them. The Teacher emphasizes responsible living on the land, while Deutero-Isaiah relates this to all nations, each in its own land.

The divine Teaching contained in the law and story of Torah has to do with the kind of life that will ensure that "it may go well with you, in the land which the LORD your God gives you" (Deut. 5:16; cf. Exod. 20:12). It included absolute loyalty to Yahweh, rejection of the false gods of a corrupt Canaanite society (Deut. 5:7-10; Exod. 20:3-8), honoring God's name by swearing "in truth, in justice, and in uprightness" (Jer. 4:2; cf. Deut. 5:11; 6:13; Exod. 20:7), protecting the rights of the weak and powerless (Deut. 5:17, 19; Exod. 20:13, 15), honoring the family (Deut. 5:16, 18; Exod. 20:12, 14), speaking the truth for the neighbor (Deut. 5:20; Exod. 20:16), and controlling greed (Deut. 5:21; Exod. 20:17). Faith in the message of the story and obedience to the commandments of God's Teaching will bring about success in the new land.

The Teacher seems to have chosen the Hebrew word *yaskil* ("to have good success") with a particular application to King Josiah. The same word is used to describe the success of David's campaigns (1 Sam. 18:5, 14, 15 and possibly 30). The Deuteronomic Historian used it in his version of David's charge to Solomon, which resembles the charge to Joshua (1 Kgs. 2:3). The great reforming King Hezekiah is also said to have been successful (RSV "prospered") in all that he did, including his religious reform and his political revolt against Assyria (2 Kgs. 18:7). The remark that "there was no king like him" among all the kings of Judah, "nor did any like him arise after him" (2 Kgs. 23:25) seems to indicate that the historian wrote those words in the early years of Josiah's reign, before the young king had proven himself. Joshua 1:7-8 would then serve as a challenge to the youthful king to emulate his great-grandfather.

After the death of Josiah, people in Judah expected a new descendant of David who would, like Joshua, "be successful" (RSV "deal wisely") in reuniting Judah and Israel, and "execute justice and righteousness in the land" (Jer. 23:5-6; cf. 22:15). This same word (*yaskil*) and the parallel expression *yitslah* ("be prosperous"), which are used together in Josh. 1:7-8, appear together again only once in the OT, in the poem about the "suffering servant." "Behold, my servant shall prosper (*yaskil*). . . . The will of the LORD shall prosper (*yitslah*) in his hand" (Isa.

52:13; 53:10). The picture of Joshua/Josiah has been reinterpreted as the one who "succeeds" by his death!

Strength for the Task (1:5-6, 7, 9)

Three times Joshua is charged to face this great task with courage, in words very similar to Deut. 3:28; 31:7, 23. The three
encouragements are for three different situations.

Courage is needed to face difficult opposition from the Canaanite kings, and for patience in working with the people to
bring them to their inheritance (vv. 5-6). Here we must recall
Moses' escape from being stoned by the people in the wilderness
(Num. 14:10). Likewise we must remember that God promised
to make Jeremiah "a fortified city, an iron pillar, and bronze
walls" (Jer. 1:18). We should also call to mind the Servant's
willing back, cheeks, and face set "like a flint" (Isa. 50:6-7).

Courage is needed as well to live personally by Covenant
Teaching and to make it a reality in the lives of the people (Josh.
1:7-8). Christians would call this the courage to take up the cross
(Mark 8:34).

Finally, courage is needed to walk with a God who may lead
in unexpected ways (Josh. 1:9). God's promise to go with Joshua
implied Joshua's readiness to go where God wanted him to go.
The courage of Jesus in the Garden of Gethsemane comes to
mind, as well as the words to Peter that he would be taken "where
you do not wish to go" (John 21:18).

Joshua would have to test the reality of the words "I will not
fail you or forsake you" (Josh. 1:5).

SECTION II. JOSHUA PREPARES THE PEOPLE (1:10-11)

A well-prepared leader must be ready to prepare his people for
the momentous events that lie ahead.

Provisions

The Teacher here begins his comparison of the Jordan crossing
with the Reed Sea crossing at the time of the Exodus. As the
Exodus generation "baked unleavened cakes" before leaving Egypt
(Exod. 12:39), so the Joshua group must make provision for the
journey. When they cross the Jordan they will eat of the fruit of

the land (Josh. 5:11). These provisions are presumably for the three-day period before that event (1:11; 3:2).

Consecration

Any great task requires spiritual as well as material preparation. The analogy with the Exodus tradition is noticeable here again. The three days allowed for preparation are a reenactment of the three days for purification and consecration at the foot of Mt. Sinai (Exod. 19:10-11). During this time of spiritual preparation, all impurities are to be removed (Exod. 19:10), because God himself "walks in the midst of your camp, to save you and give you your enemies before you" (Deut. 23:14). It is not a time for indulgence in ordinary pleasures (1 Sam. 21:4-5), but for inner discipline and dedication to the task ahead.

The People's Task: To Possess the Land

It was Joshua's task to help the people come into their inheritance. The people, on their part, must "possess" the land, as God's tenants.

The Hebrew verb *yarash* has an original and archaic meaning "to tread on" grapes, as seen from Mic. 6:15, the only surviving example. The parallel and more commonly used word *darak* can mean to tread on grapes (Judg. 9:27), or to tread on a land as conqueror (Mic. 5:5-6). It is this latter word which is used in Deut. 11:24-25 and Josh. 1:3 as symbolic action, not of a conqueror, but of a tenant receiving the land from the owner: "Every place on which the sole of your foot treads (*darak*) shall be yours."

The verb *yarash* has three meanings when used in relation to land. The first is to receive the land as a gift (Lev. 20:24; RSV "inherit"). The second is to occupy and organize the land according to God's Teaching. The Deuteronomic reform group lays great emphasis on this second meaning. Again and again they say that the commandments are to be applied "in the land to which you are going over, to possess it. . . . that it may go well with you . . ." (Deut. 6:1-3, etc.). Conversely, failure to observe the conditions of faithful tenants will mean that the rights of tenancy or "possession" will be taken away (Deut. 4:26; 28:63). The tenants may be "dispossessed" (Num. 14:12).

The third meaning derives from the first two. Receiving the right of tenancy (possessing in the sense of inheriting) and living on the land (possessing in the sense of a proper ordering of society on the land) can be effected only if there is actual control. For this reason *yarash* may also mean to take possession by force (Deut. 6:18-19) from "nations greater and mightier" than Israel, who are occupying the land. It is in this sense that the word is sometimes translated "dispossess," i.e., to take control of the land from the present tenants (Deut. 9:1; 19:1-3). This act is justified, according to the Teacher, only when the old society is wicked and corrupt (Deut. 9:5), and when the new society fulfills God's will.

The causative form of the verb *yarash* means to cause a change in the power structure on the land, i.e., to bring down the ruling kings, nobles, and rich, so that a new social order may be set up. This form of the verb has often been translated mistakenly as "destroy" (Exod. 15:9), "cast out" (Exod. 34:24), or more commonly "drive out" (Num. 33:51-56; Deut. 4:38; 9:3, 4, 5; 18:12; Josh. 3:10; 13:6, 12, 13; 14:12; 15:14, 63; 16:10; 17:13, 18; 23:5, 9, 13). These translations give the erroneous impression that entire populations were either wiped out or evicted from the land before the conquering armies of Israel. The emphasis in all of these references is not on what happened to people in the villages or elsewhere in Canaan, but to the rulers and their power.

Deutero-Isaiah used the verb *yarash* in his reinterpretation of the conquest tradition: "Your descendants will possess the nations" (Isa. 54:3). If we look at Isaiah 54 together with Isa. 52:13 – 53:12, it is apparent that the prophet does not have in mind violent conquest of the nations of Canaan. He sees the nations transformed ("accounted righteous," 53:10) by the servant people's suffering love. It is the servant people's mission to bring about a new social order of all nations under the guidance of God's Teaching and justice (Isa. 42:1-4; 51:4). The first two meanings of the verb *yarash* are dominant here. The result is not tenancy rights on the land, but the formation of a covenant family of nations. It appears that the prophet was seeking the hidden meaning of the words "have good success" and "prosper" in Josh. 1:7-8.

SECTION III. JOSHUA PREPARES THE EAST JORDAN TRIBES (1:12-15)

At this point in the narrative, a rather unexpected interlude takes place. Joshua addresses not the whole people, but the East Jordan tribes of Reuben, Gad, and the eastern half of the tribe of Manasseh. Yet the two things he says to them are of great importance for the coming struggle.

"You . . . shall help . . . your brethren . . ." (1:14)

The meaning of this passage is clear: "all this people" (v. 2) must possess the land and inherit it. No one group can inherit the land (v. 6) or possess it (v. 11) without the others. All must work together. "Mutual help among the segments of ancient Israel was a foundation of its early existence, and hence of the unity of Israel" (N. K. Gottwald, *The Tribes of Yahweh*, 253). Perhaps the Teacher was thinking of the time when Reuben and Gad refused to help their brothers west of the Jordan in their struggle for freedom from Canaanite oppression, while Machir (East Jordan Manasseh) did offer help (Judg. 5:14-19). The curse of nonparticipants in Judg. 5:23 seems to be reflected in the prose of Num. 32:23: "If you will not do so, behold, you have sinned against the LORD."

There may, however, be more to this special mention of the East Jordan tribe than the simple lesson of cooperation. David had made the East Jordanian territories an integral part of the greater kingdom (2 Sam. 8:12). His census had begun at Aroer, the southern limit of Gad's territory, and extended north to Gilead and Dan (2 Sam. 24:5-6). Solomon had officers stationed in three administrative districts in East Jordan (1 Kgs. 4:13, 14, 19).

At the time of Josiah, however, the whole area had fallen to Assyria (2 Kgs. 15:29). Most of it was organized into the Assyrian province of Gal-aza. Ammonite worshipers of Milcom were living there (Jer. 49:1), and according to 1 Chr. 5:22 most of the East Jordan Israelites were taken into exile in 732 or 722 B.C. When a psalmist said that the Jabbok Valley (Vale of Succoth) and the whole of Gilead belonged to Yahweh (Ps. 60:6-7), he may have been calling for the recovery of those territories by Josiah (D. L. Christensen, *The Transformation of the War Oracle in OT Prophecy*, 121-27). The call for the cooperation of the East Jordan tribes appears in Numbers 32, Deuteronomy 3, as well as here in vv. 12-15. In the 7th cent. B.C., this could have been a call to members of these tribes, who were living under Assyrian domination, to join the renewal movement for the sake of all their brothers. Along with this, of course, there would be the hope and

11

expectation that the renewal movement would incorporate the East Jordan territories into the new kingdom.

". . . *until the* LORD *gives rest to your brethren as well as to you" (1:15)*

"Rest" is the third important word relating Israel to the land. The Hebrew word *menuhah* means security from disruption or enemy attack on land which has been given as an inheritance (Deut. 12:9-10). A condition of rest, security, and peace is thus a sign and evidence of God's presence with his people (Exod. 33:14), as well as his gracious provision for them (Josh. 1:13). Rest is a reward for the right stewardship of the land according to God's Teaching. It is associated in Israelite tradition with the reign of good kings such as David (2 Sam. 7:1), Solomon (1 Kgs. 5:4; 8:56; 1 Chr. 22:9, 18), Asa (2 Chr. 14:2-6; 15:15), and Jehoshaphat (2 Chr. 20:30).

Looking ahead to the close of the Joshua story, we see all Israel in peace and security (21:44; 22:4; 23:1). "Rest" is thus an implied promise or hope for the outcome of Josiah's renewal program. In the actual situation of the late 7th cent. B.C., however, there was a pronounced lack of such "rest" (see Mic. 2:10; Jer. 45:3; Lam. 5:5 among the prophetic literature of the period). For this reason, the prophets spoke of a future "rest" —

> For lo, I will save you from afar,
>> and your offspring from the land of their captivity. (Jer. 46:27)
> Jacob shall return and have quiet and ease,
>> and none shall make him afraid. (Jer. 30:10)

Restless Israel must wait

> until the Spirit is poured upon us from on high,
>> and the wilderness becomes a fruitful field, . . .
> Then justice will dwell in the wilderness,
>> and righteousness abide in the fruitful field.
> And the effect of righteousness will be peace,
>> and the result of righteousness, quietness and trust for ever.
> My people will abide in a peaceful habitation,
>> in secure dwellings and in quiet resting places. (Isa. 32:15-18)

Against the 7th-cent. B.C. background, the conditional phrase "until the LORD gives rest" contains the hope of a future transformation of the troubled land into "a peaceful habitation" for the people.

"Rest" as a gift of God is further stressed in the New Testament. It is to be received through a living relationship with Jesus in the actual places where people "labor and are heavy laden" (Matt. 11:28). Faith and obedience in real-life situations are conditions for accepting the gift (Heb. 4:3, 11). The "sabbath rest for the people of God" (v. 9) is to be sought not only in the heavenly spheres, but also in the land where they struggle, suffer, and hope. Moreover, as in the case of the Transjordan tribes, the perfection of rest cannot be sought in isolation from brothers and sisters in other places and times (Josh. 11:40).

SECTION IV. THE PEOPLE'S OBEDIENCE (1:16-18)

Obedience

The absolute obedience offered by the people at the beginning of the Joshua story contrasts sadly with their rebelliousness in the wilderness (Exod. 15:23; ch. 32; Num. 14:2-3; ch. 16; Deut. 9:22-23). Therefore it is surprising to hear the words, "Just as we obeyed Moses in all things, so we will obey you." In fact, they did not obey Moses. Perhaps the explanation of the apparent contradiction can be found in the two possible translations of the Hebrew word *shama'*: "hear" or "obey." The book of Deuteronomy is largely an appeal to "hear" the words of God through Moses (e.g., Deut. 6:4). Having *heard* Moses' preaching and kept it in their hearts (Deut. 6:5-9), they were now ready to *obey* the commands of Joshua (Josh. 1:17).

There are three chains of command in the Joshua story. In the first, Yahweh commands Moses, who commands Joshua (11:15); Joshua in turn commands the officers and people (1:10, 16). Everything has been determined in advance before the crossing of the Jordan. All Joshua does is to carry out the divine command given by Moses (8:31, 33, 35). In the second line of authority, Yahweh speaks directly to Joshua in particular situations for which the Mosaic teaching was not sufficient (4:15-16; 8:1-2; 11:6; 13:1). And in the third, Joshua uses his own initiative and skill to accomplish the goal disclosed through Mosaic revelation or directly from Yahweh (1:10; 8:4-8; 18:3-7).

We may find here a paradigm for fulfilling the will of God. The biblical revelation gives us the broad outlines and goals for the kingdom struggle and the kingdom society. Yet we need to seek fresh inspiration in specific situations as they arise. And we must use our own initiative and skills to meet the particular challenges of each crisis.

"Wherever you send us we will go" (v. 16). Joshua's commissions to the officers or to Israel were of two kinds: (1) He sent men to destroy oppressive power and win freedom in the kingdom struggle. He sent out spies (2:1; 7:1), and dispatched men to battle (8:3, 9). (2) He also sent them to maintain the health of the kingdom society — to help in the administration of justice in the case of Achan (7:22) and to assist in the right management of the land by surveying it (18:4-8). Isaiah promised to go where God would send him (Isa. 6:8). Jesus also sends out his disciples to participate in the kingdom struggle and the kingdom society.

The commands found in Joshua, whether given by Yahweh, Moses, or Joshua, are all under the primary command found in 22:5 and again in 23:8, 11 — to love, serve, and cleave to Yahweh with absolute commitment, and to walk in his ways. All other commands — whether concerning the crossing of the Jordan (3:3, 8; 4:3, 15-16), or military strategy (6:10; 8:4, 8, 27), or the treatment of the inhabitants of Canaan (9:24; 10:40; 11:12, 20) — are secondary and must be interpreted in relation to this primary command.

Discipline

The only incident in the Joshua story that involves the death sentence referred to in 1:18 is that of Achan (ch. 7). However, it recalls the episode of Dathan, Abiram, and Korah (Num. 16) in the wilderness. Because of human sin, discipline is needed. Thus, too, there are punishments as well as rewards (23:12, 16). Hence this mention of death in an otherwise bright picture of possessirg the land is a kind of shadow in which we can see the ruins of Samaria and Jerusalem, the loss of the land, and the death of the nation that is just being formed.

Support

The people's words of support echo God's own words to Joshua earlier in the chapter, and form a fitting conclusion to this introductory part of the story. Their wish for Joshua is God's continual presence. As God goes with him he will give him courage and persistence in carrying out the kingdom struggle and building the kingdom society.

CHAPTER 2

ALLIES IN CANAAN
Joshua 2:1-24

The tax collectors and the harlots go into the kingdom of God before you.
— Matthew 21:31

Rahab was well known to the NT writers as a woman of exemplary faith (Heb. 11:31) whose help to the spies was acceptable to God (Jas. 2:25). She was also revered as one of four women (the others are Tamar, Ruth, and Bathsheba) mentioned by Matthew in the genealogy of Jesus (Matt. 1:5). Jewish tradition also held Rahab in high esteem as a non-Jewish convert to Judaism. According to Jewish legend, she married Joshua and was the mother of priests and prophets in Israel.

Modern commentators have asked questions about the origin, composition, and historical reliability of the story, but have not shown much interest in the theological dimensions of the narrative. Without doubt, the story served to explain the existence of a clan of Rahab, perhaps living near the ruins of Jericho in later times. The narrative is certainly part of the oldest traditions and is not simply the product of someone's imagination. The words of Rahab in 2:9-11 may have been expanded by later writers from a simpler, earlier version. Yet both the narrative and the person of Rahab have important theological dimensions. Following are a few suggestions to help the reader grasp the significance of the story.

THE GOOD CANAANITE

Rahab was a Canaanite who, with her extended family ("father's house," v. 12), became a part of Israel, because of her bold act of befriending the spies. This is an indication that the Canaanites were not all to be labelled as "wicked" (Deut. 9:4). The Rahab group is a reminder of the fact that there were large bodies of potential allies in that decadent and corrupt city-state society. The "wickedness" lay in the system in which some oppressed others. Many, however, could find freedom by crossing over to join the kingdom movement.

THE POOR CANAANITE

Rahab and her family seem to have been from the poorer segment of Jericho society, who welcomed an opportunity for freedom. The flax kept on her roof (v. 6) suggests that her family lived by agriculture outside the city, and that the flax bundles were hauled up on the roof through the window and by the rope mentioned in v. 15. We may surmise that they were working the land of some noble to supply flax for linen workers such as "the families of the house of linen workers" mentioned in 1 Chr. 4:21. These in turn would produce linen for priests' garments, and for the upper-class people of Jericho (see Isa. 3:16, 23). Rahab's house on the wall would serve as a place for the family to stay when they were in the city. From the words of Rahab in v. 10, it is possible to conclude that the presence of the Joshua group in the region was not unnoticed, and that it would have aroused hopes among the alienated for a better life.

THE MARGINAL CANAANITE

Rahab had, probably out of economic necessity, earned a living as a prostitute. She was on the edge of Canaanite society. In ancient cities, certain occupational groups were tolerated but, because of the nature of the work, entirely without a recognized place. Among these groups were prostitutes and slaves. We are reminded of the scheduled castes in India, the Mihaiho Burakumin ghettoized group in Japan, and leprosy colonies in many countries. Rahab had joined this kind of outcast group because of the poverty of her family. In later Israel this was not allowed (Lev. 19:29). Becoming a prostitute because of poverty is a common thing in many countries of Asia in our own time. Of course, Rahab was not caught in a system of highly commercialized prostitution as it is known today. Yet we can see in her a woman who found dignity and fulfillment by choosing a different kind of society where there was no economically compelled degradation or dehumanization of sex.

PARADIGM OF HOPE FOR "HARLOT" ISRAEL

Rahab, a harlot in Canaan, left her former gods who, it was believed, gave bread, water, wool, flax, oil, and wine (Hos. 2:5), and put her faith in Yahweh who in truth gave these things (Hos. 2:8). She is a paradigm for an unfaithful Israel (or Church) who could still turn away from false gods. We read that Israel "played the harlot" already at Shittim (Num. 25:1), the very place from which the Joshua group would enter the land of Canaan (Josh. 2:1; 3:1; Mic. 6:5); and that they "played the harlot" in Canaan (Judg. 2:17), in northern Israel (Hos. 4:10, 12, 14-15), and in Judah (Jer. 3:1). Isaiah described the city of Jerusalem as a harlot (Isa. 1:21).

Rahab was a paradigm of hope, showing that the old idols, the old corrupt ways of the past, could be given up. What Rahab did just before the fall of Jericho, Israel could do before (or after) the fall of Jerusalem. The contrast between Rahab at the bottom of the social scale and the king and nobles of Jericho at the top illustrates well what Jesus said: "Harlots go into the kingdom of God before you" (Matt. 21:31).

THE FAITH OF A CANAANITE BELIEVER

Rahab's confession of faith begins with the confident assertion "I know" (v. 9), and comes to a climax with the affirmation "The LORD your God . . . is God in heaven above and on earth beneath" (v. 11). What this Canaanite woman knew was what Israel had been taught: "Know therefore this day, and lay it to your heart, that the LORD is God in heaven above and on earth beneath; there is no other" (Deut. 4:39).

It was Israel's desire and prayer that all peoples would come to this knowledge as well: "Know that the LORD is God!" (**Ps.** 100:3). The prayers of both Solomon (1 Kgs. 8:60) and Hezekiah (2 Kgs. 19:19) contain the same aspiration, "that all the peoples of the earth may know that the LORD is God; there is no other." Rahab is thus the first representative in Canaan of "all the peoples of the earth" to say "I know that the LORD your God is God indeed."

We may put beside this confession of faith others of a similar nature:

Jethro of Midian: "Now I know that the LORD is greater than
all gods" (Exod. 18:11).

The repentant Israelites on Mt. Carmel: "The LORD, he is
God" (1 Kgs. 18:39).

Naaman of Syria: "Behold, I know that there is no God in all
the earth but in Israel" (2 Kgs. 5:15).

Caravan merchants from Egypt, Ethiopia, and South Arabia:
"God is in your midst, and there is no other God besides
. . . the God of Israel, the Savior!" (Isa. 45:14-15, following
the Chinese Kuoyü version).

Yahweh the God of Israel shows himself to be the true God
by his mighty works of delivering his people, giving them victory
in battle (Josh. 2:10), answering with fire (1 Kgs. 18:24), healing
sickness (2 Kgs. 5:14), keeping covenant and steadfast love, pun-
ishing those who hate him (Deut. 7:9-10), and carrying out justice for the widow, orphan, and sojourner (Deut. 10:18).

The corollary of declaring faith in the true God is "put away
foreign gods" and turn to him (Josh. 24:23). In other words, it
is to begin a new way of life. We can imagine Rahab beginning
this change when she made a covenant with the spies, and com-
pleting it with all her father's house at the great covenant at
Shechem (Josh. 24).

RAHAB AND ACHAN: A STUDY IN CONTRASTS

Rahab stands in studied contrast with the only other individual
to receive extended treatment in the book of Joshua: Achan.

The one was a poor Canaanite woman; the other a well-to-do
man of the tribe of Judah (Josh. 7:24).

The one *took* the spies to the roof and *hid* them from the king
of Jericho (2:6); the other *took* the forbidden things and *hid* them
from Joshua (7:21-22).

The one showed kindness and loyalty to the Israelite spies and
helped them achieve victory (2:12); the other brought trouble on
Israel by his greed (7:11, 25).

The one covenanted with the Israelites (2:12-14); the other
broke covenant with God (7:11).

The one saved her whole family alive, and they became respected members of the kingdom society (2:13-14; 6:22-23, 25); the other condemned his family to death and oblivion (7:25).

The contrast between the unfaithful Israelite and the faithful foreigner is remarkable. King Ahab was a kind of Achan figure, and the prophets described Israel in terms of unfaithfulness reminiscent of Achan. We can find counterparts of Rahab in Ruth the Moabitess (Ruth 2:2), the widow of Zarephath in Sidon (1 Kgs. 17:9), Naaman the Syrian (2 Kgs. 5:1), the people of Nineveh (Jonah 3:6-9), those described in Isa. 44:5; 45:14, 22-23; 49:7; 55:5, King Cyrus (Isa. 44:28; 45:1), the centurion of Capernaum (Matt. 8:5, 10), the Canaanite woman of Phoenicia (Matt. 15:22, 28), the centurion at the cross (Matt. 27:54), and Cornelius in Caesarea (Acts 10), as well as the great multitude "from every nation, from all tribes and peoples and tongues, standing before the throne" (Rev. 7:9).

The contrast between Rahab and Achan is well illustrated in Jesus' words: "Many will come from east and west and sit at table with Abraham, Isaac, and Jacob in the kingdom of heaven, while the sons of the kingdom will be thrown into the outer darkness" (Matt. 8:11-12).

HISTORICAL NOTES

Jericho, about 8 km. (5 mi.) W of the Jordan River, guards the main southern ford across the Jordan. It thus commands a key defense position in the Jordan Valley. From its position as the eastern gateway to the land, it would be a good place to get an overall impression of the entire land, or at least the central part of it (vv. 1-3). The hills where the spies concealed themselves for three days, doubtless with the help of provisions supplied by Rahab, lie about 4 km. (2.5 mi.) W of the city.

It has been suggested that *Rahab's house* was built across the gap between an inner and an outer wall, which would explain the peculiar phrase "in the wall" (v. 15), i.e., "between the walls."

The story of the spies in ch. 2 seems to reflect a *now lost account of an actual battle,* in which the Israelite forces infiltrated the city by Rahab's window, and the "men of Jericho fought against" the main forces outside the city (24:11). That hint of an actual battle is supported by a variant LXX reading of 2:18. Instead of the Hebrew "when we come into the land," the LXX reads "and if we succeed in penetrating into a part of the town" (J. A. Soggin, *Joshua*, 38). The problem remains that if the "wall fell down flat" (6:20), this would have demolished Rahab's house as well, whereas obviously this did not take place.

CHAPTER 3

CROSSING JORDAN
Joshua 3:1 – 5:1

O my people, remember . . .
what happened from Shittim to Gilgal,
that you may know the saving acts of the LORD. — Micah 6:5

Sacred history may be described as an attempt to see the past in the present tense. — A. J. Heschel, *God in Search of Man,* 211-12.

The record of "what happened from Shittim to Gilgal" found in Joshua 3 – 4 remains one of the key passages in Israelite self-understanding. The 9th-cent. B.C. Narrator probably used liturgical traditions from a spring festival held each year at Gilgal to "remember what happened," and to "see the past in the present tense." We have here the narrative of the last stage in the long march from Goshen to Gilgal.

The journey began in Goshen near Rameses (Exod. 12:37 where the Hebrew verb *nasa'* is translated "journeyed"). It continued from the shore of the Reed Sea where the Hebrews were commanded to "go forward" (Heb. *nasa',* Exod. 14:15). They "set out" again and again (Exod. 16:1; 17:1; 19:2 and eighty-nine times in Numbers). Their journey was thus a constant "going onward" (*nasa',* Exod. 40:36-37). In the book of Joshua, however, this word occurs only three times, once when Joshua and the people "set out" from Shittim (3:1), and twice when they "set out" from the east bank to cross the Jordan (3:3, 14). Crossing the Jordan meant the *arrival* toward which the Exodus *departure* and the wilderness experience of covenant and training had been preparation. More than that, it was the fulfillment of the promise made to the fathers at the very beginning.

CROSSING OVER

The Hebrew word *'abar,* meaning "to cross over," or "to pass over," is used twenty-one times in this passage. Besides empha-

22

sizing the decisive nature of this moment in the history of the Hebrew people, it distinguishes this event from what happened at the Reed Sea. This word is never used to describe the passage through the waters of the sea. Two other words for crossing over are used in Exod. 14:22 and 29; they mean "enter," or "walk." The reason for this is that the verb *'abar* implies crossing over a boundary, whether physical like a river valley (Deut. 2:13-14), political like a nation's border (Deut. 2:18), or moral, as to enter a covenant (Deut. 29:12) or transgress a commandment (Deut. 26:13; Josh. 7:11, 15).

While walking through the waters of the Reed Sea was both an escape and a liberation, crossing over Jordan meant entering a new kind of life in the Promised Land. The physical boundary formed by the deep rift of the Jordan Valley and River had to be crossed. More than that, the crossing marked a decisive transition which involved inheriting (acquiring tenancy rights) and finding "rest" (see above, pp. 5, 12-13).

The land of Canaan was not some kind of earthly paradise, or a transcendent existence in which there would be no problems. It was not the kingdom of God, but rather the place where the meaning and discipline of being God's people must be worked out, with the pain of failure and the joy of success. Thus the common Christian identification of "Canaan" with heaven is not really correct, if we use the OT perspective. Of course, the ultimate goal of this transition is never completely realized. The problems of "life in Canaan" mean a constant postponement of the hope of the final "arrival." In the NT we read of "an inheritance which is imperishable, undefiled, and unfading, kept in heaven for you . . ." (1 Pet. 1:4). With insights from the NT, we can see that the decisive transition ("we have been born anew to a living hope," 1 Pet. 1:3) does not take us out of the "land of Canaan" where God has given us living space, but gives us strength to live the life of discipleship where we are.

THE ARK

The centerpiece of the entire narrative in these two chapters is the ark, mentioned fifteen times. The instructions given (3:2-4, 6, 8, 12-13), the description of the solemn procession and the miracle at the water's edge (3:14-16; 4:10-13, 15-18), the setting up of the stones (4:2-3, 5, 8, 9, 20), and the catechetical questions (4:6-7, 21-23) surely show traces of the actual liturgy at Gilgal, in which the ark must have been central. Rather than try to find out what the ark meant in the original event (probably impossible), it is better to look at its accumulated meaning as the story was told and retold.

Titles of the Ark

The simplest description is "the ark" (3:15; 4:10), which could mean simply a sacred box containing some objects. When the terms "ark of the LORD" (4:11) and "the ark of the LORD your God" (4:5) are used, the reference is to the ark as the portable throne of the invisible God. God was described as "seated on the cherubim" (Pss. 80:1; 99:1). The cherubim were represented as winged lions with human faces and were placed on either side of the ark (Exod. 25:18-19), in the royal style of ancient West Asia. The ark of Yahweh, carried as the people journeyed, symbolized their belief that Yahweh went with them, guiding them to places of rest (Num. 10:33). The ark was thus a symbol of the mysterious and awesome presence of God in their midst as they crossed over into the new land. It was this presence, symbolized by the ark, that made this people unique: "Is it not in thy going with us, so that we are distinct, I and thy people, from all other people that are on the face of the earth?" (Exod. 33:16).

A more frequent expression is "the ark of the covenant" (3:3, 6, 8, 11, 14, 17; 4:7, 9, 18), or, more specifically, "the ark of the testimony" (4:16). It was believed that Yahweh gave commands to his people from the ark (Exod. 25:22). More importantly the tablets on which the Ten Commandments were written (Deut. 10:1-5), or even the whole "book of [Covenant Teaching]" (Deut. 31:24-26), were to be carried in the box. The "book of [Covenant Teaching]" was also called the "book of the covenant" (2 Kgs. 22:8; 23:2). Thus the ark of the covenant symbolized the story and the commands of the covenant which formed the people Israel. This whole covenant relationship and way of life went with them as they crossed over Jordan (see above, pp. 6-7).

The ark of the covenant also contained a jar of manna (Exod. 16:33-34), which was a reminder of the grace of God in the wilderness, and the dependence of the people on this grace for physical and spiritual food.

24

He humbled you and let you hunger and fed you with manna, which you did not know . . . that he might make you know that man does not live by bread alone, but that man lives by everything that proceeds from the mouth of the LORD. (Deut. 8:3)

Finally, the term "the ark of the LORD, the Lord of all the earth" (3:13; cf. v. 11) gives a cosmic dimension to the whole event, already hinted at in Rahab's confession of faith (Josh. 2:11). When the Lord of all the earth (Gen. 19:25; Exod. 19:5; Ps. 24:1) chose a people for himself "out of all the peoples that are on the face of the earth" (Deut. 7:6), it was for his purposes, which are as wide as the earth. This is suggested by the words of Joshua (4:24): "that all the peoples of the earth might know that the hand of the LORD is mighty." This verse is in turn linked to God's purpose in calling Abraham, that "in you all the families of the earth shall be blessed" (see p. xii above).

Following the Ark

The ark, then, was a symbol serving as the religious, ethical, and social center of the people as they went through this dramatic transition. Without that center, the crossing of the Jordan would have been simply a power struggle for control of land. We notice how carefully the meaning of the symbol and the relationship of the people to the reality it represented are dramatized in the liturgy.

Only when the ark itself moves are the people allowed to begin the crossing (3:3). The ark is positioned "before" the people, meaning "in their sight" (3:6). Further, only by "following" the ark of the covenant will they be able to "know the way that they should go" (3:4), i.e., the kind of life they should lead, and the decisions they should make in the new domain they are about to enter. Only by following God's Teaching will they be able to keep from going "after other gods, . . . the gods of the peoples who are round about you" (Deut. 6:14, etc.).

The Holiness of the Ark

The distance to be maintained between the people and the ark (about 1 km. or .6 mi. — a sabbath-day's journey) symbolized the holiness and unapproachability of "the Lord of all the earth."

The LORD of the covenant was not subject to manipulation. This holiness was also expressed by the fact that only authorized people, the priests, could carry the ark. It was the priests who were responsible for "handling," or interpreting, God's Teaching (Jer. 2:8).

The Power in the Ark

The Teacher uses the title "the ark of the LORD, the Lord of all the earth" in connection with the subduing of the waters of the river. The "soles of the feet" of the priests (3:13; 4:18) are described as having power to divide the Jordan waters so that "the waters coming down from above stood and rose up in a heap," and "those flowing down toward the sea of Arabah . . . were wholly cut off" (3:16). The king of Assyria boasted that the soles of his feet dried up the rivers of Egypt (2 Kgs. 19:24). An idiomatic way of speaking about a king's victory was to say that the LORD had put his enemies "under the soles of his feet" (1 Kgs. 5:3). Only when the ark-bearers lifted the soles of their feet out of the dried-up riverbed was the water permitted to flow again. This interpretation is supported by the words of 4:7 where the waters are said to be cut off "before the ark of the covenant of the LORD." This, then, is a rather low-key version of the taming of the waters recorded in Habakkuk 3 and Exodus 15, and is reflected in the poetic words "Jordan . . . turn[ed] back . . . at the presence of the God of Jacob" (Ps. 114:5, 7).

Recollections of the landslide that may have been the physical cause of the damming up of the waters for the original crossing are found in 3:16. Adam is known today as ed-Dâmiyeh, and there are records of the waters being stopped there by landslides in A.D. 1267 and A.D. 1927. Regardless of the means used, however, there was never any question in the minds of the Israelites that this was a miracle wrought by the powerful presence and purpose of the LORD.

This demonstration of Yahweh's power over the waters of the Jordan is presented as a sign that Yahweh would take control of the land from the seven nations mentioned in 3:10. "Hereby [by the subduing of the waters] you shall know that the living God is among you." This sign meant that complete victory had already been won. The Lord of all the earth (3:11) has power over the waters of the river (the unruly powers of nature) as well as over the nations, who are "like the roaring of many waters" (Isa. 17:12-13).

THE NEW PEOPLE

The other major theme of this passage is the reconstitution of Israel in the new land following the failures of the older generation (Num. 14:27-35). The number twelve, used for men or stones "according to the tribes of Israel" (4:5), is found seven times (3:12; 4:2, 3, 4, 8, 9, 20). It is likely that this was a recollection of the Sinai covenant ceremony in which twelve pillars were set up around the altar (Exod. 24:4). There was probably a renewal of the covenant and a new commissioning of the people during the annual festival at Gilgal in ancient times. Elijah was using the same kind of symbolism when he "took twelve stones according to the number of the tribes of the sons of Israel" and built an altar of them on Mt. Carmel (1 Kgs. 18:31-32).

Again, after the Babylonian exile, it was necessary to "raise up the tribes of Jacob" (Isa. 49:6) for their new tasks in the post-Babylonian world. In the NT we find Jesus gathering twelve disciples around him to represent a new people for the new age of the kingdom of God which he came to proclaim (Mark 3:13-14). It was perhaps these memorial stones on the bank of the Jordan that inspired the words of John the Baptist that "God is able *from these stones* to raise up children to Abraham" (Matt. 3:8-9; Luke 3:8; see O. J. F. Seitz, "What Do These Stones Mean?" *JBL* 60 [1960]: 247-54).

The fact that the Narrator preserved the memory of two sets of stones, the one in the riverbed (4:9) where the priests stood, and the other at Gilgal where they first camped (4:20), only served to show the importance of the renewal of all Israel (3:1, 7, 17; 4:11, 14) in the radical transition which was taking place. Later readers may have thought here of Israel as it was to become in the days of David when the twelve-tribe structure was well established. At the time of the first crossing, many who later became a part of Israel, including some of the northern tribes, were not yet incorporated.

The important message of the twelve stones is that every transition, every new task, requires a renewal of the whole, undivided people of God.

THE TWELVE AND THE SEVEN

The present narrative places the instructions of Joshua to "take *twelve* men" (3:12) immediately after the statement that God himself will take the power away from (not drive out; see above, pp. 9-10) the *seven* nations (v. 10). In this way the seven and the twelve are placed in relationship to each other. The twelve symbolize the new covenant society of freedom and justice that was God's intention for the land. The seven symbolize the entire number of the oppressive and corrupt authorities presently ruling the land (see below, pp. 180-86). When the "Lord of all the earth" had taken power away from the seven and given it to the twelve, the people who had been under the oppressive rule of the seven would be free to join the new society of the twelve. In fact, this is what happened in the course of the struggle for the land (see above, pp. xvii, xix, xx-xxi).

JOSHUA AS SPIRITUAL LEADER

In this narrative of the great crossing, Joshua is presented not as a military commander and strategist, but as the spiritual leader of his people. In constant communication with God, he instructs the officers as to what they should say to the people (1:10; 3:2-4), calls on the people to sanctify themselves (3:5) and explains to them the meaning of events about to happen (3:9-13), directs the priests (3:6; 4:17-18) and the twelve men (4:4-5), personally sets up the memorial stones (4:9, 20), and prepares the parents for the task of educating their children in the faith (4:6-7; 21:24). His role as liturgist is different in some ways from that of Moses, who had to act as a "nurse" (Num. 11:12) for undisciplined children (Hos. 11:1-3). The narrators present Joshua as the leader of trained and disciplined adults, "causing them to inherit the land" (1:6). It was this careful spiritual leadership that caused the people to "[stand] in awe of him . . . all the days of his life" (4:14).

DEPARTURE AND ARRIVAL

The Exodus departure and the Jordan arrival are often combined in the Old Testament. The earliest description is found in the "Song of the Sea" (Exod. 15:1-18), which may have been part of the liturgy of the spring festival at Gilgal (F. M. Cross, *Canaanite Myth and Hebrew Epic*, 123). There we read how "Pharaoh's chariots and his host he cast into the sea" (v. 4), how the people of Canaan "melted away" (v. 15; cf. Josh. 5:1), and how God's people "crossed over" into the land of Canaan (v. 16; cf. Josh. 3:17; 4:23).

In Ps. 66:6 the two events are combined very briefly: "He turned the sea into dry land, men passed through the river on foot." The whole of Psalm 114 is devoted to God's victory over the sea and the Jordan. The "song of the arm of the LORD" (Isa. 51:9-11) speaks of the drying up of the sea (cf. Josh. 4:24), and making "a way for the redeemed to pass over" — meaning the path through the Jordan waters — "to Zion."

Because of the limitations of geography, the first crossing could take place only once, while the Jordan crossing might be repeated. We think of Saul, who after the victory at Jabesh-gilead crossed the Jordan to be crowned at Gilgal, as a preparation for the liberation of the land from Philistine oppression (1 Sam. 11:14-15). David also crossed the Jordan to the east in his escape from Absalom's forces (2 Sam. 17:22), and then crossed again to the west after the victory had been won. "So the king came back to the Jordan; and Judah came to Gilgal to meet the king and to bring the king over the Jordan" (2 Sam. 19:15). Elijah crossed the Jordan from Gilead to carry out his ministry, and then crossed to the east to be received up by God. Elisha crossed to the west again in circumstances recalling the crossing under Joshua, to continue his master's ministry (2 Kgs. 2:6-14).

Crossing Jordan is an important motif in the New Testament. Jesus' ministry begins when he is baptized "into" (Gk. *eis*) the waters of the Jordan, marking a decisive "crossing over" to a new task and ministry. When he "came up" out of the waters (Mark 1:10; cf. Josh. 4:19), he heard the voice from heaven ordaining him to his mission: "Thou art my beloved Son; with thee I am well pleased" (Mark 1:11). This recalls the words of God to Joshua, "This day I will begin to exalt you in the sight of all Israel" (Josh. 3:7; 4:14). This in turn calls to mind the words of the Johannine Jesus, "Now is the Son of man glorified. . . . Glorify . . . me in thy own presence. . . . I am glorified in them" (John 13:31; 17:5, 10). The reference here is to Jesus' death and resurrection, which could be described as a "baptism" (Luke 12:50).

29

At the end of his ministry, Jesus was indeed on the east side of the Jordan (Matt. 19:1; John 10:40), and had to cross to the west for the last decisive struggle of his life. In John 11:6, we read that he delayed "two days longer" (cf. Josh. 3:2), before crossing Jordan to reveal God's power to raise Lazarus from death. Thomas' remark, "Let us also go, that we may die with him" (John 11:16), carries with it the suggestion that crossing Jordan is a symbol of the final transition of death (cf. Elijah's crossing referred to above).

This symbolism may have been suggested by the physical nature of the Jordan Valley, which is a deep cleft in the surface of the earth. There are three levels which must be crossed. The upper level, called the Ghor in Arabic, is possible to cultivate and, especially at Jericho, is fertile and green. The middle level is desolate, with gray soil of clay, unfit for habitation or cultivation. The lowest level, called the Zor, is thick jungle (Jer. 12:5). In ancient times wild animals lurked here (Jer. 50:44). The crossing would mean going down from the cultivated land, passing through the desert area, penetrating the jungle, going through the water, then coming up out of the jungle, crossing the desert, and entering the green and fertile area "on the other side."

Crossing Jordan as a symbol of death is found in Christian hymns. The influence of Josh. 3:15-17 is obvious in the following words:

> When I tread the verge of Jordan,
>   bid my anxious fears subside.
> Death of death, and hell's destruction,
>   land me safe on Canaan's side.
>   (William Williams, 1717-1791)

However, it is sounder to see the Jordan crossing as pictured in Joshua 3 – 4 as the last stage in the long march toward full maturity. This maturity begins with liberation, proceeds to covenantal formation and wilderness training, and comes to completion in an entrance to the life of the kingdom. All this, of course, comes about only on the condition that God's people "follow the ark."

CHAPTER 4

COMING OF AGE IN CANAAN
Joshua 5:2-15

. . . that we may present every person mature in Christ.

Colossians 1:28

This chapter describes how, at the full moon of the first month of the year, the wilderness generation became the new Israel, ready for the kingdom struggle.

In every society, each new generation is introduced into the ways of thinking and acting which define that society's view of social, personal, and transcendent reality. The new generation is introduced to this corporate identity by education and ritual. Education extends from birth to the dawn of adulthood. Ritual marks the transition from childhood to adulthood.

In a Theravada Buddhist society like Thailand, each young man is expected to spend at least three months in a monastery. The purpose is to shape him according to the Thai Buddhist ideal of a man. The hair on his head and eyebrows is shaved off to mark his withdrawal into another dimension of life. He discards ordinary clothes to put on the white initiation robe for the ordination ceremony, and then exchanges it for the saffron robe to be worn during his period as a *bikku* (monk). Instead of earning his living like ordinary people, he lives very simply on the contributions of food from the faithful. The goal of his meditation is to "cross the river" to true enlightenment so that he can control his emotions and desires and live with detachment from the corrupting effects of desire and the painful conflicts of life. After this period of inner discipline, he is ready for marriage and the responsibilities of adulthood.

The analogy to the wilderness period and the Jordan crossing in the history of Israel is striking. It was in the wilderness that

Yahweh disciplined his people "as a man disciplines his son" (Deut. 8:5). The Jordan crossing was from one kind of life to another.

THE WILDERNESS GENERATION

In this sequel to the Jordan crossing, we find a focus on the new generation which God "raised up" in place of the former one (Josh. 5:7). They were "born on the way in the wilderness" (v. 5), and we may call them "the wilderness generation." Their parents, "who came out of Egypt" (v. 4), may be called "the Exodus generation," because they knew the "broken spirit and . . . cruel bondage" of slavery (Exod. 6:9), the excited joy of an impossible breakthrough to freedom (Exod. 15:1-2), and the solidarity of covenant bonding (Exod. 24:4-8), none of which their children had experienced. They had also tasted the bitterness of idolatry (Exod. 32), greed (Num. 11:32-34), jealousy (12:1-6), disobedience (14:1-12), and rebellion (ch. 16). That whole generation had "died on the way in the wilderness" (Josh. 5:4), an apparently failed generation.

In their preoccupation with the problems of freedom and survival, they had neglected their children, who "had not been circumcised on the way" (5:7). The parents had not introduced their children to the underlying structures of their own corporate existence. The wilderness generation was in need of education and initiation as God's people. Only in this way could they succeed in establishing the new society in the land of Canaan. This new society would then show the world what it means to live under the rule of "the Lord of all the earth" (3:11).

This kind of "generation gap," which concerned the Teacher who wrote vv. 4-7, must have had some significance for his time. He may have been thinking of the way in which the work of the great reforming king, Hezekiah (2 Kgs. 18:3-7), was completely negated by the long rule of his son Manasseh (2 Kgs. 21:1-16). Hezekiah would be something like the "Exodus generation," while Manasseh would correspond to the sinful side of that generation. In the early years of the reform of Josiah, the "wilderness generation" who had grown up in the time of Manasseh's rule would have to undergo a radical transformation to become the force that would bring renewal and reform to Israel.

Continuing along this same line of thought, we can understand the major part of the book of Deuteronomy as a sermon to both "wilderness generations" — the group who were about to cross over the Jordan in the 13th cent. B.C. *and* those who were about to embark on the momentous reform led by Josiah in the 7th cent. B.C. It was intended for those "who are all of us here alive this day" (Deut. 5:3; 29:10), who face decisions of life or death "this day" (30:15), as well as for those who live in every "wilderness generation."

THE "SECOND" CIRCUMCISION

The first thing that happened after the crossing of the Jordan and the setting up of the twelve memorial stones was the circumcision of "the people of Israel," meaning, of course, the "wilderness generation." Circumcision was the rite by which all males became members of Israel. The ceremony at Gilgal apparently included adult males (Num. 14:29, 33) as well as small boys. The mention in 5:2, as well as in Exod. 4:25, of flint knives shows that circumcision was an ancient custom. Originally, perhaps, it was performed before marriage, but at a later time the act was transferred to childhood.

The mention of "Circumcision Hill" (5:3 TEV) indicates that there must have been an annual ceremony performed on new members of the Israelite tribal league at the spring festival at Gilgal. Circumcision was practiced by the Egyptians and by all of Israel's neighbors in Canaan except the Philistines. For this reason, it is important to try to understand what made Israelite circumcision different from that of their neighbors.

The First Circumcision

A careful reading of Exodus 12 gives no evidence of a "first" circumcision in Egypt. By mentioning the "second time," the Teacher was probably thinking of the "first time" as the circumcision of Abraham and all the men of his household, recorded in the priestly tradition of Genesis 17. The distinctiveness of the Hebrew rite is evident. It was "a sign" of God's "everlasting covenant" (vv. 11, 13). The Teacher wanted to emphasize the importance of this ceremony in Canaan as a new beginning similar to that made by Abraham. By this rite, the "wilderness gen-

33

eration" would become the new Israel, descendants of Abraham, the first generation in the Promised Land.

Restored to Life

We find two reflections on the meaning of circumcision in the Joshua story. The first is implied in the words, "till they were healed" (v. 8). The Hebrew original has a double sense: (1) *healed from the wounds* of the operation, as in the case of Hezekiah who was healed from illness (2 Kgs. 20:7; see Gen. 34:25 for the recovery period necessary after circumcision); (2) *restored to life,* as in the case of those fallen in the wilderness who looked on the bronze serpent and lived (Num. 21:8-9). The same verb is used in Deut. 30:6 to describe the purpose of circumcision, "that you may *live*" (Deut. 30:6). Here, then, circumcision is presented as a wounding and recovery, almost like a death and resurrection, with obvious connections with the NT description of baptism (Rom. 6:3-5; Col. 2:11-13). The words of Hosea are appropriate:

> Come, let us return to the LORD;
> for he has torn, that he may *heal* us. . . .
> After two days he will *revive* us;
> on the third day he will *raise us up*
> that we may *live before him*. (Hos. 6:1-2; cf. Deut. 32:39)

The End of "Reproach"

The second reflection is: with the circumcision in Canaan, God removed "the reproach of Egypt" (v. 9). The "reproach of Egypt" was probably the humiliation of slavery in Egypt that made them subject to insult and disgrace from all the nations (Zeph. 2:8-9). It was this humiliation that came to an end when they became a free people in the land of Canaan. The words of Lev. 26:13 come to mind: "I have broken the bar of your yoke and made you walk erect." Circumcision meant freedom and dignity instead of servitude.

In later generations, the word "reproach" could refer to the shame and disgrace resulting from dependence on false support, like that of Egypt (Isa. 30:5), or the defeat of 597 B.C. or 587 B.C. (Jer. 24:9). Thus, the words "remove the reproach" could have a future reference to coming deliverance during the years of exile or defeat: "I will not let you hear any more of the reproach of the nations, and you shall no longer bear the disgrace of the peoples" (Ezek. 36:15). Deutero-Isaiah also looked forward to the time when it would be said of Israel: "The reproach of your widowhood you will remember no more" (Isa. 54:4). The result is a paradox. If Israel's "uncircumcised heart is humbled" (Lev. 26:41), they can stand erect without fearing insult or disgrace (cf. Isa. 50:4-5, 7-9).

The Circumcised Heart

In the later years of the Jerusalem monarchy, about the time of the Teacher, there was growing attention to the inner meaning of circumcision. The physical operation on the flesh was seen as an analogy to a spiritual cutting away which opens the heart to allow a person or a people to love and obey God. Jeremiah pointed to Israel's neighbors who practiced circumcision as examples of the possibility of being "circumcised, but yet uncircumcised." He then declared that "all the house of Israel" were "uncircumcised *in heart*" (Jer. 9:25-26). For this reason, he pleaded with his people: "Circumcise yourselves to the LORD, remove the foreskin of *your hearts*" (4:4). Only this spiritual cutting away would permit a return to God and a restoration of the integrity of personal and social life (4:1-2). Possibly applying words of Isaiah (Isa. 6:9-10), Jeremiah also spoke of *uncircumcised ears* that made it impossible to hear, and even led the people to scorn God's word (Jer. 6:10).

Deuteronomy, like Jeremiah, called on the wilderness generation to "circumcise . . . the foreskin of your heart, and be no longer stubborn" (Deut. 10:16), so that they could fear, love, and serve God and walk in his ways (10:12-13). Yet he saw that the problem of rebelliousness was so severe (31:27) that God himself would have to do the cutting away. Only in this way could Israel's heart be opened to God, so that they might live and not die (30:6). Without this inner transformation of the individual Israelite, the presence of the ark of the covenant in their midst would not be effective (see above, pp. 24-26).

Paul's Views

It is of interest to see how Paul carried the thought of Jeremiah and the Teacher further. He reminded his readers that circumcision becomes "uncircumcision" through disobedience (Rom. 2:25; cf. Jer. 9:25-26). Real circumcision, he said, was "a matter of the heart, spiritual and not literal" (Rom. 2:29; cf. Jer. 4:4; Deut. 10:12-13). He recognized that the people of God included both circumcised and uncircumcised, i.e., both Jews and Gentiles (Gal. 2:7). He held, however, that physical circumcision was not the true distinguishing mark of the covenant people. It was rather the heart opened to God (faith) and to other people (love, Gal. 5:6). Those who bore this mark were the new creation, or the new people of God (Gal. 6:15). This interpretation of the inner meaning of circumcision could apply of course to females as well as males (Gal. 3:28).

True circumcision, we read in Colossians, is not a physical operation "made with hands," but a supernatural operation to remove the rebellious nature ("the body of flesh") that separates us from God. This very painful operation can be described as being "crucified with Christ" (Rom. 6:6; Gal. 2:20; 6:14), but the result is that those who die with Christ are raised and made alive with him (Col. 2:11-13). The true sign of membership in the covenant people is the "crucified mind" (see K. Koyama, *No Handle on the Cross: An Asian Meditation on the Crucified Mind*).

THE FIRST PASSOVER IN CANAAN: MEMORY AND HOPE

The "chosen time" for the renewal of Israel in Canaan was not an isolated moment, but was related to other "times" in the past and the future. According to the tradition recorded by the priestly writers in Exodus 12, the sacrificial lamb was selected on the tenth day of the first month and the Passover meal was held on the evening of the fourteenth day. It may be that the Teacher had this in mind when he noted that the Israelites came out of the river on the tenth day of the month (Josh. 4:19), and celebrated the Passover on the fourteenth. Perhaps, at the annual festival, the crossing, the selection of the lamb, and circumcision all took place on the tenth day. The first Passover in Canaan was a "memorial" (Exod. 12:14) of the night "forty years" earlier when God began to deliver the slaves (v. 29). It was also a momentous new beginning which opened up the future.

Six Passovers

We find six great Passover festivals in the OT, each of which marks a turning point between past and future.

The *first* Passover meant the end of slavery and the beginning of the long march from Goshen to Gilgal (Exod. 12:27-29). The *second*, exactly a year later, was held at the end of the sojourn in Sinai when the covenant bond had been completed by the giving of the Covenant Teaching, and when the next stage of the wilderness journey from Sinai to Kadesh-barnea and the plains of Moab was about to begin (Num. 9:5). The *third* was in Canaan at the end of the wilderness journey and the beginning of the process of inheriting the land (Josh. 5:10). For the first three hundred years of the monarchy, there is no record of any official celebrations of the Passover. This adds emphasis to the *fourth*, reported by the Chronicler, the feast held by King Hezekiah marking the end of a period of disobedience and the beginning of his reform movement (2 Chr. 30). The *fifth* was held in 622 B.C. by King Josiah as a continuation of Hezekiah's reform, following the dark age of King Manasseh. It was the beginning of a national revival at a time of international crisis brought about by the collapse of the Assyrian empire (2 Kgs. 23:21-23). The *sixth* was in 515 B.C. when Zerubbabel and Joshua the high priest were in Jerusalem, and it marked the completion of the second temple. This took place in a time of international crisis brought about by the Babylonian revolt against Persia (Ezra 6:19-20). As we know from the books of Haggai and Zechariah, the completion of the temple was expected to mark not only the end of the Exile, but the beginning of the messianic age.

Jesus' Passover

Jesus' Passover meal with his disciples looked back across all of the previous passovers of the OT, in Goshen, Sinai, Gilgal, and Jerusalem, and pointed to the fulfillment of them all in the kingdom of God (Luke 22:15-16). The Passover in Gilgal would have been especially important to him because of its relationship to the kingdom of God which was "at hand" (Mark 1:5). Perhaps the tradition of the messianic banquet found in Isa. 25:6-8; 55:1-2; Luke 14:12-24; and Rev. 19:9 is an application of the Passover tradition.

It seems likely that the readers of the Joshua story, whether at the time of Josiah's reform, during the Babylonian exile, at the time of the rebuilding of the temple, or in Jesus' time, would see in this feast at Gilgal the same sacred meal which bound them to the past and turned them in hope toward the future.

UNLEAVENED BREAD AND THE FRUIT OF THE LAND

In accordance with what became a fixed tradition, Josh. 5:11 tells of the celebration of the Feast of Unleavened Bread (*matsoth*) the next day, after the Passover.

That Very Day

The words "on that very day" (Josh. 5:11; cf. Exod. 12:17) link this feast with the actual beginning of the journey out of Egypt, which is also said to have happened on the 15th of the first month (Exod. 12:51; Num. 33:3). It was a memory of the haste of their departure (Exod. 12:39) and the bitterness of their oppression (Deut. 16:3).

"That very day," however, carried other connotations. In the agricultural cycle of the land of Canaan, it was "the time you first put the sickle to the standing grain" (Deut. 16:9), i.e., the beginning of the barley harvest. It is quite probable that this was a Canaanite festival which was adopted by the Israelites in Canaan. They gave it an additional meaning by associating it with the Exodus tradition, which was specifically Israelite. Their "coming of age" was marked, then, not only by their renewed covenant with Yahweh, symbolized by circumcision, and their appropriation of past memories and future hopes as found in the Passover, but by their eating of the fruit of the land, and their new responsibility: the care of the land.

The End of Manna

The new period in their history was marked by the end of the manna, also on "that very day." The jar of manna carried in the ark (see p. 24), however, was a reminder of God's provision of food in the wilderness, and a warning against mismanagement of food on the land. "He that gathered much had nothing over, and he that gathered little had no lack; each gathered according to what he could eat" (Exod. 16:18). No acquisitiveness or selfish accumulation was possible, because whatever was gathered in excess of need "bred worms and became foul" (v. 20).

Food Management on the Land

Management on the land would involve dealing with the problems of removing a neighbor's landmark to get his land (Deut. 27:17), coveting fields and seizing houses (Mic. 2:2), as well as acquiring field after field from the poor (Isa. 5:8). Eating the fruit of the land immediately raised the matter of justice. The manna tradition of food management was a mark of the new society that attracted many of the Canaanite lower classes who were suffering from the greediness of the royal and noble segments of Canaanite society (W. Brueggemann, *The Land*, 46-51).

A Welcome in Canaan?

The liturgical tradition from which the narrator of the Joshua story took his material was not interested in the question of how the group under Joshua got the parched grain and the unleavened cakes. For those who are interested there are three possibilities: (1) They brought it with them from Shittim in Moab as "provisions" (see Josh. 1:11; see also above, pp. 8-9). Probably the Teacher who wrote the note about the manna in 5:12 did not consider this possibility. (2) They took the ripe grain from the fields in the plains of Jericho, ground it up to make cakes, and roasted the fresh ears themselves. (3) Friendly Canaanites like Rahab's "father's house" (Josh. 2:13; 6:25) were expecting them, and had prepared provisions like those brought by David to his brothers (1 Sam. 17:17), or by Abigail or Barzillai to David (1 Sam. 25:18; 2 Sam. 17:28). A variation of this third possibility is that the farmers around Gilgal were celebrating their firstfruits-of-the-harvest festival and invited the newly arrived groups of friendly liberators to take part with them.

JOSHUA'S TEST (5:13-15)

The three brief episodes described thus far in this chapter have all dealt with the preparation of the "wilderness generation" for their new responsibilities on the land. They reflect the procedures of an annual festival at Gilgal in the days of the judges to commemorate the original events of the Exodus and the entry into the Promised Land. In the final episode there is no mention of the people, who had presumably gone to their tents after the feast.

The Mysterious Stranger

We see Joshua alone at evening, like Jacob on the banks of the Jabbok River (Gen. 32:22). The sun was setting over the highlands of Canaan, to which the people must go. Meanwhile the moon was rising over the hills of Moab, from which they had come a few days earlier.

As the only survivor of the "Exodus generation" (Num. 14:30) and the successor to Moses, Joshua faced the task of causing this "new" people to inherit the land. Suddenly he encounters a mysterious stranger with a drawn sword in hand.

This episode is linked with the tradition about "the angel of the LORD" who would lead the people through the wilderness to "the place" prepared by God (Exod. 23:20; 32:34; cf. Josh. 5:15), and defeat their enemies (Exod. 23:23; 33:2; cf. Josh. 6:2). Since the Teacher uses other ways of saying that God was with his people (Josh. 1:9), or among them (3:10), and since he does not again mention any angelic figure, we must ask why this particular tradition was included.

The Anxious Question

The theological reason for its inclusion is found in the brief conversation between Joshua and the divine warrior. Joshua's question expresses the anxiety of Israel about her relationship to her God. "Are you for us, or for our adversaries?" (5:13). Another translation is possible: "To which side do you belong — ours or our enemy's?" Israel wanted and expected full support from her covenant God.

The simple answer to this question from God's angel is "No!" It is a warning against a misinterpretation of the words "with you" and "among you." There can be no relief from the anxiety out of which the question comes, because the covenant LORD is free, not subject to attempts "to get him on our side," to make him a kind of "idol" that would always do our will (cf. Isa. 48:5). The covenant LORD is free to become an adversary (Hos. 13:8; Lam. 2:5) or to allow Israel's adversaries to do their work (Isa. 10:5-6). This "no" is especially important in time of war, which arouses emotions of hatred, fear, revenge, and the demand that whatever is done must be blessed by God.

On the eve of the struggle for the land, this incident reminds

Joshua and later generations that the struggles in which they are engaged must be subordinated to God's greater purpose for the whole earth. Joshua's reply, "What does my lord bid his servant?", reminds us of Jesus' prayer before his final confrontation with the power of evil: "Not what I will, but what thou wilt" (Mark 14:36).

Once Again, God's "Now"

The time-freighted word "now" has already been used as God's designation of the right moment for action by Joshua and Israel at Shittim (1:2; see above, p. 4), and on the bank of the Jordan (3:12). Here (5:14) it refers to the time of God's own coming to guide and direct his people in the perilous and testing days ahead. The words "I have *now* come" remind us of the coming of God to save his people in Egypt (Exod. 3:8-10). They also make us think of God's question: "Why, when I came, was there no man? When I called, was there no one to answer?" (Isa. 50:2). The words in Josh. 5:14 also point to the advent of the LORD at the fulfillment of history. "Behold, the Lord GOD comes with might, and his arm rules for him . . ." (Isa. 40:10).

A Holy Place for the LORD in Canaan

The final word spoken by the angel recalls Moses at the mountain of God (Exod. 3:5). The force of the command here, however, is not simply to identify Joshua with Moses. It is to transform what may have been a Canaanite holy place into a Yahweh shrine in the Promised Land.

Gilgal may have been a Canaanite shrine before the arrival of the Joshua group in Canaan. The "sculptured stones" (the Hebrew word can also be translated as "idols") mentioned in Judg. 3:19, 26 may be evidence of this. The process by which it became a Yahweh shrine does not interest the narrator of the Joshua story. It is quite clear that it did become such, however. A "house of the LORD" is referred to in Josh. 6:24 (but in the LXX). If this refers to a sanctuary of Joshua's time, it must have been at Gilgal (Soggin, *Joshua*, 88). The victory poem of Moses and Miriam makes mention of "the place" or "sanctuary" which Yahweh made for his abode (Exod. 15:17). Although this was later interpreted as Jerusalem, its meaning in the 13th cent. B.C. was doubtless Gilgal (Cross, *Canaanite Myth and Hebrew Epic*, 182).

41

Saul was crowned king, offered sacrifice, and quarreled with Samuel there (1 Sam. 11:14-15; 13:8-12; 15:12-35). In the days of Amos and Hosea, the Gilgal shrine had become a place of apostasy where false oaths were taken (Hos. 4:15), and empty sacrifices were made by insincere Israelites (Amos. 4:4; Hos. 12:11). Yahweh had in fact abandoned it, even though the people thought they were seeking him there (Amos 5:5). Amos said that Gilgal, where the first Passover on the land of Canaan had been held, would be the first to go into exile (Amos 5:5). Apart from the historical reflection in Mic. 6:5, there is no later mention of Gilgal in the Old Testament.

The history of the Gilgal sanctuary would lead us to believe that the emphasis of the Teacher was not on that particular place, but rather on what happened there: Israel's military leader bowed down before the covenant LORD and accepted the divine guidance. The message was for other leaders, too, like King Josiah. Jesus himself went through a similar struggle after he came up out of the waters of the Jordan (Mark 1:12).

PART II

DETHRONING THE POWERS IN THE LAND

Joshua 6– 12

CHAPTER 5

VICTORY AT JERICHO
Joshua 6:1-27

*The weapons of our warfare are not worldly but have divine power
to destroy strongholds.* —2 Corinthians 10:4

*The kingdom of God bursts history open, sets it in motion . . . toward
the liberation of men in all the many stratifications in which they are
endangered or enslaved.* —J. M. Lochman, "The Kingdom of God,"
Reformed World 36(1980): 10, 103

"THE BATTLE OF JERICHO"

"The battle of Jericho" is a well-known and often told story which
not only entertains, but questions and challenges the attentive
reader. One NT writer found in it two examples of faith (Heb.
11:30-31). A chronicler of the Maccabean wars reported that the
Jericho story inspired Judas to attack an impregnable fortress
with inferior forces and slaughter the inhabitants (2 Macc.
12:15-16). Rabbis of other years discussed the problem of whether
the seventh day in the story was a sabbath, and if so, whether
Joshua violated the sabbath commandment, or again, whether
the sparing of Rahab was justified in view of the Deuteronomic
command to destroy the seven nations of Canaan. For one early
Christian writer, the action of Joshua on the seventh (sabbath)
day amounted to the abrogation of the Mosaic law (L. Ginzberg,
The Legends of the Jews 6:174).

Modern readers come with questions too. Some of these are
historical: Did the walls really collapse as reported? If so, would
not Rahab's house have been destroyed? Was there any battle at
all?

Other more serious questions are ethical and religious. Did
God really command, and did Joshua carry out, the slaughter of
all the inhabitants of Jericho, including old people, boys and girls,

45

little babies, and their mothers? Does this story not encourage fanaticism that knows no other solution to human problems than to exterminate the enemy, as the forces under Hitler actually did to the Jews in Europe in the 1930s and 1940s? Does it not give us a wrong model of triumphalism for the work of God's kingdom today?

HISTORY REMEMBERED THROUGH LITURGY

It is obvious that we cannot look at Joshua 6 as a simple factual account of things as they actually happened in the late 13th or early 12th cent. B.C. What we find is rather history remembered through liturgy. The narrative as we have it reflects the annual Gilgal festival, in which a ceremonial procession of people taking the part of warriors, priests, ark-bearers, and rear guard circled the ruins of ancient Jericho over a period of seven days, climaxing in the ritualized destruction of "the city." The ritual served to recall and actualize the original event and its meaning. The narrative depends on the liturgical tradition for its description of events, and thus preserves the meaning well, but leaves us wondering about the original events themselves.

Clues

There are some clues. We find in Josh. 24:11 the suggestion of an armed clash between Jericho's "mighty men of valor" (6:2) and Joshua's "men of war" or "armed men" (vv. 3, 7, 9, 13). Again the scarlet cord hanging from Rahab's window (2:18) seems to hint at a secret mode of access by infiltrators into Jericho. The repeated processions around the walls may preserve the memory of an actual military strategy to deceive and confuse the enemy as well as to reduce the level of vigilance in preparation for a frontal attack. Such a strategy is known to have been used in the ancient world.

Archeology

Archeology gives us only a negative contribution. The ruin-mound (known today as Tell es-Sulṭân) which stands beside the copiously flowing spring that waters the plains of Jericho was undoubtedly standing in the late 13th cent. B.C., more or less as it now appears. It is about 2 km. (1.2 mi.) from Khirbet Mefjer, the probable site of ancient Gilgal. The strong walls of mud brick which were found by the archeologists, however, cannot be later than 1500 B.C. In the 14th cent. B.C. an unfortified village was located on the mound, but beginning with the last quarter of the 13th cent. B.C. it was unoccupied. We cannot tell whether the battle, remembered in the liturgy, involved a temporary fort for guarding the water source, or another site in the region of Jericho. Our historical questions must remain unanswered, at least until more evidence is found. Fortunately, these questions are not the major key to an understanding of this narrative.

The liturgical background of this chapter encourages us to search for symbolic meanings that open up the theological message in the wider context of other parts of the Bible.

THE DOOMED CITY

Jericho, meaning "moon city" (as Beth-shemesh, Josh. 15:10, means "sun city"), is mentioned by name only three times in this chapter. In v. 1 it is described as tightly closed up, afraid of God's new people in the land. In v. 2 Joshua is told that Yahweh has given Jericho, with its king and military aristocracy, into his hand. Finally, in v. 26 the city is condemned to remain an uninhabited waste. Jericho is a doomed city.

Outside these verses, the reference is always to "the city" or "this city" (fifteen times). Elsewhere in the Joshua story, we find that Jericho's fate strikes fear into other kings and cities (9:3; 10:1), and is a pattern to be followed in the treatment of other cities (10:28, 30). Its name heads the list of the conquered cities in Canaan (12:9-24). Thus Jericho appears as "the city," representative of the other cities in Canaan.

Other Doomed Cities

If we look for antecedents of this doomed city, we may identify Cain's city (Gen. 4:17), Nimrod's city (10:9-11), Babel (11:4), and the destroyed city of Sodom (19:4-29). Doomed cities in subsequent references are Nineveh, "the bloody city, all full of lies and booty" (Nah. 3:1), the mighty, renowned Tyre which was laid waste and uninhabited (Ezek. 26:17, 19), and Babylon, "the hammer of the whole earth . . . become a horror among the nations" (Jer. 50:23), never to be inhabited (Isa. 13:19-20; cf.

47

47:10-11). These themes are taken up and used in the NT description of "the great city, the mighty city, Babylon," a code
name for Rome (Rev. 18:10).

Jerusalem

Jerusalem itself is presented as a doomed city by Jeremiah. He
says that it is given by Yahweh into the hand of Babylon (Jer.
32:3; 38:3; cf. Josh. 6:2) with all its wealth (Jer. 20:5; cf. Josh.
6:19), to be burned with fire (Jer. 32:29; 34:2; 37:8; cf. Josh.
6:24), "a desolation, a waste, a hissing, and a curse" (Jer. 25:18;
cf. Josh. 6:26) for all the nations of the earth (Jer. 26:6), to remain
with no inhabitants (Jer. 44:22). We might call this theme "Je-
rusalem-become-Jericho." Jeremiah also saw the reverse of this
theme, a New Jerusalem to be for God "a name of joy, a praise
and a glory before all the nations of the earth" (Jer. 33:9; cf. Rev.
21:10).

   Jericho as the doomed city is a paradigm of a society which
can no longer survive as it is.

THE KING AND HIS MIGHTY MEN OF VALOR

If the liturgical drama were to be performed in Asian lands today,
the king of Jericho and his military aristocracy would wear masks
or special costumes to show their stylized role. They would represent the old oppressive, stratified, feudal society of the Canaanite city-states. Significantly, there is no mention in the story
of the Canaanite gods of Jericho. The gods were in fact part of
the system symbolized by the king, not above it. The ruling elite
were responsible for the "abominable practices" of the Canaanite
feudal society that were doomed to be destroyed (see above,
p. xix).

The Strong Man

When Jesus spoke of "the strong man guarding his palace," a
model close at hand would have been Jericho of OT history. The
king of Jericho then becomes a mirror image of Satan, challenged
by the NT "Joshua" as "one stronger than he," who "assails him
and overcomes him, takes away his armor in which he trusted,
and divides the spoil" (Luke 11:21-22). Also, we may see the king
and the military aristocracy of feudal Jericho as symbols of the

48

historical powers of evil entrenched in social systems, oppressive structures, and destructive relationships.

THE WALLS OF JERICHO

City walls "up to heaven" (Deut. 1:28; cf. 3:5; Num. 13:28) are symbols not only of impregnability, but of collective pride against which God's judgment must come (Deut. 28:52). The collapsed walls of Jericho anticipate the day of judgment "against every fortified wall" (Isa. 2:15), the "high wall, bulging out, about to collapse" because of the iniquity of Judah (30:13), or "the high fortifications of his walls [which] he will bring down, lay low, and cast to the ground, even to the dust" (25:12). Ezekiel seems to have used the fallen walls of Jericho as a paradigm for all the cities of the world in the final struggle, when "every wall shall tumble to the ground" (Ezek. 38:20).

The author of Hebrews used the story of Jericho to illustrate the power of faith (11:30). In our day we may see in the walls of Jericho the political, military, and economic defenses which give an illusion of security to the rich and powerful, but which must fall down in the day of God's coming.

THE KINGDOM PEOPLE

God's alternative to the doomed city is "the people of Israel" and their new society (v. 1). The procession that performs the ritual encirclement of the city is made up as follows:

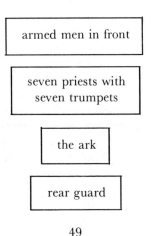

armed men in front

seven priests with
seven trumpets

the ark

rear guard

The narrative makes clear that the military men form a guard of honor for the priests with their trumpets. Although v. 15 gives the impression that the ark alone was carried around the city, the priests and their trumpets are by far the most prominent part of the story as it now exists.

THE RAMS' HORN TRUMPETS

From a study of other texts about the use of rams' horns in the OT, we can select two meanings that this story illustrates.

Warning

First, the trumpets sound a warning to those in Jericho and in the whole land of Canaan that God is about to act.

> Is a trumpet blown in a city,
>   and the people are not afraid?
> Does evil befall a city,
>   unless the LORD has done it? (Amos 3:6)
>
> All you inhabitants of the world. . . .
>   When a trumpet is blown, hear! (Isa. 18:3)

The trumpets announce the coming of "the Lord of all the earth" (Josh. 3:11) against the doomed city. The blast on the ram's horn (6:5) is presented by the Teacher as an echo of the same "long blast" which preceded the theophany of Yahweh on Sinai (Exod. 19:13). It is only in these two passages that this phrase occurs. He was saying that the same covenant God was about to fulfill his promise to his people at this solemn moment.

Herald

The trumpets also herald the new age of God's kingdom. The victory at Jericho is set in the first month of the year, when the trumpets sounded to announce the joyful celebration of the New Year (Num. 10:10). Even today, the central feature of the Jewish Rosh Hashanah (New Year) services is the sound of the ram's horn trumpet. The seven days and seven trumpets also recall the "seven times seven years" (Lev. 25:8) marking the jubilee year, when the trumpets would sound throughout the land to "proclaim liberty" (v. 10) and restoration of rights to the poor, the slave, and the landless (vv. 13-55).

The Trumpets of Jericho

The trumpets of Jericho have taken on symbolic meanings in later writings. A prophet's message is compared to a trumpet that warns the people to repent of their oppression, let the oppressed go free, feed the hungry, and clothe the naked (Isa. 58:1, 3, 6-7). The Chronicler seems to have used Joshua 6 as a model for his description of a battle between Judah and Israel.

> "Behold, God is with us at our head, and his priests with their battle trumpets to sound the call to battle. . . ." And they cried to the LORD, and the priests blew the trumpets. . . . And when the men of Judah shouted, God defeated Jeroboam. . . . [and] gave them into their hand. (2 Chr. 13:12, 14-16)

The trumpet marking the coming of the Lord and the resurrection of the dead (1 Thess. 4:16; 1 Cor. 15:52) sounds like the seventh trumpet of Jericho.

The author of the book of Revelation uses the seven trumpets to describe the events of the last days. The first six trumpet blasts are followed by disaster after disaster (Rev. 8:7, 8, 10, 12; 9:1, 13). Finally, when the seventh trumpet sounds, "The kingdom of the world [becomes] the kingdom of our Lord and of his Christ, and he shall reign for ever and ever" (11:15).

THE WAITING SILENCE AND THE VICTORY CRY

The guard of honor preceding and following the trumpeters and the ark have a ceremonial rather than a military function. Their only duty is to keep silent until the blast of the seventh trumpet on the seventh day (v. 10): "You shall not shout or let your voice be heard, neither shall any word go out of your mouth, until the day I bid you shout." At the final moment, they are to raise "a great shout" (vv. 5, 20). With the last trumpet and the great shout, the walls fall down and they all "go up" to Jericho.

The Victory Cry

The great shout may originally have been a battle cry as in the case of Gideon's band, who also blew trumpets (Judg. 7:18-21). In its present liturgical setting, however, where there is no battle, it is more like the ceremonial shout in the procession of the ark, as when it was carried up to Jerusalem (2 Sam. 6:15). Understood in this way, the shout seems to be a cry of victory at the coming of the LORD. We find a similar cry in Psalm 47, celebrating God's victory over the peoples and his "going up" to reign (Ps. 47:3, 5).

Suffering Silence

Joshua's command of silence until the final moment of victory seems to have been developed by Deutero-Isaiah into a waiting, suffering silence. He describes the servant of the LORD as one who would not "let his voice be heard" (using the same Hebrew words as those occurring in Josh. 6:10), or cry out (Isa. 42:2), or "open his mouth" (53:7). When the right time comes, then God himself will "shout aloud" (42:13) like a warrior, and the victory cry will come from "the depths of the earth" (44:23) — perhaps symbolizing the places of the poor, oppressed people who will be redeemed.

Messianic Joy

Other writers speak of a cry of joy at the coming of the messianic king (Zeph. 3:14; Zech. 9:9), and some look forward to the time when all the peoples of the earth will join in the victory cry (Pss. 66:1; 98:4, 6; 100:1).

THE SOLEMN BAN

Just before the seventh trumpet blast on the seventh day, Joshua pronounces the solemn ban on the city of Jericho "and all that is within it" (v. 17). This is followed by the "utter destruction" of all people and animals (v. 21). Here lies the major ethical problem of this chapter, and the entire book of Joshua. We should try to understand the meaning behind it.

Herem

The Hebrew word *herem* applies to something separated or banned from ordinary use by a ritual act. A field (Lev. 27:21), the first-fruits (Num. 18:14), or any other object could be dedicated to the LORD as *herem*. Such things were set aside for the use of the priests (Lev. 27:28; Ezek. 44:29).

Objects or people which threatened to "pollute" the faith and practices of Israel were declared *herem*, i.e., banned from ordinary use or contact. Anyone who took a banned thing into his house would be polluted or infected by it, and therefore subject to the same ban (Deut. 7:26, where the RSV translates *herem* as "accursed thing" and the polluted person as "cursed").

A city which has turned away from Yahweh (Deut. 13:12-14) becomes *herem*, and must be *"heremized,"* i.e., "utterly destroyed." This would include its inhabitants, cult objects, cattle, and all spoil, as a "whole burnt offering to the LORD" (v. 16). It would never be rebuilt, but would remain a ruin-mound forever (v. 16).

The idea and practice of *herem* as found in Deuteronomy and Joshua may well contain a recollection of methods of warfare in a period before the monarchy, but it is not certain whether all details found, e.g., in Deuteronomy 20 were actually in use in this period.

Theology

The Teacher was more interested in the theological meaning of *herem* than in its actual practice. After all, in his time there were no more Canaanites as such, for they had been assimilated into Israelite society. For him, the solemn ban pronounced on Jericho and other Canaanite cities symbolized what he thought should be a radical break or discontinuity between the old Canaanite and Assyrian ways and the new covenant society of Israel. The seven nations (Deut. 7:2) must be destroyed because "they would turn your sons away from following me" (Deut. 7:4), and "teach you to do according to their abominable practices which they have done in the service of their gods, and so to sin against the LORD your God" (Deut. 20:18).

The theological rigor of the Teacher is seen in the number of cities where Joshua is said to have applied the *herem*-destruction: Jericho, Ai (Josh. 8:26), Makkedah, Eglon, Hebron, Debir (10:28, 35, 37, 39), Hazor and the cities of the northern confederacy (11:11-12), the Anakim and their cities (11:21), in fact the whole land (10:40; 11:20).

Radical Discontinuity

The principle of radical discontinuity must be seen not in the simple terms of a theoretical syncretism or ethnocentric intolerance, but rather as a difference in belief and practice. The "abominable practices of the nations" did in fact "pollute" Israelite society, as we know from the judicial murder of Naboth that enabled the king to seize his land (1 Kgs. 21); child sacrifice by the kings of Judah (2 Kgs. 16:3; 21:6); perversion of sexual relations in the name of religion (2 Kgs. 23:7); the use of magic and necromancy (2 Kgs. 21:6); the murder of prophets of Yahweh (Jer. 26:20-23); and grave injustice to the poor (Amos 2:6-7; Mic. 3:1-3). In the 7th cent. B.C., the practice of *herem* would mean a thorough cleansing of the whole nation of these "abominable practices," best described in 2 Kgs. 23:4-20.

When we read of the "utter destruction" of Jericho, the cities of Canaan, and the entire land, we should keep in mind the purpose of the Teacher *in his time,* and not take these verses in Joshua as a report from a war correspondent. No doubt there was bloodshed and violence. We know, however, from a study of the history of the time that there was no mass "genocide" committed by the Israelites (see Judg. 3:5; Gottwald , *Tribes of Yahweh,* 555-83).

A SAVED REMNANT

The climax of the story of the victory at Jericho is not the destruction of the doomed city, but the salvation of the entire extended family of Rahab from the flames. They are at first placed "outside the camp" at Gilgal (v. 23). Later, when fully instructed in the ways of the new society, they are accepted as full members of Israel (v. 25). For this saved Canaanite remnant the trumpet blast heralded the day of salvation.

OUR BATTLES

As we look for the message of this part of the Joshua story for our own time, we should think along these lines: (1) The battle is not ours, but God's; we must subject our wills and our methods to him (Josh. 5:13-15; see above, pp. 40-41). (2) We must try to discern the social, political, and religious points at which radical discontinuity is called for, i.e., at what points we must separate ourselves from the "abominable practices" of the society around us. (3) God's purpose in calling his people and giving them living space is that all families of the earth should be blessed (Gen.

12:3). This stands behind and above all conflicts and struggles in which we may be engaged.

The story of God's victory at Jericho warns us against fatalism and fanaticism. Fatalism, which gives up hope because of "high walls" and powerful structures, is ruled out because it is God himself who brings down the walls and shows up the weakness of structures based on "abominable practices." Fanaticism which seeks a quick and final solution on one's own terms is to be rejected because the timing is God's. We may have to wait and suffer in quiet action with appropriate "weapons of our warfare," or proclaim God's coming to judge and save.

At times we may raise a victory shout when the echo of the "long blast" sounds again in our time to "burst history open," in anticipation of the day when the kingdom of the world shall become the kingdom of our Lord.

CHAPTER 6

TROUBLE VALLEY
Joshua 7:1-26

An individual's misdeed can be the beginning of a nation's disaster. The sun goes down, but the deed goes on. . . . Even a single deed generating an endless set of effects . . . may place the lives of countless men in the chains of its unpredictable effects. . . .
— A. J. Heschel, *God in Search of Man,* 284

I will . . . make the Valley of Achor a door of hope. —Hosea 2:15

LESSONS IN STONE

This section of the Joshua story (chs. 7 – 8) tells of four stone monuments in the Promised Land. The pile of stones in the Valley of Achor (Trouble Valley), which marks the conclusion of ch. 7, is a reminder of the inner struggle in the heart of Israel against temptation and corruption. The pile of stones at the ruin-mound of Ai, referred to in 8:29, tells of a victory over outside forces. The stone altar of vv. 30-31 symbolizes reconciliation between God and the people, while the monumental stones (v. 32) bearing the Covenant Teaching emphasize the primary importance of righteousness in the land.

THE FALL IN THE PROMISED LAND

Achan's story may well have been handed down as a part of the Gilgal shrine tradition. Pilgrims would go on an annual ritual journey from Gilgal south across the Wadi Mukallik to a valley-plain known today as the Buqei'ah, or in ancient times as the Valley of Achor, west of the hills of Qumran, above the Dead Sea. It was a distance of about 15 km. (10 mi.). Joshua's challenge to Achan, "Why did you bring trouble on us?", would have been said by the pilgrims as they threw stones to make the pile higher and higher, year by year. Muslim pilgrims to Mecca today throw stones at the pillars of Mina to reenact the struggle of Abraham and Ishmael against the temptation of Satan.

The Teacher has taken this ancient tradition about a taboo violation by a member of the tribe of Judah and developed it into a profound study of the first sin in the Promised Land. Achan is presented as an archetypal figure of the dark side of Israel, which was first hinted at in 1:18 (see above, p. 14).

The Canaanite Background

In 7:1, we see Achan not as a lone individual, but as a member of the prominent family of Zerah of the tribe of Judah. The point is significant if we think of the relation of the Joshua story to the period of King Josiah's reform which had to contend with deep corruption in the heart of Judah (Jer. 3:12-14). The Teacher may have known of the tradition that Zerah's mother was a Canaanite woman named Tamar (1 Chr. 2:4; cf. Matt. 1:3), who had disguised herself as a woman dedicated to the fertility god Baal in order to bear a son for her dead husband (Gen. 38:12-26).

The Rich Farmer

In 7:24, Achan appears as a rich man, with oxen for plowing his fields, sheep for cash income, and donkeys for transportation. The equivalent today would be tractors, marketable products, and trucks. In this he was something like the virtuous Abraham (Gen. 13:1) or Job (Job 1:2). It is possible that his family owned the entire valley-plain of Achor (R. de Vaux, "The Settlement of the Israelites in Southern Palestine," *Translating and Understanding the OT*, 130-31). If this is true, it means that the story of Achan was not originally part of the Joshua story, but was combined with the account of the battle of Ai by the 9th-cent. B.C. Narrator. Like the rich in ancient Israel and the wealthy and powerful of today, Achan had no need of the things he took.

The Public Effects of the Private Sin

Although Achan acted in secrecy, the effects of what he did were public. By his act he caused Israel to become involved in sin and guilt, as warned in Josh. 6:18 and repeated in ch. 7. It was the people of Israel who broke faith (7:1), sinned (v. 11), trans-

gressed the covenant, took, stole, and lied (v. 11). Because of one
man's sin, a whole people could not stand before their enemies
(vv. 12-13).

Achan thus foreshadows the kings who "caused Israel to sin,"
words which the Deuteronomic Historian applied to fourteen
kings of Israel from Jeroboam to Pekah, and one king of Judah,
the infamous King Manasseh, grandfather of Josiah (2 Kgs.
21:16-17).

Achan in the Garden Land

The "devoted things" (*herem*; see above, pp. 52 – 53) are mentioned seven times in this chapter (vv. 1, 11, 12, 13, 15). The
effects of Achan's act are to make Israel "a thing for destruction"
(v. 12). Achan's sin was to take for his own use that which was
reserved for God. Although this is presented as a violation of a
cultic taboo, the wording used by the Teacher reveals its wider
significance.

Achan's confession contains three verbs: "I saw . . . I coveted
. . . [I] took" (7:21). This verse is closely related to Gen. 3:6,
where the same three verbs are used. We may paraphrase the
Genesis passage and apply it to the case of Achan in the garden
land:

> When Achan *saw* that the culture of Canaan was useful for
> satisfying personal needs and ambitions, and that its prod-
> ucts were extremely beautiful, and were to be *desired* (or
> coveted, using the same Hebrew word as in Josh. 7:21) to
> make himself successful (another possible translation of the
> word *yaskil* which the RSV of Gen. 3:6 translates as "to be
> wise"; see Josh. 1:7-8), he *took* a luxurious imported coat,
> and some gold and silver.

Coveting. The final and most inward of the words of the
Decalogue refers to the corruption of the heart. The primary problem of Israel in Canaan according to the Joshua story was not
the fertility cult, but the people's greed for what belonged to their
neighbors. We may see its ruinous effects on society from the
words of the prophets who spoke of how the rich "covet fields
and take them. . . , oppress a man and his house" (Mic. 2:2).
This was the reason for the solemn warning of Deuteronomy:
"You shall not *covet* the silver or the gold . . . or take it for your-

selves, lest you be ensnared by it; for it is an abomination to the
LORD your God" (Deut. 7:25). A similar warning was given by
Jesus to "beware of all covetousness; for a man's life does not
consist in the abundance of his possessions" (Luke 12:15). In
fact, covetousness is nothing more than idolatry, according to
one NT writer (Col. 3:5). Israel at its best believed that God's
Teaching is to be desired (coveted) more than "much fine gold"
(Ps. 19:10).

Stealing. The act generated by the corrupted heart is the taking
of forbidden things. Achan's small act of taking (vv. 1, 11, 21)
mirrors the powerful takers of Israelite society. The description
of the king in 1 Sam. 8:10-17 is dominated by the verb "take."
The king will *take* the sons and daughters, fields and orchards,
grain and wine, sheep and goats, male and female servants, work
animals of the people, and will finally *take* the people themselves
as his slaves. The prophets spoke of the rich, who "trample upon
the poor and *take* from him exactions of wheat . . . and buil[d]
houses of hewn stone" (Amos 5:11), or who *take* fields and houses
of the poor (Mic. 2:2, 9). "From the least to the greatest of them,
every one is greedy for unjust gain, and from prophet to priest,
every one deals falsely" (Jer. 6:13).

The act of taking is called "stealing" in Josh. 7:11, and this is
seen as one of the signs of a society in deep crisis by both Hosea
(4:2) and Jeremiah (7:9). What was considered legitimate "taking" in Canaanite society, by right of kingship, noble station, or
the power of wealth, is here called "stealing."

Violence. Taking also involves violence and murder, as in the
cases of Uriah (2 Sam. 12:9) and Naboth (1 Kgs. 21:13-14, 16,
19). Dishonest gain may lead to the shedding of innocent blood
(Jer. 22:17), so that bloodshed multiplies more and more (Hos.
4:2). The fall of Jerusalem, in the opinion of the Deuteronomic
Historian, was due to the innocent blood with which King Manasseh filled Jerusalem, and which the LORD would not pardon
(2 Kgs. 24:3-4).

Lying. Covetous desire and greed lead to the deceptive cover-
up. The stolen things were hidden (vv. 21, 22), concealed "among
their own stuff" (v. 11) in the family dwelling (v. 21). This was

an acted lie to cover up the crime. The analogy with Gen. 3:8-10, where the guilty pair hid themselves, comes to mind.

The word translated "lie" (v. 11) has two meanings: (a) to deceive people (Lev. 19:11), and (b) to deal falsely with God (Josh. 24:27), or lie about him in words (Jer. 5:12) or conduct (Isa. 59:13).

The socially destructive effects of lying are detailed by the prophets. Lies spoken about God are a barrier to redemption (Hos. 7:13; 11:12). The fruits of such lies are iniquity, injustice, violence, and national disaster (Hos. 10:13; 12:1; Mic. 6:12). Lying on a national scale can lead an entire generation astray (Amos 2:4-5), until they imagine that these massive structures of deception really protect them (Isa. 28:15).

The ones most responsible for such lies are the prophets who teach lies about God (Isa. 9:15) and preach lies in God's name (Jer. 14:14; Mic. 2:11). Such lies surely bring God's "great name" (Josh. 7:9) into disrepute just as much as the defeat of God's people in battle.

Idolatry. Achan's theft of gold and silver presents a problem. Presumably the spoil permitted to the Israelites in the case of Ai (8:2, 27) included silver and gold along with other things (cf. 22:8). It seems as though Achan was condemned for something declared quite legal after his death! We must recall, of course, that the spoil of Ai was taken by Israel as a whole (8:27), and presumably distributed according to the principles of fairness as in Num. 31:12, 26-31. Achan took the silver and gold designated for the treasury of the LORD for his own use. It is even possible that the beautiful coat from Mesopotamia was intended for his wife as a luxury garment such as those used later by the haughty upper-class women of Jerusalem (Isa. 3:18-20).

The stern words of Deut. 7:25 about coveting mention in particular silver and gold, which might "ensnare" the people, and hence become "an abomination" and bring the terrible *herem*-destruction down on the entire nation. It is not the silver and gold by themselves that are the problem here. They are God's gifts (Hos. 2:8; Gen. 13:1), and the results of God's covenant blessing (Deut. 8:13). The problem comes when the accumulation of silver and gold causes the rich and powerful to forget God and the lessons of the Exodus liberation and wilderness training (8:14-16), and turn to other gods (8:17-19).

The snare of silver and gold is its temptation to idolatry. The images themselves were often covered with these metals (Deut. 7:25). Israel's use of God's gifts of silver and gold "for Baal" (Hos. 2:8) may have included the actual making of idols, or the manufacture of articles used in their cultic practices. The effects of this idolatry would be national destruction (Hos. 8:4). Thus we find the stern warning to the king against "multiplying for himself silver and gold" (Deut. 17:17).

It is possible that the story of Achan lies behind the description, in Deut. 17:2-7 and 29:18-21, of an Israelite who is attracted by the silver and gold of the Canaanite idols (29:17), or who deceives himself by saying "I shall be safe, though I walk in the stubbornness of my heart" (v. 19), thus arousing God's anger. That person would be singled out from all the tribes of Israel for calamity (v. 21), and his name would be blotted out from under heaven (v. 20). Achan also seems to fit the description of the person who has done "what is evil . . . transgressing the covenant" (17:2), who has gone to serve other gods (v. 3), and who must be stoned to death (vv. 5-7).

True, Achan as he appears in Joshua 7 does not conform completely to these two pictures. Nothing is said about idols or other gods. The opinion of the prophets, however, was that whether the metals are used for idols (Isa. 2:8, 20; 30:22; 31:7; Hos. 13:2), or in the treasuries of the wealthy elite (Isa. 2:7; 39:2), the result is idolatry, in which the poor are oppressed "for silver" (Amos 2:6; 8:6). The silver and gold belong to God (Hag. 2:8), and must be used according to his will for "justice, and only justice" (Deut. 17:20).

A Shameful Thing. The term "shameful thing in Israel," which describes Achan's act in 7:15, is used elsewhere in the OT only to describe violations of sexual ethics. The bride who comes to her marriage without evidence of her virginity has committed "folly in Israel by playing the harlot in her father's house" and must be stoned to death (Deut. 22:21). The adultery of Shechem and Dinah (Gen. 34:7), the sexual crimes of the Gibeathites (Judg. 19:23-24; 20:6), the rape of Tamar by Amnon (2 Sam. 13:12), and the adultery of certain prophets in Babylon with their neighbors' wives (Jer. 29:23), are all characterized by the same

61

Hebrew word, variously translated "wantonness," "wanton folly," and "folly." It seems clear that the Teacher wished to establish some connection with the sexual liberties practiced by the Canaanites. He is suggesting that the sin of Achan would certainly lead to participation in the fertility rites and the destruction of family life, and could thus be termed "a shameful thing in Israel."

Covenant Breaking. Besides the all-inclusive term "sin" (vv. 11, 21), there is the summary expression "they have transgressed my covenant" (vv. 11, 15), a phrase probably borrowed by the Teacher from Hos. 6:7; 8:1. The consequences of the broken covenant are very serious.

First, there is the active opposition of God, here called his burning anger (v. 1). The negative way of describing this is to say that God is absent: "I will be with you no more" (v. 12). This means that he will not intervene to save, even though he is passionately concerned about his people's failures.

Second, there is trouble in Israel, brought on by Achan the troubler (v. 25). This refers to the disintegration of community because of selfishness. King Ahab, like Achan, was a "troubler of Israel" (1 Kgs. 18:17-18), but the trouble was so deep-seated that even Jehu's revolution could not overcome the destructive forces in Israelite society.

Third, there is defeat in battle. Joshua 7:2-5, if read in isolation from the rest of the chapter, seems to point to overconfidence and poor planning as the causes of the defeat at Ai. But by placing it in the context of the first sin in the Promised Land, the Narrator clearly relates it to the curse attendant on covenant breaking: "The LORD will cause you to be defeated before your enemies" (Deut. 28:25).

Fourth, there is the threat of the complete destruction of God's chosen people by victorious enemies, and with it the failure of God's plan to bring blessing to the nations of the earth. Israel's name and God's name are closely related in a common venture (v. 9). The success of the common venture was contingent on Israel's faithfulness.

RESPONSE TO JUDGMENT

This chapter includes four steps required for a repentant Israel, in order that they might seek God's grace once again, and rejoin the common venture with God.

First, lamentation. The acts described in v. 6 are ritualized symbols of the kind of shock which disintegrates the inner person (tearing the garment), the sickness that lays one low (lying prone on the ground), and the nearness of death (dust on the head). Lament enables us to come to terms with the real hurts in our lives, even though these may not be completely rational. Joshua's question to God shows his pain, and even radical doubt: "Why hast thou brought this people over the Jordan at all?"

Joshua pouring out his heart to God foreshadows David (2 Sam. 1:11; 3:32; 13:36), Hezekiah (2 Kgs. 19:1), and Josiah (2 Kgs. 22:12, 19).

Second, searching for the causes. To Joshua's question of doubt, God counters with his own question of impatience (v. 10): "Arise, why have you thus fallen upon your face?" The experience of shock, brokenness, and morbidity must give way to honest analysis.

"Godly grief produces a repentance that leads to salvation and brings no regret, but worldly grief produces death" (2 Cor. 7:10). "Godly grief" bears the fruits of repentance and thus changes the situation. The existence of corruption in the midst of Israel requires that the source be found and dealt with. Since the attempt to locate the cause of the disaster is contingent on purity of motive, it is necessary that the people be "sanctified" (v. 13; see above, p. 9) to be sure that no selfish interests affect the process of analysis.

Third, confession. In vv. 20-21, we see Achan making a full, frank confession of his sins, which is promptly verified by the messengers. He begins by stating that he is going to tell the truth (as opposed to the lie), and thus confesses that his sin is "against the LORD God of Israel." By this confession, Achan restores moral integrity to Israel, thus showing that this dark side of Israel and of mankind is redeemable.

Jewish legend pictured Achan as a hardened criminal who had taken banned things and committed other crimes, such as adultery and sabbath-breaking in the days of Moses. But it was only after his theft of an idol and its paraphernalia at Jericho that God took action. When the lot fell on him, the legend goes, he brazenly rejected the charges. He attacked Joshua as unjust and demanded two witnesses. When Joshua urged him to face the issue squarely, he called on his fellow tribesmen of Judah. In the ensuing fight there was much bloodshed and destruction. It was at this point that Achan decided to make his confession. His confession cost him his life, concluded the rabbis, but it saved him from losing his share in the world to come (Ginzberg, *Legends of the Jews* 4:8-9).

Fourth, cleansing action. In the thought of the Teacher, it was necessary that Achan and his family should die. Israel was at the crossroads and had to choose between life, good, and blessing on one side, and death, evil, and curse on the other (Deut. 30:15-20). By Achan's confession and death, he chose life for Israel, and accepted death for himself. He was like Jonah, who accepted death in the sea, "for I know it is because of me that this great tempest has come upon you" (Jonah 1:12). In a strange way, Achan in his death makes us think of the words of Caiaphas to his fellow priests: "It is expedient for you that one man should die for the people, and that the whole nation should not perish" (John 11:50). God forgave Israel in his love because of Joshua's repentance, Achan's confession, and the cleansing action of Achan's death.

Like the story of Rahab, the story of Achan ends on a note of hope. This note was taken up by Hosea: Trouble Valley could become Hope's Door (Hos. 2:15). The story of Trouble Valley was an appropriate lesson from the past for King Josiah, for countless generations of the ancient people of Israel, and for both Jews and Christians in our own day.

At the same time, we can recall the near death by stoning of great leaders, such as Moses (Exod. 17:4), Joshua and Caleb (Num. 14:10), David (1 Sam. 30:6), Jesus (John 10:31-33), and Paul (Acts 14:19; 2 Cor. 11:25). Innocent people such as Naboth (1 Kgs. 21:10), a prophet named Zechariah (2 Chr. 24:21), and Stephen (Acts 7:58-59) were stoned to death. People claiming to be Christians have burned those believed to be heretics or witches, lynched blacks, and gassed Jews. These sad incidents warn us that wrong decisions, unjust laws, mass hysteria, or misguided zeal for God may add bloodshed to bloodshed and so pollute the earth. The execution of Achan can be properly understood only in relation to the renewal of the people under God's Covenant Teaching (Josh. 8:30-35).

CHAPTER 7

THE OPEN DOOR
Joshua 8:1-35

*. . . to open doors before him
  that gates may not be closed.*   —Isaiah 45:1

Those who wait for the LORD shall possess the land.   —Psalm 37:9

Behold, I have set before you an open door. . . .   —Revelation 3:8

FROM DEFEAT TO VICTORY (8:1-29)

The pile of stones in Trouble Valley (7:26) reminds readers of the man from Judah who caused trouble for all Israel by his greed and deception, but whose confession and death made a new beginning possible for Israel. The pile of stones at the ruin-mound of Ai (8:29) recalls the beginning and the end of the old order in Canaan, and points to a new kind of society under the guidance of God. Neither the inner victory over corruption in the heart nor the outer victory over external enemies was an end in itself. Both were steps in the process of inheriting the land (see above, p. 5).

Unlike the Achan story, the defeat and victory at Ai had no particular spiritual significance. They were physical, having to do with control of the road from Jericho to the highlands, and gaining access to the land on which they were to live. As Jericho was the gateway to the Jordan Valley, so Ai was the gateway to the central part of the land. This campaign against Ai is more like the present-day struggles for a just social order, involving political, social, economic, and military issues.

THE SETTING

The story of the conquest of Ai through a clever stratagem inspired by God and executed by Joshua is told in a vivid and

65

exciting way. A visit to the ruins of Ai at et-Tell, just above the town of Deir Dibwan, makes it easy to recognize the following topographical details:

(1) the probable location of the ambush to the west of Ai, out of sight behind a hillock (8:9, 12, 13).

(2) the camping place of Joshua's army on a valley-plain (v. 13) across a ravine (v. 11).

(3) the site of the first defeat near the ruins of the corner gate (7:4), and the place where they would "come out against us, as before" (v. 5), known as "the appointed place" (8:14, where the RSV translation "descent" should be corrected).

(4) the "descent" (7:4) where the land goes down sharply toward the dry chalk hills known as the "Arabah" (v. 14), and the "wilderness" of the Jordan Valley at the upper end of the Dead Sea (v. 15).

These details help us to visualize the battle as it is described in Joshua 8.

A COMPLEX SITUATION

Archeological excavations at et-Tell, the site of ancient Ai, have taught us that the account of the battle of Ai is a simplification of a complex historical situation. The Narrator not only simplified the story, but used his artistic skills to glorify Israel's part in a rather triumphalistic way. He wanted to emphasize God's decisive part in the victory.

Archeologists all agree that the large city whose ruins have been excavated at et-Tell, and which covers 11 ha. (27.5 acres), flourished in the Early Bronze period, roughly the same time as the pyramids of Egypt and the Syrian city Ebla. This city was destroyed about 2300 B.C., and the site was unoccupied until the end of the Late Bronze or the beginning of the Iron I Age. About 1200 B.C., a small, unwalled village was built on the site, covering only one-tenth of the area of the Early Bronze Age city. This village was destroyed about one hundred years later, in 1125 B.C. One large building was burned down. A second village was built on the ruins of the first; it existed for another seventy-five years. At that time the site was abandoned, and the village was never rebuilt (J. A. Callaway, "Ai," *IDBS*, 14-16).

From this we may attempt an explanation of the information

in ch. 8 as follows: What is there called a "city" may in fact have been the first Iron Age village, a conclusion confirmed by the report of the scouts (7:3). The head of the village is rather grandly described as a "king" by the 9th-cent. B.C. Narrator, since quite likely he was so represented in the hero tales of the ancient days. The "gate" mentioned in 7:5 and 8:29 could have been the ruins of one of the Bronze Age city gates. Finally, the conquest of Ai seems to have been a much smaller operation than is implied in the Joshua story.

OTHER SITES

Additional information from other sites in the general vicintiy of Ai helps us to fill in more details and draw some further tentative conclusions. It appears that there were other new settlements established at approximately the same time as the first Iron Age village at Ai.

Gibeon, the chief city of the Hivite league (Josh. 9:17), was rebuilt in the Early Iron Age on Middle Bronze Age ruins (J. B. Pritchard, "Gibeon," *IDB* 2:291-93). *Khirbet Raddana,* on the edge of modern el-Bireh (biblical Beeroth of the Hivite league), 4 ki. (2.5 mi.) SW of Ai, shows evidence of a new settlement built on bedrock at the end of the 13th cent. B.C. This first phase was expanded by a second occupation. After this the city was violently destroyed. Among the ruins of this second phase archeologists found a jar handle with Hebrew letters on it, dating not long after 1200 B.C. (E. F. Campbell, "Moses and the Foundations of Israel," *Interpretation* 29 [1975]: 152-53; J. A. Callaway and R. E. Cooley, "A Salvage Expedition at Raddana in Bireh," *BASOR* 201 [1971]: 9-19; D. N. Freedman, "An Inscribed Jar Handle from Raddana," *BASOR* 201 [1971]: 19-22). If the second phase was Hebrew, it shows a peaceful occupation followed by destruction at the hands of an unknown force. *Gibeah* (Judg. 19:12), now known as Tell el-Fûl, 10 km. (6 mi.) S of Raddana, was built as a new settlement on bedrock at about 1200 B.C. (C. Graesser, "Gibeah (of Benjamin)," *IDBS,* 363-64). *Bethel* (Josh. 7:2), about 2.25 km. (1.4 mi.) W of Ai, was destroyed at the end of the 13th cent. B.C., and then rebuilt and destroyed several times during the next hundred years. One of these destructions is recorded in Judg. 1:22-26, but the biblical account tells us nothing about the others (J. L. Kelso, "Bethel," *IDB* 1:391).

Conclusion: The coming of the Hebrews was not as simple as the Joshua story describes it. There were minor engagements like that at Ai. There may also have been cases like that at Raddana, where the Hebrews apparently integrated politically with the people living in a village who were attracted by their style of life and society.

OTHER PEOPLES

Some scholars have suggested that the founders of the first Iron Age village at Ai were the Hivites who founded Gibeon about the same time, perhaps Raddana and Gibeah, as well as other settlements still unknown to us (J. A. Callaway, "New Evidence on the Conquest of Ai," *JBL* 87 [1968]: 318). The Hivites, who according to biblical evidence settled in the area of western Lebanon (Judg. 3:3), Shechem (Gen. 34:2), and Gibeon (Josh. 9:7; 11:19), seem to have originated in Cilicia of Asia Minor. Many of the names in the list of cities of Benjamin (Josh. 18:21-27) are not Semitic, but show associations with Syro-Hittite and Cilician peoples in Asia Minor (G. E. Mendenhall, *The Tenth Generation*, 145-71).

Conclusion: Many peoples were moving about in Canaan and elsewhere in the Late Bronze and Early Iron Ages. Among these were the Hivites, as well as the Hebrews. It is the Hivites, one of the traditional seven nations, who are the chief actors in the next two chapters, following the important interlude on Mt. Ebal near Shechem.

WHAT DOES THE LORD REQUIRE? (8:30-35)

Jewish legend tells how the Israelites crossed the Jordan and on the same day marched all the way to Shechem, where the levitical priests recited twelve blessings toward Mt. Gerizim and twelve curses toward Mt. Ebal. Then, with the twelve stones taken from the Jordan, they built an altar, plastered it with lime, and wrote the Covenant Teaching on it in seventy languages so that the non-Jewish nations might have the opportunity of learning the law (L. Ginzberg, *Legends of the Jews* 4:6-7).

Though not credible as history, and overlooking many details of the Joshua story, this legend is theologically correct. It links together the twelve stones at Gilgal, symbols of the new people (pp. 27-28 above), and the stone altar and monumental stone on Mt. Ebal, themselves symbols of the renewal of the people. A parallel passage in Deuteronomy has these words: "This day you have become [once again] the people of the LORD your God" (Deut. 27:9).

The Teacher has placed vv. 30-35 at this particular point in the Joshua story as the climax of the Achan-Ai sequence and as a preparation for the new life in the land. Trouble Valley could become Hope's Door for every generation.

THE RIGHT TIME

An emphatic Hebrew word is used to emphasize the theological significance of the timing of this event: "*Then* Joshua built an altar. . . ." Only after the opened doors at Achor and Ai were the people ready to pause and reflect by ritual action on who they were and how they should act.

THE ALTAR

The altar and the ark both relate to God's presence and will, but there are important differences. The ark goes with the people. It is surrounded by the people. The altar stands on the land as a witness to a meeting between God and man. It is not portable. It marks a holy place. The first act of Israel on reaching the heart of the land was to erect an altar (cf. Deut. 27:5) to remind successive generations of God's presence in the land.

The altar, as the Hebrew root *zabah* ("to sacrifice") makes clear, is the place of sacrifice. The purpose of sacrifice is not to appease an angry God. The anger of God had already been turned away after the death of Achan (Josh. 7:26). Rather, the sacrifice is to maintain and enhance the relationship of solidarity between God and man.

Burnt Offering

The burnt offering (literally, that which goes up) was wholly consumed on the altar, a symbol of the total self-giving of the congregation (see v. 35) to God. Paul expressed the inner meaning of the burnt offering when he appealed to Christians to "present your bodies as a living sacrifice, holy and acceptable to God, which is your spiritual worship" (Rom. 12:1).

69

Peace Offering

The peace offering (literally, that which makes for wholeness or well-being) included a meal together. The fat pieces of the animal were burned on the altar to symbolize God's part in the meal, while the meal itself both symbolized and created the solidarity, or *shalom*, of the group. With this mutual support and the assurance of divine blessing the meal was naturally a time of rejoicing (Deut. 27:7).

Yet the altar, closely related to the land, remains ambiguous, because it may also express relations with other gods. In the narrative of the golden calf, we read that Aaron built an altar and the people "offered burnt offerings and brought peace offerings . . . sat down to eat and drink, rose up to play . . . and corrupted themselves" (Exod. 32:5-7). The prophets said that sacrifices alone without obedience were unacceptable to God (Isa. 1:11-13; Amos 5:21-22; Hos. 6:6). What happens at the altar may sanctify or pollute the land (Hos. 8:11; 10:1-2; 12:11; see below, pp. 168-69). Amid the temptations of life in the land, God's Teaching is essential.

THE MONUMENTAL STONE

Although it is the same Teaching, there is a difference between what was written on the stone and what was carried in the ark. In the ark God's Teaching is the treasure of the people, which it is their particular task to preserve and apply to their own lives. The monumental stone is set up, planted as it were, on the land. The words written on it are no longer the exclusive treasure of God's people. They become public information, announcing to the nations living in the land what God requires of all peoples, i.e., "what is good" (Mic. 6:8). This is the meaning of the Jewish legend that the Covenant Teaching was written in seventy languages. Once the Teaching has been "planted" in the land of Canaan, it may be "transplanted" to the soil of each of the seventy nations! Thus, at harvesttime, Israel says:

> May God be gracious to us and bless us. . . .
>   that thy way may be known upon earth. . . .
> Let the nations be glad and sing for joy,
>   for thou dost judge the peoples with equity
>   and guide the nations upon earth. (Ps. 67:1, 2, 4)

RIGHTEOUSNESS IN THE LAND

It is not likely that the Teacher was thinking of the entire five books of the Pentateuch, called "Torah" by Jews, when he said that Joshua wrote "a copy of the law of Moses" on the monumental stone. For one thing, the Pentateuch was not completed until exilic or postexilic times. Also, the limitations of space would make a long text unlikely. Some have suggested that the major part of the book of Deuteronomy was written on the stone. Others favor the simple form of the Decalogue, especially in view of the public nature of this proclamation of God's Teaching. This would be a concise summary of the whole Teaching, both as story and as guidelines for conduct (see above, pp. 6-7). In favor of this suggestion are these words from Deuteronomy: "These words the LORD spoke to all your assembly [cf. Josh. 8:35] at the mountain . . . and he added no more. And he wrote them upon two tables of stone, and gave them to me" (Deut. 5:22).

As we have seen, the sin of Achan/Israel is presented in ch. 7 as a violation of many of the covenantal conditions in the Decalogue. It is natural to think of this concise summary of the Teaching as being part of the renewal of the people after the defeat and victory at Achor and Ai.

Exclusive loyalty to Yahweh, forsaking of idols, and honoring Yahweh's name by swearing "in truth, in justice, and in righteousness" (Jer. 4:2) are all implied in the dedication of the altar and people to "the LORD, the God of Israel" (8:30; cf. 7:19, 20).

The guidelines for conduct found in the Decalogue have a particular relevance to the powerful — the elders, officers, and judges. The "homeborn" or native Israelites are warned against exploiting the sojourner — the foreigner, guest worker, or refugee — in their midst. The presence of women and little children emphasizes the provision in the law for the protection of the weak — widows, orphans, and sojourners. The disintegrated and defeated community of ch. 7 is now reintegrated at the meal of the peace offering, and bound to each other with a common commitment to the observance of God's Covenant Teaching.

BLESSING

The solemn gathering around the ark, the altar, and the monumental stone comes to a climax with the blessing of the priests on the entire congregation. Blessing is power to live. It insures the continuity of generations through the birth of healthy children, and the well-being of the community. Blessing gives wisdom for successful living and the enhancement of the quality of life. Victory in battles, like those at Jericho, Ai, Gibeon, or Merom, comes by the divine intervention of God's saving hand. The building of strong families, righteous communities of *shalom*, comes by God's presence, which gives blessing day by day, week by week, year by year, and from generation to generation. Blessing is related to life on the land received as a gift of God.

HISTORICAL CONSIDERATIONS

From a historical point of view, this passage presents several problems. The mention of "sojourners" assumes a situation where foreigners are resident in a stable community with towns and villages, rather than a newly arrived group as assumed by Joshua 1 – 8. The presence of women and little children at Shechem is strange, since the main camp continued to be in Gilgal (9:6; 10:6). Again, there is no mention of the journey of the entire community from Ai or Gilgal through what would have been hostile territory.

It seems clear that this passage has been put here by the Teacher for theological reasons, which have been suggested above. At the same time it is not likely that he simply "made it up" out of his imagination. It is probable that he was making use of ancient traditions of an actual ceremony in the years before the monarchy, held either annually or, as we read in Deut. 31:10-13, every seven years.

What did this incident have to do with events in Joshua's time? One suggestion (H. W. Hertzberg, *Josua, Richter, Ruth*, 62-63) is that the original incident was a ceremony held at the Bethel shrine, just outside the town of Luz/Bethel now called el-Burj. As the theophany at Gilgal sanctified that place as an Israelite holy place, so this ceremony at the Bethel shrine would sanctify it. It was here, according to his hypothesis, that the early Israelites came to celebrate their festivals, just as they did at Gilgal (Amos 5:4-5). It is possible that the Passover and the Feast of Unleavened Bread were celebrated at Gilgal, the Feast of Weeks at Bethel, and the Feast of Tabernacles at Shechem. When Jeroboam built an altar on the high place at Bethel (1 Kgs. 12:29-33), the Bethel shrine fell into disrepute along with the shrine at Gilgal. Josiah destroyed the altar and shrine at Bethel as part of his reform (2 Kgs. 23:5). For this reason, the Teacher might have transferred the Bethel gathering for covenant renewal to Ebal and Gerizim without mentioning Shechem, since he wanted to reserve that for the final covenant ceremony recorded in ch. 24.

A SACRED CHRONOLOGY

It is possible that the Teacher has arranged the Joshua story around the three agricultural feasts of the year, as in Deuteronomy 16. If this was his intention, he would have linked the agricultural year not only with the Exodus, but with the process of inheriting the land. Passover and Unleavened Bread at the beginning of the barley harvest would recall the entry into the land. The Feast of Weeks at the end of the wheat harvest would remind them of their arrival in the highlands and the reading of the Covenant Teaching. The fruit harvest, the Feast of Booths, at the climax of the year would remind them of Joshua's covenant at Shechem.

CHAPTER 8

A HAZARDOUS COVENANT
Joshua 9:1-27

She did not know
that it was I who gave her
the grain, the wine, . . . the oil, . . . wool, and . . . flax.
— Hosea 2:8-9

I would rather be a doorkeeper in the house of my God
than dwell in the tents of wickedness.
— Psalm 84:10

The life of Israel in Canaan, like the life of Christians in every nation, is characterized by a tension between faith and practice on the one side, and the demands of living in the world of different cultures and values on the other. We have seen two models in the Joshua story so far. The "Jericho model" stresses the radical discontinuity between the revolutionary new society of Israel and the old, corrupt society of Canaan. The "Ai model," preceded by the solemn warning of the Achan story, modifies this position. There can be a continuity of material things (spoil), as long as it is used fairly for the common good. Any relationship with the people and culture, including religion, is still strictly forbidden.

In this chapter we find a third alternative. In the "Gibeon model" the revolutionary community meets a friendly group from Canaanite society who seek an alliance with them, and offer great strategic benefits to the newly arrived company. Outright rejection of this request and offer on the sole ground that these are Canaanites ("Jericho model") is ruled out. Acceptance of the benefits while rejecting the alliance ("Ai model") would be cynical opportunism. The "Gibeon model" means finding a way of living side by side for mutual benefit.

For Christians or Jews in a modern city like Singapore, the

"Jericho model" would mean cutting themselves off from Hindus, Buddhists, Muslims, and secularists. Their offer of friendship would have to be rejected because they are a danger to the purity of faith. The "Ai model" would mean accepting the material benefits of the culture around us, but having nothing to do socially with non-Christian or non-Jewish people. The "Gibeon model" offers some guidelines for living side by side in peace with the friendly neighbor.

GIBEON

Since the "Gibeon model" involves an actual city of the ancient world, we must first look at the historical setting for the story. The site of ancient Gibeon has been identified as ej-Jib. It lies about 10.5 km. (6.5 mi.) NW of Jerusalem, and about 4 km. (2.5 mi.) W of er-Râm (ancient Ramah) on the main ancient communication road between the central highlands and the coastal plain. Excavations on the site have revealed a strong wall from the Early Iron Age (Iron I), an elaborate water system, and an underground storage area capable of holding 25,000 gallons of wine in jars. It is surrounded by fertile fields and vineyards. About 1 km. (.6 mi.) to the south is the imposing height known today as Nebi Samwil, which in biblical times may have been the location of the shrine of Gibeon. It is visible from Jerusalem and all the surrounding countryside.

The Gibeonite Quadrangle

Gibeon was the chief city in a league of four cities (9:17) occupying a strategic segment ("our country," v. 11) of the land of Canaan. Beeroth was probably situated about 2 km. (1.25 mi.) to the south, while Chephirah and Kiriath-jearim were located about 10 km. (6 mi.) to the west and south. This quadrangle controlled the vital east-west road which extended from the seacoast by way of Ai and Bethel to the Jordan Valley at Jericho. An alliance with these four cities would give the Israelites many economic, political, and military advantages, which they could hardly refuse.

Cities without Kings

Unlike other cities in the Joshua story, these four cities did not have kings. They did have "elders" (v. 11), and possibly "rulers."

75

The word translated "inhabitants" (those sitting or living in the land) may in the proper context also be rendered "rulers" (those sitting in positions of authority). We find these "rulers" referred to in vv. 3, 11, 24, as well as 2:9, 24 and 7:9.

That no kings are mentioned may well signify a vassal relationship with the Jebusite king of Jerusalem. This would explain his consternation over the alliance of his vassals with an invading power. Such a vassal relationship with the older and more established city-state a short distance to the south would fit in well with the hypothesis that the Hivites were comparative newcomers on the land (see above, p. 68). A decision by the four vassal cities to break ties of dependence with their overlord would explain the urgency of their request for a covenant (vv. 6, 11).

A Shrine City

The Gibeonite high place must have been an important shrine in pre-Israelite times. Although we do not have any evidence of this, we do know of its importance in the early days of the monarchy. Before the construction of the temple in Jerusalem, it was known as "*the* great high place" (1 Kgs. 3:4). According to priestly tradition, Zadok, one of David's priests, served there at the "dwelling place" of Yahweh (1 Chr. 16:39). An altar at this place dated from the time of Moses (1 Chr. 21:29; 2 Chr. 1:5). It was at the royal shrine at Gibeon that the young king Solomon met Yahweh in a dream at the beginning of his reign (1 Kgs. 3:3-14). It was only after the building of the temple in Jerusalem that the high place of Gibeon was reduced in importance (see 1 Chr. 22:1).

If we are right in assuming that the Israelite royal shrine was formerly a Canaanite shrine (the high place of Gibeon), then Gibeon would have been a city of great feasts and celebrations. There is every reason to suppose that the worship of Baal and Asherah took place there. It is probable that Gibeonites served as shrine attendants to supply fuel and water for the sacrificial cult, and that they became attendants at the Yahweh shrine that was later established there. We read of "a thousand burnt offerings" being offered there (1 Kgs. 3:4). It is possible that the numerous group of attendants known as "temple servants" (literally, "dedicated ones"), mentioned among the returned exiles, included Gibeonites (Ezra 2:43; 8:20; Neh. 7:73).

This story of Gibeon's alliance with the Israelites served to explain to later generations why Gibeonites were serving in the temple.

A Contested City

The Gibeonite quadrangle was contested territory between the forces of Saul and David, and between the Philistines and the Israelites. When the Philistines established their camp at Michmash with a chariot force, they must have controlled the route beside Gibeon (1 Sam. 13:5). It was down that road to Aijalon that Saul and Jonathan pursued them (14:31). In a contest between Abner's men from the north and Joab's men from Judah at Gibeon (2 Sam. 2:12-14), the Benjaminites were loyal to Saul's house against David's forces (vv. 24-25).

For some unknown reason, the Gibeonites fell into disfavor with Saul, and he tried to destroy them and drive them off their land in violation of the covenant made in the days of Joshua (2 Sam. 21:2, 5). Perhaps the Gibeonite who was one of David's heroes (1 Chr. 12:2, 4) escaped Saul's wrath to join David at this time, as Abiathar the priest had escaped from another of Saul's violent purges (1 Sam. 22:19-23). Beeroth suffered in the same purge as Gibeon, and this may explain why two men from Beeroth assassinated Ish-bosheth, Saul's son (2 Sam. 4:2-3). From this it seems probable that Saul's anger was due to his belief that the Gibeonites were siding with David. No doubt it was Saul's preoccupation with pursuing David that gave the Philistines an opportunity to come up the same invasion route again. It was necessary for David to defeat them "from Geba to Gezer" (2 Sam. 5:22-25; cf. 1 Chr. 14:16 where Gibeon takes the place of Geba).

It is remarkable indeed that such a contested area should have been offered to Joshua as a gift.

THE ORIGINAL STORY

With this background in mind, we can see three stages of development. The original events may have resembled the following reconstruction: The elders and vassal rulers of the four cities decided to break their ties with the Jebusite king of Jersualem, Adoni-zedek, on condition that they could make an alliance with the newly arriving Israelites, camped at Gilgal. In order to de-

ceive the Jebusite agents living in their midst, the messengers
disguised themselves as a band of poor merchants or travelers.
They took a detour north toward Shechem, then down to the
Jordan Valley by the Wâdī Farah, and south to Gilgal.

At Gilgal they explained the reason for their disguise, and
their urgent need for an alliance to support their strike for freedom. Delighted at this unexpected breakthrough in a hostile
front, the Israelites concluded the alliance. As a result, the Gibeonites received protection from Jebusite attack (Josh. 10:5-6),
as well as territorial rights in Israel (2 Sam. 21:5). Their shrine
was probably converted to a Yahweh sanctuary with Gibeonite
functionaries. On their part, the Israelites gained an agricultural
heartland, an economic base, and a position of power in the
middle of the land.

THE NORTHERN NARRATOR'S VERSION

The Narrator took over the story as told and retold, and included
it in the Joshua story as a folktale around the popular theme "the
trickster tricked." His hearers were not interested in the political
or sociological situation in the period before the monarchy. They
enjoyed the story of how the tricky Gibeonites fooled the Israelites, but then were themselves put to forced labor as David
(2 Sam. 12:31) and Solomon (1 Kgs. 9:21) had done to other
foreign peoples. This story explained why some peoples were
working as slaves, and why others were working as temple
servants.

THE TEACHER'S INTERPRETATION

The Teacher added his own interpretation to the Narrator's version of the story. He wanted to make it more relevant to the
situation of Israelites living in the days of Josiah's reform. His
words could later be applied to those living in exile in Babylon
or elsewhere. He stressed the hazards, the responsibilities, and
to some extent the opportunities of an alliance with friendly
neighbors. His ideas appear at different levels of understanding
which we must try to uncover.

The Strangers from a Far Country

At one level, the words of the Gibeonite messengers that they
came from a very distant land (vv. 6, 9, 13) relate to the more

lenient law of warfare with "the cities which are very far from you" (Deut. 20:15). If they sued for peace, their lives would be spared, but they would be put to forced labor (v. 11). At this level, the messengers were trying to establish a false identity in order to avoid the terrible destruction suffered by the people of Jericho and Ai (Josh. 9:3), as well as the Transjordanian kingdoms (v. 10).

A second level of meaning appears when we read of the temptations from the gods of distant peoples (Deut. 13:7), which could corrupt Israel's faith and practice. Perhaps the Teacher was thinking of the Assyrian altar which King Ahaz brought from Damascus to put in the temple (2 Kgs. 16:10-16), or the delegation to King Hezekiah "from a far country, from Babylon" (Isa. 39:3). In addition, there was a strong tradition, beginning with Isaiah, of great danger and destruction to come from distant lands (Isa. 5:26; 10:3; Jer. 4:16; 5:15; cf. Deut. 28:49). At this level, the arrival of an embassy from a distant land should have alerted the Israelites to danger.

A third level may be seen by looking at the prayer of King Solomon at the time of the dedication of the temple. There we see a reference to "a foreigner, who is not of thy people" (cf. 2 Sam. 21:2) and who comes "from a far country for thy name's sake (for they shall hear of thy great name, and thy mighty hand, and thy outstretched arm. . .)" (1 Kgs. 8:41). The foreigner comes to pray toward the temple, and Solomon's prayer, which shows evidence of the Deuteronomic Historian's hand, goes on to ask God to answer the foreigner's prayer, "in order that all peoples of the earth may know thy name and fear thee, as do thy people Israel" (1 Kgs. 8:43).

At this level, we see the arrival of friendly foreigners from afar as an opportunity for the Israelites to tell them more about the great name of Yahweh. This is the dimension of the mission of Israel among the nations which is further developed by the great exilic prophet Deutero-Isaiah, as well as by the New Testament.

Because of the Name (9:9)

The first level is one of fear. The Gibeonites have come because of the success that God gives to his people against his enemies. At a deeper level, we can see here the hope of claiming the protection of this great God by entering into a covenant with his

people (v. 11), and of gaining a place to live in the land promised
to Israel. Knowledge of the name gave them courage to break
the old chains and claim a new freedom under a God "who is
not partial and takes no bribe . . . executes justice for the fatherless and the widow, and loves the sojourner, giving him food and
clothing" (Deut. 10:17-18).

"Acted with cunning. . . ." (9:4)

By using this phrase to describe the Gibeonite rulers, the Teacher
linked this story with Gen. 3:1, where a word from the same root
is used to describe the serpent as "cunning" (NAB). The Teacher's
intention is not to attribute evil motives to the Gibeonites, but
to suggest that hidden within this request for an alliance is the
fatal attraction of Canaanite culture, especially Baalism. We have
already seen how he used this theme in the story of Achan. Here
he returns to it, to emphasize the hazardous quality of the alliance about to be formed between Yahwist faith and Canaanite
culture. The appearance of the word "cursed" at the end of the
story (v. 23) reinforces the intention to associate this encounter
with the Eden narrative (see Gen. 3:14).

A Worn-Out Society and Religion

The most entertaining part of this story is the description of the
preparations to deceive the Israelites (vv. 4-5, 12-13). Behind the
humor, however, we may detect the purpose of the Teacher: he
is not suggesting deception but revealing the "worn-out" nature
of the Canaanite culture.

The worn-out clothing would remind the hearers of the fact that,
under God's care in the wilderness, their clothing did *not* wear
out (Deut. 8:4; 29:5). Canaanite religion taught, and many Israelites believed, that the wool and flax from which garments
were made were gifts of the Baals (Hos. 2:5). Israel's prophets
reminded them that clothing "to cover their nakedness" came
from Yahweh (v. 9).

The dry and moldy provisions included bread and oil. These were
supposed by many Israelites to come from Baal, but in fact grain
and olives were gifts of Yahweh (Hos. 2:5, 9). The people did not
eat bread in the wilderness (Deut. 29:6), but God supplied their
needs with manna to make them know "that man does not live

by bread alone, but . . . by everything that proceeds out of the mouth of the LORD" (Deut. 8:3).

The wine, appropriate for a wine-producing shrine city, would call to mind the "feast days of the Baals" (Hos. 2:13), when wine and new wine "take away the understanding" (Hos. 4:11). At these feasts prophet and priest would reel, stagger, and vomit (Isa. 28:7). The leaders who joined the feasting competed in drinking, while they accepted bribes to let the guilty go free (Isa. 5:22), and made schemes to bring down their kings (Hos. 7:5). They gave no thought to God's cause (Isa. 5:11-12). This wine of the Baal feasts was called "the poison of serpents . . . from the vine of Sodom, and from the fields of Gomorrah" (Deut. 32:32-33).

The Deuteronomist reminded his people that they had no wine in the wilderness (Deut. 29:6). It was this memory that motivated the Rechabites to refuse to drink wine (Jer. 35:5-7). In this way they could avoid the corruptions of the Canaanite fertility cult as well. The warning for the reader was this: beware of the poison in the wine of the strangers from another culture and religion.

The torn, mended, burst wineskins may be understood by reading Ps. 119:83, where the psalmist compares himself to a "wineskin in the smoke." In the verses which follow he describes himself as persecuted, slandered, and near death. Perhaps the Teacher was thinking of Canaanite religion as a worn-out wineskin, unfit to hold the new wine of the Yahwist faith. As Jesus said, "No one puts new wine into old wineskins" (Mark 2:22).

The worn-out clothing, the moldy provisions, the poisonous wine, and the patched and leaky wineskins all symbolize the breakdown of the economic, social, and religious order of Canaan. Behind these humorous pictures lies a warning. Despite the great advantages brought by the messengers, their offer of an alliance contains serious dangers. If Israel forgets God's Teaching, their clothing will wear out, their bread will grow stale, and their wineskins will hold no wine. Only when they keep covenant with God will the earth become fertile with grain, oil, wine, wool, and flax (Hos. 2:15, 22), and will they be blessed "in the city, . . . and in the field" (Deut. 28:3). The blessing will affect the "fruit of your ground . . . your beasts . . . cattle . . . basket and kneading-trough" (Deut. 28:4-5).

The Covenant of Peace (9:15)

The humorous picture of the representative of Israel reluctantly tasting the moldy provisions of the Gibeonites probably conceals some kind of covenant meal. The strange comment that they "did not ask direction from the LORD" (v. 14) seems to suggest that God would have repeated the stern injunction: "You shall make no covenant with them, and show no mercy to them" (Deut. 7:2). However, the Teacher's view of God's will comes out in his description of what Joshua did. This was just the opposite of the expected command.

"Joshua made peace with them" (9:15). They were no longer considered enemies. In the condensed time frame of this narrative, Israelite and Hivite are already seen as living side by side (v. 16). Peacemaking transforms physical proximity into peaceful coexistence. This goes far beyond the line taken in Deut. 20:11, where the terms of peace for foreign people are forced labor. Set as it is in close succession to the battles of Jericho and Ai, Joshua's act of making peace is indeed remarkable. By this act, the ones who claimed to be "far away" were brought near. This verse anticipates the words of the postexilic prophet who wrote: "Peace, peace, to the far and to the near, says the LORD" (Isa. 57:19). This verse from Isaiah was, in turn, used to describe the work of the NT Joshua: "Now in Christ Jesus you who were once far off have been brought near in the blood of Christ. . . . he came and preached peace to you who were far off, and peace to those who were near" (Eph. 2:13, 17).

He *"made a covenant with them . . ."* (9:15). The end of enmity is sealed by a formal agreement binding the two parties together. This was more than peaceful coexistence, for it included mutual defense, mutual assistance, and mutual responsibility. Israel accepted the Hivites on terms similar to those used in the NT: "no longer strangers and sojourners, but . . . fellow citizens with the saints and members of the household of God" (Eph. 2:19). We must assume that on their part the Hivites declared their loyalty to the God of Israel.

". . . to let them live" (9:15). At the first level, this means simple survival, a decision to refrain from killing them. On a deeper level, it must be related to the same options that Israel had for

life or death. Only by keeping God's commands could they "live and multiply" and be blessed on the land (Deut. 30:16; cf. 4:1; 5:33; 16:20). Like Rahab (Josh. 6:17), the Hivites of the Gibeonite quadrangle are allowed to share the life and blessings of Israel on the land.

Three Reactions

Having described what is believed to be God's will, i.e., to make a hazardous covenant with the Hivites, the Teacher went on to outline three reactions.

First, narrow nationalism motivated the people to go up to the four cities in a mob spirit to kill the foreigners and take their property as spoil (9:16-18). When they were prevented from carrying out this rash action of hate and greed, they turned on their leaders and "murmured against" them as the people in the wilderness had done to Moses (Exod. 15:24, etc.).

Second (9:19-21), the wise counsel of the leaders convinced the people that since an oath had been taken "by the LORD, the God of Israel," Yahweh himself was the protector of the foreigners in their midst! But the leaders thought of a compromise solution that would satisfy the terms of the oath and at the same time appease the prejudice of the people against the foreigners in their midst. They should be put to menial labor, cutting wood and carrying water for the Israelites. The only other place in the OT where these tasks are mentioned is Deut. 29:11, where it is the sojourner who cuts the wood and carries the water. He is still in the covenant community, but reduced in status. There had been no suggestion of lower status in v. 15.

Third (9:23, 27), the intervention of Joshua finally saved the foreigners from slaughter by an inflamed mob (v. 26). At the same time, he changed their position from that of slaves of the people to the honorable status of attendants in the worship of Yahweh, providing wood and water for the sacrifices. Other Gibeonites who are not involved in this service to God are presumably allowed to live as equals among the Israelites.

The "curse" on the Gibeonites (v. 23) seems to have been meant as a lesson to the Israelites rather than as a condemnation of a whole people. "You are cursed" might be interpreted as follows: Canaanite culture as it is must die, and be transformed through incorporation into the worship of Yahweh. Those who foolishly follow the Canaanite gods will come under this curse, as Deutero-Isaiah said about foreign gods during the Exile: "Behold, you are nothing, and your work is nought; an abomination is he who chooses you" (Isa. 41:24). The true relationship between Yahweh faith and Canaanite culture must begin with rejection of the Canaanite gods and "abominable practices." Only then can Canaanite culture enrich the service of Yahweh at the altar.

THE GIBEON MODEL

From our study we may summarize some of the points of the "Gibeon model" for relationships between Israelite (Jewish and Christian) faith and Canaanite (or any other) culture.

(1) There are occasions when an alliance between faith and culture may be mutually beneficial. Faith may aid in liberation from oppression. Culture may open important opportunities for faith.

(2) The "Israelite" side of the alliance should keep constantly aware of "the poison in the wine" on the "Canaanite" side. They should enter the alliance with open eyes to discern and reject the "gods" of "Canaan."

(3) Blind prejudice, hatred of the "Canaanites," and greed for their goods are likely to break out in "Israel" and spoil the chances of a fruitful alliance. Only wise leadership can prevent this.

(4) The true evaluation of "Canaanite" culture comes in the context of "Israelite" worship, which must be ready to accept foreign values and customs in the service of God.

CHAPTER 9

WHEN GOD FOUGHT FOR ISRAEL
Joshua 10:1-43

*Those who war against you
  shall be as nothing at all.* — Isaiah 41:12

*He disarmed the principalities and powers
  and made a public example of them.* — Colossians 2:15

This chapter is a story of the Day of the LORD, in which those who cry for help (the Gibeonites) are saved, and the oppressing powers are decisively defeated in a way that signifies the ultimate defeat of evil. The oppressing powers are the nine cities and nine kings which appear in this chapter. Those who gather to attack Gibeon include the five cities of the Amorite coalition—Jerusalem, Hebron, Jarmuth, Lachish, and Eglon (v. 3)—and four others: Azekah (v. 10), Makkedah (v. 29), Libnah (v. 29), and Debir (v. 38). The nine kings are from the coalition cities plus Makkedah, Libnah, Debir, and Gezer.

The well-told story proceeds rapidly in three stages: the rescue of the Gibeonites (vv. 1-15), the ritual subjugation of the Amorite kings (vv. 16-27), and the southern campaign against six cities in southern Canaan (vv. 28-43). Both the rescue and the campaign stories conclude with the same formula: "The LORD fought for Israel." This is then followed by the notice of the return to the camp at Gilgal, where the struggle to inherit the land began.

SECTION I. THE SALVATION OF GIBEON (10:1-15)

At the center of this story is the urgent cry of the Gibeonites to Joshua: "Come up to us quickly, and save us, and help us; for all the kings of the Amorites . . . are gathered against us" (v. 6).

The cry for help comes from the recent Hivite converts to Yahwism, who claim the help of Joshua as their right under the covenant agreement. Their Savior is in fact Yahweh himself, who intervenes through his agent, Joshua/Israel. God "fought for Israel" when Israel was going to the rescue of oppressed people in the land of Canaan.

The Big Five (10:1-5)

The five kings of the Amorites have their counterparts in the five kings of the plains (Gen. 14:2), and of Midian (Num. 31:8), and in the five lords of the Philistines (Josh. 13:3). These parallel references suggest a symbolic meaning for the number five, which is confirmed by the summary phrase "all the kings of the Amorites" (v. 6, cf. vv. 40, 42). The same terminology is used in Jer. 25:20-26 in a portrayal of "all the kingdoms of the world which are on the face of the earth."

In Joshua's time these were the petty kings of the city-states of Canaan in the Late Bronze and Early Iron Ages, who in theory were vassals of the Egyptian pharaoh. In fact, these kings, with their nobles and priestly entourage, were the real rulers of the decaying and corrupt society of Canaan.

Their fear (v. 2) was natural. The Yahwist revolutionaries under Joshua had succeeded in winning over the Hivites who controlled the strategic area north and west of Jerusalem. This was a direct threat to their system and their power structures. The marching of their massed armies against Gibeon was the predictable result.

The Rescue Expedition (10:6-11)

The striking thing about this story of the rescue mission is the way in which God and Joshua work together. First, Joshua responds immediately to the call from the allies in the hill country (v. 7). Then God announces in advance that he has already decided to bless the expedition with victory (v. 8).

At the end of the all-night march of about 25 or 30 km. (15 or 20 mi.), along a road which rises some 1000 m. (3300 ft.) above Gilgal, the ill-armed, outnumbered army of Israel wins an initial victory, because God throws the armies of the five kings into a panic (v. 10). Their success is presumably due to the psychological advantage given by the predawn darkness, the unexpected direction of the attack from the rear, and quite probably a violent storm with thunder and lightning.

In the final scene, Joshua's forces press their advantage by hot pursuit along the only possible escape route to the west, past Upper and Lower Beth-horon, and then south to Azekah and Makkedah near Jarmuth (v. 10). In the midst of the wild chase, God intervenes again by sending down large, death-dealing hailstones to make the victory complete (v. 11, continued in v. 20).

The Long Day (10:12-14)

"Was it not through him [Joshua] that the sun stood still, and made one day as long as two?" (Sir. 46:4 NEB).

The tradition that the "sun stood still" at Joshua's command is widely known but often misunderstood. Some have tried to make this passage a test of belief in the literal sense of the Scriptures. Others have tried to reconcile it with natural phenomena, such as an eclipse of the sun, or planetary disturbances causing a "lost day" in terrestrial chronology. Still others say that it is impossible to understand it as anything other than the creation of a pious writer's imagination. In our consideration of the meaning of the verses, the following points should be kept in mind:

(1) The length of "a whole day" as understood in biblical times was twenty-four hours, from sunset to sunset or, more probably in this case, from sunrise to sunrise. This would suggest that the sun and moon stopped their normal activity for a twenty-four-hour period.

(2) The prayer of Joshua is set at Gibeon (v. 12), and hence in the predawn darkness *before* the battle, rather than during the course or at the end of the battle, which has already been described in v. 11. We have here, then, *an alternative version of what happened in the one battle.*

(3) The time of the prayer is just before the rising of the sun "at Gibeon," and the setting of the moon "in the valley of Aijalon." This corresponds to the time of Joshua's arrival after the night march from Gilgal. Such a juxtaposition happens only at the time of the full moon, which would give maximum illumination on a normal night.

(4) The intent of the prayer is that the sun and moon "be silent" (a more accurate translation of the Hebrew word *damam* than the RSV "stand still"). Since the two heavenly bodies can-

not speak, to "be silent" means that they should stop shining whether by day or by night, so that the enemy could not recover from the panic caused by the surprise attack in the darkness and storm. The first part of v. 13 should then read, "the sun refrained from shining, and the moon ceased (to shine)." In the latter case, the Hebrew word *'amad,* which usually means "to stand still," may also mean "to cease doing something" (see, e.g., Gen. 29:35; 30:9; 2 Sam. 2:28; 2 Kgs. 4:6; cf. NIV "stopped glowing," Josh. 3:16).

(5) The prayer is addressed to God (v. 12), rather than to the sun and moon. The natural way for God to keep the sun and moon from shining is to cover the sky with a heavy cloud for a period of twenty-four hours. We may suppose that thunder and lightning would enhance the sense of mystery and dread, prolonging the panic of the enemy. Thus, even at noon when the sun was "in the midst of heaven" (v. 13), the day was as dark as night, while the darkness of the night would be complete without the light of the full moon. It was not until the following day that the sun "rose" as usual, since the darkness prevailed "for about a whole day" (v. 13).

It is natural that people of ancient times would think of the sun "going down" in its supposed orbit around the earth. They did not know that the apparent movements of the sun and moon are caused by the revolutions of the earth on its axis. Most present-day readers would find it difficult to accept the idea that God would respond to Joshua's request by stopping the earth from revolving. The words of a later writer who told of God's "darkening the sun" by "cloth[ing] the heavens with blackness" (Isa. 50:3) would be more understandable.

The Vengeance of God's People (10:13)

The meaning of the statement that the Israelites "took vengeance" on their enemies is not to be understood as "taking revenge," like that practiced by Lamech (Gen. 4:24), Samson (Judg. 15:7; 16:28), the jealous man (Prov. 6:34), Edom (Ezek. 25:12-14), or Philistia (Ezek. 25:15-17). Taking revenge is not sanctioned by God (Lev. 19:18; Deut. 32:35).

The true meaning of the Hebrew word *naqam,* translated "to take vengeance," is to right a wrong or to restore a condition of peace by taking action against those who have done the wrong,

or violated the peace. In this case, it is the violation of peace by
the Amorite kings who were threatening to destroy those with
whom Joshua had "made peace" (Josh. 9:15; 10:1, 4). The words
of a psalmist bring out the correct meaning of the word, including
the primary truth that it is God who sets right the wrong and
restores the condition of peace.

> O LORD, thou God of vengeance, . . . shine forth! . . .
> How long shall the wicked exult?
> They pour out their arrogant words, . . .
> They crush thy people, O LORD,
>   and afflict thy heritage.
> They slay the widow and the sojourner,
>   and murder the fatherless! (Ps. 94:1, 3-6)

God Fought for Israel (10:14)

The battle of Gibeon gives us several important insights into
God's "warfare." *First,* we see God's direct intervention through
natural events, causing them to occur at the right time. In this
case it was a storm, with heavy clouds and hailstones. See also
Exod. 9:22-26 (hail), 14:21 (wind), 1 Sam. 7:10 (thunder), Judg.
5:21 (heavy rain), and Josh. 3:16 (landslide).

Second, there is God's indirect intervention through his agents,
Joshua and the armies of Israel. *Third,* we see God and Israel
working together on behalf of covenant allies, to "save" and "help"
them.

SECTION II. THE SIGN OF THE END OF THE OPPRESSING POWERS (10:16-27)

The theological center of this passage is vv. 24-25. The ritual of
placing the feet of the victors on the necks of the defeated kings
has a prophetic quality: "Thus the LORD *will do to all your enemies*
against whom you fight" (v. 25). The victory at Gibeon is a sign
and promise of more to come. Perhaps the 9th-cent. B.C. Narrator was thinking of the victories of David over his enemies,
when "the LORD put them under the soles of his feet" (1 Kgs.
5:3).

A psalmist saw present victories as a promise of the day when
God would make "your enemies your footstool" (Ps. 110:1). Jesus
saw in the small-scale victories over demonic powers a sign of

the final defeat of Satan (Luke 10:17-18). Some of the NT writers applied the words of Psalm 110 to the NT "Joshua" (Acts 2:34-36; Eph. 1:22; Heb. 1:13). Paul saw in Jesus' resurrection from the dead an anticipation of the end, when Jesus will "deliver the kingdom to God the Father, after destroying every rule and authority and power. For he must reign until he has put *all his enemies* under his feet" (1 Cor. 15:24-25).

SECTION III. CLEANSING THE LAND (10:28-43)

This section shows a marked difference in style from the previous two sections. The theological message is contained in certain frequently repeated key words and phrases describing the conquest of the six cities, as well as in the summarizing statement at the end.

The Harsh Words

The following seven phrases appear again and again in these verses.

The *herem* destruction (RSV "utter destruction") of the population—vv. 28, 35, 37, 39, 40.

Every person *(nephesh)* in it—vv. 28, 32, 35, 37, 39.

None remaining—vv. 29, 30, 33, 37, 39, 40.

Fought against—vv. 29, 31, 34, 36, 38.

Took it in battle—vv. 32, 35, 37, 39.

Smote it—vv. 28, 30, 32, 33, 35, 37, 39, 40, 41.

With the edge of the sword—vv. 28, 30, 32, 35, 39.

The strong impression given by these "harsh words" is of a mass slaughter of every human being not only in the six cities, but in the entire land (see v. 40). The statement that Joshua had done this at the express command of the LORD makes the account even more shocking. At first glance, this seems to imply that God condones the most terrible bloodshed if it is done by his people.

We may cite here the example of the attack on Jerusalem by the Crusaders in A.D. 1099. When they finally forced their way into the city, they carried out a massacre "such as has seldom been paralleled in the history of war. The troops ran amok through the streets, stabbing and slaying everyone they encountered. . . . The Jewish community, gathered in the central synagogue, were shut in by the Crusaders and burnt alive. . . . The massacre aroused horror among the Crusaders themselves" (M. Benvenisti,

The Crusaders in the Holy Land, 38; cited by R. G. Boling, *Joshua,* 211).

We must conclude that whatever the message intended by the Teacher, it cannot have been approval of this kind of shocking cruelty done under the banner of faith in God. What, then, is the message behind these "harsh words"?

In the first place, we should take very seriously the strong probability that Josh. 10:28-43 comes in its present form from the hand of the Teacher himself, who lived at least six hundred years after the events he is describing. Important corollaries follow from this basic understanding:

(1) In the 7th cent. B.C. there were no Amorite kings in the territory of Judah, nor were there any ethnic groups corresponding to the seven nations of Josh. 3:10 (see above, p. 53). The message of this story for the reform movement led by King Josiah was certainly not a summons to conduct a mass slaughter of minority people in the kingdom.

(2) The chief concern of the Teacher was the moral and spiritual breakdown of his time. To describe the conditions that prevailed he used certain code words such as "abominations," "abominable practices" (2 Kgs. 21:2, 11), "wickedness" (Deut. 9:5), and "defilement" (Jer. 7:30; 16:18; 32:34-35). In his view, a thorough and radical cleansing process was necessary if complete disaster, including loss of the land, was to be avoided. As the land had "vomited out" the previous rulers with their oppressive structures (the nine cities and the nine kings) because of the terrible evil they had done, so it would again "vomit out" its Israelite rulers and people (Lev. 18:24-30).

(3) The term *herem* "destruction" (RSV "utter destruction") should be seen as a code word referring to the cleansing of the land of idolatry, with its "abominable practices."

(4) The reference to "every person" could also be a code word referring to all those who lead or participate in the Baal cult, especially the priests functioning in the high places of Samaria, who were in fact killed by King Josiah in the course of his reform (2 Kgs. 23:19-20).

City Rulers and Oppressed Villagers

In the second place, we should keep in mind the sociological profile of the Canaanite cities (see above, p. xviii). The "inhabitants" (see above, pp. 75-76) of the cities were the rulers — kings, nobles, priests — who had dominated the social and religious structures of the land. The villagers outside the cities were an oppressed majority. Nothing is said about them in the conquest narrative. It is these villagers who would, like Rahab and the Gibeonites, rise up against their overlords to join the Yahwist revolutionary movement.

GEOGRAPHY

As in the case of the battle of Ai, the geographical setting of this chapter is very clear. All but one (Makkedah) of the sites mentioned has been identified with more or less agreement among archeologists.

IMPORTANT SITES IN JOSHUA 10

Of the five coalition cities, Jerusalem and Hebron are well known today, controlling the north-south road along the hill country of Judah. Jarmuth (Khirbet Yarmûk) and Lachish (Tell ed-Duweir) guard roads leading from the coastal plain along the Valley of Elah to Bethlehem and another valley road to Hebron. Eglon (probably Khirbet ʿAiṭûn) lies between Lachish and Hebron.

Azekah (Tell ez-Zakariyeh), Makkedah (not yet identified), and Libnah (Tell Bornat) are west and south of Jarmuth, while Debir (Tell Rabûd), the largest and most important city south of Hebron, lies about 14 km. (8.5 mi.) away. Gezer, whose king is mentioned in v. 13 as leading an unsuccessful relief expedition to help Lachish, is another strategically located city on the edge of the coastal plain, controlling the road to Gibeon.

HISTORY

With such a clear geographical setting, it would be natural to assume that the account in Josh. 10:28-39 is an accurate picture of events as they happened. Unfortunately, the evidence at hand does not support such a conclusion.

The Nature of the Text

(1) The stereotyped expressions already referred to in the descriptions of the conquest of each of the six cities indicate a symbolic, theological kind of writing, rather than factual reporting.

(2) The lack of any report of casualties on the Israelite side, or survivors on the Amorite side, suggests that we are dealing with teaching material rather than a careful report of the actual battles.

(3) The conquest of the six cities in a single campaign lasting only a few days gives the impression of condensation, and possibly rearrangement of original events.

(4) References to "all Israel" (vv. 15, 31, 43) reflect a view that the whole of the Israelite tribal league as it later became, was working together in the conquest of this part of the land. Yet, as we have seen, the Joshua group probably included only a part of what later became "all Israel" (see above, p. xx). This suggests an idealized rather than a sober factual account.

Other Biblical Evidence

The conquest of Hebron, here attributed to Joshua, is elsewhere said to have been accomplished by Judah (Judg. 1:10), or Caleb (Josh. 15:15-19; Judg. 1:11-15). Both Caleb and his nephew Othniel were Kenizzites (Josh. 14:6), a group which later became part of Judah. The Kenites, another tribal group who later became a part of Judah, entered the territory (later assigned to Judah) from the south, and settled around Arad (Judg. 1:16; cf. Num. 21:1-3). This seems to suggest that the conquest of the Negeb, claimed by the Narrator for Joshua, was a much more complicated process than is assumed in the final summary statement in Josh. 10:40.

Archeology

Archeology has done little to clarify this situation aside from identifying the sites. Lachish is the only one of the nine cities whose excavated ruins show a destruction occurring in the early years of the Iron Age. Even there, however, it is impossible to determine who destroyed the city at that time, whether Egyptian, Philistine, Canaanite, or Israelite forces. In any case, the site was abandoned for more than 100 years after its destruction.

An Echo of David's Conquests?

Eight of the nine cities mentioned in this chapter are included in the list of cities belonging to Judah (Josh. 15:35, 39, 41-42, 49, 54). If, as many scholars maintain, this list comes from the period of the united kingdom, the cities located in the lowland area (shephelah) bordering on the coastal plain may be related to David's campaigns against the Philistines (2 Sam. 5:18-25; 8:1; 23:9-12), and his fortifications of these key locations may be for protection against incursions from them. We read in 2 Chr. 11:9-10 that Rehoboam fortified three of these cities (Lachish, Azekah, and Hebron) along with several others, probably against Egypt which favored his northern rival, Jeroboam.

A Suggested Explanation

With this information in hand, we may consider the following possible explanations:

The 9th-cent. B.C. Narrator in the north expanded the already existing narrative of Joshua's victory over the southern coalition at Gibeon to include the conquest of six strategically located Judean cities as an extension of the Gibeon campaign. His purpose as a northerner, writing after the division of the kingdom, was to emphasize that all of the territory of Judah had been brought under Israelite control by the Ephraimite Joshua. David's work, then, would be viewed as a consolidation of what had already been achieved by Joshua.

The 7th-cent. B.C. Teacher developed this conquest story to emphasize the role of Joshua as Moses' successor. His work of cleansing the land according to God's Teaching would be a model for the reformers under King Josiah. The summary statement in vv. 40-41 seems to be particularly relevant for Josiah and for later generations who would return to the land of Judah. Josiah's religious reform and national renewal should include the hill country, the lowlands (shephelah), the Dead Sea slopes, and the Negeb all the way south to Kadesh-barnea (Tell el-Qudeirat). This latter point, 160 km. (99 mi.) SW of Hebron, was the southernmost point in the territory of Judah (Josh. 15:3), as well as the entire land of Canaan (Num. 34:4). It was only in David's time, however, that a permanent settlement was established there. A fortress was erected in the 9th cent. B.C., probably by King Jehoshaphat (873-849 B.C.). Kadesh-barnea is not relevant to the Joshua story, but very relevant to Josiah's national renewal movement. Its importance as the southern boundary is seen again in Ezekiel's map of the idealized land to be restored after the Exile (Ezek. 47:19; 48:28).

The Divine Warfare

We have already looked at how God "fought for Israel" in the battle of Gibeon (see above, p. 89). In v. 42 the reference seems to be not to a single battle, nor even the six battles, but the entire first half of the Joshua story, which is related to Deut. 1:30. More than that, this theological assertion puts the battles of the Joshua story in the wider setting of God's warfare *against* the powers of evil, *for* the victory of righteousness and the establishment of peace. It is this struggle that is so prominent throughout the entire Bible.

The Liberation — Formation — New Land Phase

The most obvious setting for the words "God fought for Israel" is the entire story which began in Egypt and ended in the land of Canaan. God's contest with the deified Egyptian pharaoh was the first step in the liberation of the group of slaves who would form the beginnings of Israel. God's energetic intervention was necessary because "the king of Egypt [like all tyrants] will not let you go unless compelled by a mighty hand" (Exod. 3:19). The result of the contest was to be judgment "on all the gods of Egypt" (Exod. 12:12).

At the Reed Sea, Moses promised that "the LORD will fight for you" (Exod. 14:14), a reality which, according to the narrative, the Egyptian forces recognized only too late (v. 25). The victory at the sea (Exod. 15:4-10) was followed by a triumphal march through the wilderness, across the Jordan, to the land chosen by God for his people to dwell in (vv. 13-17).

In this setting, the words "God fought for Israel" mark the climax of a long series of interventions by God on behalf of his people.

The Creation — New Creation Phase

Another phase of God's "warfare" is found in the poetic description of creation as a struggle against the forces of chaos and death in the world. Although the element of conflict is not clearly brought out in Genesis 1, other descriptions of the act of creation refer in semimythological terms to the forces of chaos as a dragon who is conquered by God (Job 26:12-13; Pss. 74:13-14; 89:10; Isa. 27:1; 51:9). The idea behind this kind of poetic language is that

God is engaged in a constant struggle with "dragonlike" forces all over the world. This is the struggle for a new creation.

In this setting, the statement "the LORD . . . fought for Israel" means that the warfare with the forces of destruction and death in Canaan is part of the age-old conflict which God is waging with evil in the entire world.

A Stereoscopic View

These two phases of God's warfare are both necessary background for understanding the meaning of God's support for the forces of Israel in the "conquest" of Canaan. God fights for Israel as part of his battle against the powers of death, and for 'salvation" in the whole world (Ps. 74:12). The same may be said of the reverse, when God "turned to be their enemy and . . . fought against them" (Isa. 63:10). This means that God's people have joined the forces of chaos and destruction, and are no longer on the side of the new creation (e.g., see Isa. 5:8-30).

At the same time we may say that the struggle for a new creation in any society or nation is part of the same struggle by which God fought for Israel. The nine cities and nine kings of Joshua 10 have their counterparts in "all the rulers of the earth . . . their nations . . . nation by nation" who come under God's judgment (Jer. 25:30-32; cf. Isa. 24:1-23). The massing of the five kings against Gibeon is reflected in the gathering of all the forces of evil into a single army against God (Ezek. 38– 39). God is at work in Israel as well as in the whole world to bring down the tyrant Assyria (Isa. 14:24-27), or the Babylonian oppressors (Jer. 51:54-58), and to support the liberator, King Cyrus of Persia (Isa. 45:1-2).

The Agents of God's Warfare

Although God is free to use the forces of nature in his warfare against evil, he more commonly employs human agents, like the Assyrian emperor, "the rod of [his] anger" (Isa. 10:5); the Babylonian army, his "sword" (Jer. 25:29), or "hammer . . . to break nations in pieces" (Jer. 51:20); or Cyrus, to "set my exiles free" (Isa. 45:13). This does not mean that the cruelty, terror, and destruction of war are either God's doing or God's will. God's "warfare" is his concerned, costly effort to create righteousness and peace. In some mysterious way, God's will may be accom-

plished even in the midst of the brutalities of war. The human
agents probably do not realize or intend what God wills (Isa.
10:7). In fact, it is God's will that wars come to an end (Ps. 46:9),
and that nations should not make war with each other (Isa. 2:4).

God's Servant

The Teacher presents Joshua and Israel as God's chosen agent
for his "warfare" in the land of Canaan, to cleanse the land of
idolatry and "abominable practices," and prepare it for the new
society of peace and justice to be established there. The death of
Josiah led to the apparent failure of the religious reform and
national renewal movement, and the end of the monarchy. New
reflections were necessary concerning the role of God's people in
his "warfare" against evil.

Deutero-Isaiah, prophet to the exiles, reflected deeply on the
issues of the "conquest," and included many of its themes in his
message to his fellow exiles. First, he assured them that God
himself would oppose those who made war against them as had
the five kings against Gibeon (Isa. 41:11-13; cf. Josh. 10:5). On
the other hand, the prophet compared the renewed Israel to an
instrument to be used in God's "harvest" of the nations. Israel
would "thresh" the nations. The "mountains and hills," symbolizing the nations, recall the nine cities on their mounds in
Joshua 10 (E. J. Hamlin, "The Meaning of the 'Mountains and
Hills' in Isaiah 41:14-16," *JNES* 13 [1954]: 185-90). The picture
in Isa. 41:15-16 is reminiscent of the southern campaign of Josh.
10:28-39. The useless "chaff" of idolatry is carried away by the
storms of history (cf. Isa. 40:24), while the precious seed (Rahab,
Gibeonites) is separated out (cf. Isa. 28:28) as "seed for the
sower" (Isa. 55:10). This gives great joy to the harvester (Isa.
41:16; cf. 9:3) because the seed may be sown for God's new planting (60:21; 61:3, 11). God may use Cyrus the Persian emperor
to "lay waste mountains and hills" (Isa. 42:15) of the Babylonian
empire, but he uses his servant Israel to take the great invitation
to the "survivors of the nations" (the new planting, Isa. 45:20),
to turn to Yahweh for true salvation (v. 22).

Except for Babylon the great tyrant, Deutero-Isaiah saw the
other nations not primarily as enemies of God, but as helpless
stubble (Isa. 41:2), trembling in fear during a time of vast his-

torical change (v. 5), trampled like clay in a pit (v. 25), bruised reeds and smoking wicks (Isa. 42:3), in the darkness of prison (v. 7), dazed and confused by their fate (49:9), borne down by grief and sorrow (53:4), alienated from each other (v. 6), transgressors against God and man (v. 8). For all people in such circumstances "warfare" is like the rescue expedition for the Gibeonites, a liberation from the yoke of the oppressive forces.

In the view of this prophet in Babylon, God's agent is not a victorious conqueror like Joshua, but a humble suffering servant. This exilic "Joshua" is blind (42:16, 19), oppressed (v. 22), despised by the powerful (49:7), walking in darkness (50:10). It is this blind, stumbling "Joshua" that God chooses (42:1) to make God's salvation real to fellow sufferers (49:6), and to implant and establish God's justice among them (42:1-4).

In this bold reinterpretation of the triumphant Joshua as the Suffering Servant, Deutero-Isaiah implies that God himself is involved in the new creation, as a woman in labor (Isa. 42:14). As one of this prophet's disciples said, "In all their affliction he was afflicted" (Isa. 63:9).

New Testament Perspectives

It is this insight that forms the background to the NT understanding of the new "Joshua." He warred against the powers of evil by his teaching, his healings, and finally by his death. By the cross God "disarmed principalities and powers" (Col. 2:15) and delivered his people "from the dominion of darkness" to "the kingdom of his beloved Son" (Col. 1:13). It is he who judges and makes war (Rev. 19:11). The sword from his mouth will "smite" the nations (v. 15). Yet he wears a robe dipped in his own blood (v. 13).

(Note: The sword issuing from his mouth may be an intentional reversal of the Hebrew idiom used in Joshua 10, "to smite with the edge [mouth] of the sword.")

CHAPTER 10

ALL THAT LAND

Joshua 11:1 – 12:24

The bows of the mighty are broken,
but the feeble gird on strength.   — 1 Samuel 2:4

He has put down the mighty from their thrones,
and exalted those of low degree.   — Luke 1:52

These two chapters form the conclusion of the first part of the
Joshua story, which tells how the "land of Canaan" (5:12) became "the land of the people of Israel" (11:22). The first part
(11:1-15) is parallel to the first part of ch. 10, with the focus
shifting to the region of Galilee. Two summary statements
(11:16-31; 12:1-24) follow, again parallel to the second part of
ch. 10, making clear Israel's relationship to the land. In the
7th cent. B.C. the first part could be understood as an encouragement to King Josiah to recover the region of Galilee as part
of the neo-Davidic state, in fulfillment of the prophecies of Isa.
9:1-4 and Jer. 30:8. The "yoke" in question at that time was that
of Assyria. The comprehensive term "all that land" (11:16) would
seem to include the entire territory controlled by David in the
10th cent. B.C. Early Christians, perhaps putting together Josh.
11:1-15 and Isa. 9:1-4, saw Jesus as the liberator at work in "the
land of Zebulun and . . . Naphtali" to bring light to the people
living in darkness. His message, "the kingdom of heaven is at
hand," was like Joshua's sudden attack on the charioteers in
Galilee (Matt. 4:12-17).

THE CANAAN GENERATION

As in the case of Gibeon, a coalition of northern kings initiated
a military campaign against "Israel" (11:5). We are not prepared
for the sudden shift from south to north, nor are we told how

"Israel" was there to excite such alarm and hostility among the Canaanite ruling elite.

Archeologists have found evidence of a series of unfortified settlements, dating to the early part of the Iron Age (ca. 1200 B.C.), in the highlands of upper Galilee. From our knowledge of Canaanite society in that period (see above, pp. xvii-xix), we can make an educated guess that these settlers were debt slaves, tenant farmers, and Habiru bands who were escaping the oppression of the city-state system which prevailed on the plains. We may further surmise that this kind of revolutionary breakaway occurred at this particular time instead of earlier, precisely because of the arrival in Canaan of the Joshua group with its revolutionary social and religious ideas and structure (see above, pp. xx-xxi). The openness of the Joshua group to Canaanites like the Rahab clan, the Hivites of Gibeon, and others would have encouraged the poor and oppressed Canaanites in the north to seek an alliance with this new force.

These breakaway Canaanites were "proto-Israelites" or future Israelites. They were the "Canaan generation" as distinct from the "Exodus generation" and the "wilderness generation" (see above, pp. 32-33). Their experience of slavery was not in Egypt under the pharaoh, but in Canaan under vassal kings (see above, p. xvii). Their experience of liberation was not a sea crossing, but an escape from the old society and its bondage. Their experience of crossing over into the new land was not at the banks of the Jordan, but in the hills of Galilee. Their entrance into the covenant society was not at Sinai, nor at Gilgal, but at a ceremony like that described in Joshua 24, when they were adopted as members of the tribal league. They were to become the Galilean tribes of Naphtali, Issachar, Zebulun, and Asher.

Evidence that at least some of these proto-Israelites were in Galilee before the time of Joshua comes from one of the Amarna Letters (see above, p. xvii), which mentions a people doing forced labor for a king in the region of Shunem in the Valley of Jezreel. If we coordinate this information with the description of the tribe of Issachar as having been in slavery (Gen. 49:15), the meaning of the tribal name as "men of hire," and the inclusion of Shunem in the territory assigned to Issachar, we may conclude that those who later became the tribe of Issachar were living in the region south of the Sea of Galilee as many as 150 years before the arrival of the Joshua group.

This picture of the proto-Israelites seems to be in tension with the following lists of the twelve tribes: in Egypt (Gen. 46:8-27; Exod. 1:1-4), in the wilderness as Moses' attendants (Num. 1:4-16), in the census of males (Num. 1:20-47), the position in the camp (2:3-31), the roster of liturgical duties (7:12-83), the tribal commanders (10:14-28), and the spies (13:4-16). We may look at these lists in two ways. First, it is possible that small numbers of all twelve tribes were with Moses and Joshua, but that membership in the tribes was expanded by allies and converts of the "Canaan generation." Another possibility, favored by many scholars today, is that the tribal structure of Israelite society was achieved only *after* arrival in Canaan as an alternative social organization to the city-state model of the old society. In later generations, when the stories were told and retold, the twelve-tribe structure became symbolic of the whole people of Israel. People forgot that there had been a period before the formation of the tribal league, and assumed that this structure was as early as the time of Moses.

THE BROKEN YOKE

These breakaway settlements in upper Galilee, as well as the new revolutionary ferment in the south, stirred the ruling elite in Galilee to concerted action. The extensive coalition of kings described in 11:1-3, while somewhat overstated, emphasizes dramatically the massive power structure that was overturned following the initial victory at "the waters of Merom." The five cities of the coalition (note the parallel with 10:5; see above p. 86) are located to the north (Hazor) and west (Madon) of the Sea of Galilee, in the Kishon Valley (Shimron), and the Mediterranean coastal plain north (Achshaph) and south (Naphoth-dor) of Mt. Carmel. The "northern hill country" designates the area around Hazor, while the "Arabah" refers to the plain south of the Sea of Galilee (Chinnereth). The six peoples mentioned in 11:3 are the same as those referred to in the summary in 9:1. Both lists find their theological purpose in 12:8. The land they formerly controlled is now placed under Israel's jurisdiction.

As background for the northern liberation campaign of Joshua's armies, we may imagine the harassment of the breakaway rebels by military forces of Hazor and Madon. This would have been the basis for an urgent call for help, as in the case of Gibeon (10:6).

The intended battlefield was probably the plains to the south of the Sea of Galilee where the war chariots (11:5) would give the Canaanite forces clear superiority. "The waters of Merom" probably refer to a spring-watered plateau between Merom (modern Meirôn or Meirûn) and Hazor. This would have been a military camp or staging area where chariots, horses, drivers, charioteer warriors, and support personnel would assemble before moving south to anticipate the arrival of Joshua's army.

The divinely inspired (11:6) pre-dawn attack on the military camp caught the sleeping charioteers unawares. The attacking forces crippled the horses by cutting their rear leg tendons (hamstrings), and burned the chariots. Deprived of their military advantage, the Canaanite forces were badly beaten. This victory and its sequel opened the way for peaceful development of towns and villages in Galilee by the "Canaan generation" without fear of harassment or subjection to the deposed kings. In poetic language, "the people who walked in darkness" saw "a great light" (Isa. 9:2).

THE DESTRUCTION OF THE OPPRESSING POWER

In the early part of the Iron Age, Hazor was a city whose glory was in the past. In the Middle Bronze Age (2000-1500 B.C.), when it was "the head of all those kingdoms" (11:10), there was a lower city covering 80 ha. (185 acres), ruled from an upper citadel of 10 ha. (25 acres). At that time Hazor's king was lord over ten to twenty vassal kings, just like other great cities of the period such as Mari, Babylon, and Larsa. Even in the Late Bronze Age (1500-1200 B.C.), the Amarna Letters speak of Hazor as dominating the eastern part of Galilee. By the 13th cent. B.C. the lower city was abandoned, and the citadel was destroyed about 1225 B.C. If the Joshua group is datable to that period, this destruction could possibly be attributed to them (11:10). It may well be, however, that what was destroyed by Joshua was a small fort built on the ruins of the Middle Bronze city. This would make it comparable to Jericho and Ai, which were also ruins of great and powerful Middle Bronze cities (R. G. Boling, *Joshua*, 309).

This view of Hazor as a small fort built on older ruins would help us understand how unwalled settlements could have been established in upper Galilee in the 13th cent. B.C. It also helps us to see the language of 11:11-14 as Deuteronomic rhetoric, or as code language which is not to be taken literally (see above, pp. 52-54, 90-91). In the mind of the Teacher, the radical reform and national renewal of Josiah should extend to Galilee. The words of the Chronicler that the reform extended "as far as Naphtali" (2 Chr. 34:6) may well reflect the historical realities of the 7th-cent. B.C. reform movement.

THE PROTRACTED STRUGGLE

The impression given of a whirlwind campaign lasting a few weeks or months (see 10:42; 11:16-17) is shown in 11:18 to be a radical condensation of actual events for teaching purposes (see above, pp. xiv-xv). The statement in 11:19 that every city had to be taken in battle may well be an exaggeration (see above, p. 68), but it supports the picture in v. 18 of a long, hard struggle lasting many years before the ruling elite could finally be overthrown and the new society firmly established. The list of dethroned kings in 12:9-24, which may well come from the period before the monarchy, shows that many details have been omitted from the condensed story. There are indications that the struggle lasted longer than the life of Joshua himself (see above, p. xiv).

Perhaps we may see in 11:18 a warning by the Teacher to the leaders of the reform and renewal movement that a purge of the shrines and a reform of the priesthood were only a beginning. A long struggle lay ahead. Subsequent events showed this to have been sound advice. In fact, the struggle still goes on.

THE STUBBORN RESISTANCE OF THE OPPRESSORS

The meaning of the protracted struggle is further elaborated in 11:20, where the hardened hearts of "all those kings" describes the stubborn resistance of oppressive institutional structures to liberating changes. The Teacher was here explicitly linking the liberation struggle led by Joshua with the Exodus struggle led by Moses. The "hardening" of pharaoh's heart indicates his refusal to heed the signs that were presented to him one after the other (Exod. 7:3, 13, 28; 8:19; 9:12), and his blind, greedy unwillingness to let his slaves go (4:21; 7:14; 9:35; 11:10). His "hard heart" even drove him to pursue the fleeing slaves into the waters of the sea (14:4, 8, 17) to his own destruction (14:27-28). The theological problem seen in the statement that Yahweh caused the hardening of the heart is placed in better perspective by the declaration in 3:19, "I know that the king of Egypt will not let you go unless compelled by a mighty hand." The same was true, according to the Teacher, of the rulers of the corrupt and oppressive city-state system of Canaan, or the entrenched imperial power of Assyria and its allies in Israel in the 7th cent. B.C. Yet it proved possible to break out of the seemingly hopeless situation to a completely new beginning.

WHAT ABOUT CENTRAL CANAAN?

It is remarkable that the northern campaign described in ch. 11 follows directly after the southern campaign of ch. 10, with no mention of the territory between Gibeon and Galilee, sometimes known as Ephraim. No battles are recorded as having been fought in Ephraim. In the list of kings in 12:9-24, there are thirteen kings from the territory of Judah, ten from Galilee, and only five from Ephraim (12:17-20, 31), none of which was mentioned elsewhere in the Joshua narrative. On the other hand, two important ceremonies are located at Shechem (8:30-35; 24:1-28), whose king is not mentioned in the list in ch. 12. Here are some possible ways of explaining this omission in the Joshua story.

(1) The neutralization of central Canaan may have been the result of Joshua's work as a mediator. Joshua was known as an Ephraimite (24:30). He may have negotiated an alliance with the king of Shechem and avoided a battle.

(2) The antifeudal revolution may have taken place in central Canaan before the arrival of the Joshua group. This seems to be suggested by references to armed struggle in Gen. 48:22 and 49:23-24. This would have made them friendly to the newcomers, and easily converted as the "Canaan generation."

(3) The Hivites living in Shechem (see above, p. 68) may have had an alliance with their relatives in Gibeon. The Gibeonite alliance with the Joshua group would have involved Shech-

emites as well. This would explain how the rescue expedition was free from interference from the north.

(4) The Northern Narrator of the 9th cent. B.C. had no need to prove that Ephraim belonged to Israel. This would be assumed. He stressed the southern and northern campaigns in order to show that the true conqueror of the land was the northerner Joshua, rather than David who came from Judah.

(5) The Teacher of the 7th cent. B.C. took over the framework of the Narrator (see above, p. xvi). He then summarized the whole story in 11:16 – 12:8 to make it include the entire land.

RECEIVING THE LAND

At the beginning and end of the first summary statement (11:16, 23), we find the expression "Joshua took all that land." The Hebrew verb *laqah* is better translated "receive" as in 13:8 and 18:7, as well as in Num. 34:14-15, than "take" (RSV) or "capture" (NAB, TEV), i.e., by force. Another Hebrew verb, *lakad*, is used for the act of capturing ten cities (Jericho, Ai, Lachish, Eglon, Hebron, Debir, Hazor, Kiriath-arba, Leshem) and "all their kings" (10:42; 11:12, 17). *Lakad* is never used to refer to the taking of *land* by force. When the verb *laqah* is used for the action of "taking" cities, it is qualified by the phrase "in battle" (11:19).

The idea that Yahweh gives victory so that his people are enabled to take *(lakad)* cities and kings is repeatedly affirmed (6:2; 8:1; 10:8; 11:6). In the case of the land, it is Yahweh who gives (1:2, 6) and Joshua as representative of the people who receives *(laqah)* the gift. Enemies may be conquered and their cities captured. The land is not to be seized but rather received. It belongs to Yahweh (see above, p. 5). As Joshua receives the land in trust, he gives it to the tribes as a grant or patrimony (inheritance; see above, p. 5) over which those who receive it have domain or tenancy rights (possession, 12:6, 7; see above, pp. 9-10).

THE LAND AT REST

The result of the long struggle was that "the land had rest from war." This idea is parallel to that of the land as resting place for the wandering people (see above, pp. 12-13). Here, however, the focus is on the land itself. Warfare appears as a violence to the

105

land because it disrupts the divinely intended relationship between the inhabitants and the habitat. The effect of this disruption is that "cities lie waste without inhabitant, houses without
men, . . . the land . . . utterly desolate . . . [with] forsaken places
. . . in the midst of the land" (Isa. 6:11-12). This reminds us of
Hiroshima or Nagasaki after the explosion of the atomic bombs,
but also of the exploitation and ruin of the land by economic
policies of nations, classes, and corporations. In Hebrew poetic
symbolism, the violated land "mourns" (Hos. 4:3), like Tamar
with ashes of death on her head, torn garments of ruined beauty,
crying with bitter lamentation (2 Sam. 13:19). The sickness of
the land may be so violent that the land will "vomit" out the
source of pollution (Lev. 18:25). Other poets have universalized
this poetic language:

> The earth mourns and withers, . . .
>   lies polluted under its inhabitants,
> for they have transgressed the laws, . . .
>   broken the everlasting covenant.
> Therefore a curse devours the earth,
>   and its inhabitants suffer for their guilt. (Isa. 24:4-6,
>   passim)

When the land is "at rest," curse is changed to blessing,
oppression to freedom, fear to confidence. Mourning is ex-
changed for joyful singing (Isa. 14:7; 35:1-2; 44:23; 49:13; 51:3).
Pollution and corruption are changed to an abundance of salvation and righteousness (Isa. 45:8).

In the Teacher's view this kind of "rest" for the land was not
permanent. It would last for limited periods like forty or eighty
years (Judg. 3:11, 31; 5:31; 8:28), and depended on wise administration and fidelity to the covenantal way of life. The urgent
task that lay ahead was the organization of life on the land (Josh.
13 – 19).

THE NEW SOCIETY ON THE LAND

Joshua 13 – 22

CHAPTER 11

A REFORMED SOCIETY
Joshua 13:1 – 19:51

. . . that you may live long in the land which the LORD swore to your fathers to give to them and to their descendants, a land flowing with milk and honey. — Deuteronomy 11:9

This is the heritage of the servants of the LORD. — Isaiah 54:17

PART III OF THE JOSHUA STORY

With Part III of the Joshua story (chs. 13 – 22), the task assigned to Joshua comes to completion. Parts I (Entering the Land) and II (Dethroning the Powers) are preparations for Part III. The ceremonial meal of the produce of the land on the west bank of the Jordan River was an anticipation of this goal (see above, p. 36), and a preparation for the attendant responsibilities of faithful land management (see above, pp. 38-39). The trumpets of Jericho heralded the dawn of the kingdom society (see above, pp. 51-52). God's Teaching, written on stone, was planted in the land as the constitution of the new society which was in the process of formation (see above, p. 70). The hills, valleys, and forests, the springs, streams, and rivers, the boundaries, territories, and regions, the cities and villages, the tribes, kinship associations, and extended families which make up the rather dull prose of these chapters are witness to the historical, social, and economic grounding of this portrayal of salvation fulfilled in the land of Canaan. Land forms a vital component in the complex interrelationship between God, people, and land of which the Bible speaks. Contemporary readers of the Joshua story can learn much about the scope and process of salvation from a study of these chapters.

THE CANAAN PATTERN OF LAND MANAGEMENT

In these chapters, and throughout the history of Israel, we find two patterns of land management. The first is the Canaan pattern. As we have seen (see above, p. xviii), the pharaoh was the ultimate landowner, but the city kings were the effective owners of the land around the city and under its power. Sociological studies indicate that the aristocracy, temple, and government officials, making up about 2 percent of the population of Canaan, had control of over 50 percent of the land as patrimonial holdings. These holdings were worked by slaves or sharecropping peasants who paid over half of their produce to the landlords. The rest of the land was tilled by villagers who paid heavy taxes to support the urban elite. This system of land management was organized for the benefit of the 2 percent at the top.

This "Canaan pattern" is very common in many parts of the world today. In these countries a small percentage of the population controls a large part of the means of production, and the great majority are exploited for the benefit of the few.

The New Society: Land Reform

According to the Israel pattern, God is the ultimate landowner. God grants the whole land not to a king but to all the people, tribe by tribe, family by family. There is no privileged class. Joshua himself receives only a small grant "among them" (19:49-50). Casting lots with representatives of the people present assured impartiality, as in the government-sponsored balloting for flats in the Singapore housing estates. The Israel pattern stood in sharp discontinuity with the Canaan pattern. It was this contrast which attracted many oppressed Canaanites to break away from their overlords and join the Israelites as the "Canaan generation" (see above, pp. 99-101).

Matching the three parts of the Joshua story, we find that the distribution of the land takes place in three phases.

Phase one: the Transjordan tribes (Josh. 13:8-33), recapitulating Num. 32:33-42.
Phase two: A. Judah (Josh. 15:1-63).
             B. Joseph, i.e., Ephraim and Manasseh (16:1–17:18).
Phase three: A. Benjamin, differentiated from Judah (18:11-28).

     B. Simeon, differentiated from Judah (19:1-9).

     C. The four northern tribes, and the migratory tribe of Dan (19:10-48).

R. G. Boling has suggested that phases two and three may reflect the actual historical situation. Phase two, which could have taken place at Shechem, fits well with the situation following the treaty with the Hivites of Gibeon and Shechem (see above, pp. 68, 104-5), and the defeat of the coalition of southern kings described in Joshua 10. If this phase took place after these events, the result would have been the consolidation of the southern and central parts of the land. This would have encouraged breakaway movements in the north, and given cause to the northern kings to prepare for a major battle to stop the movement then and there (Josh. 11).

According to this view, phase three would have taken place at Shiloh, considerably later (18:1), to bring the northern group into the new pattern of land management (Boling, *Joshua*, 425).

Beginning with Judah

The Teacher used these ancient materials with the 7th-cent. B.C. situation in mind. The territories represented by phases 1 and 3C were lost to Assyria in 732 B.C. (2 Kgs. 15:29). The territory of Joseph (phase 2B) was lost to Assyria in 721 B.C. (2 Kgs. 17:6). This left Judah as the centerpiece of the land distribution scheme, exactly as in the time of the great reform movement of the 7th cent. B.C. King Josiah's national renewal program proceeded from Judah (2A; 2 Kgs. 23:4-14) to Joseph (2B) and the northern territories (3C; 2 Chr. 34:6-7), and perhaps across the Jordan (1; see above, p. 11). Behind the land distribution scheme in Joshua we may discern a program for land recovery and redistribution in the 7th cent. B.C.

The Expanding Arena of the New Society

Perhaps the Teacher was thinking of God's dream-promise to Jacob at Bethel: "You shall spread abroad to the west [i.e., the seacoast; Josh. 13:2-6] and to the east [phase 1] and to the north [phase 3C] and to the south [phase 3B]" (Gen. 28:14). It was this promise which Deutero-Isaiah repeated in the days of the Exile in a way which extended the scope of salvation to the ends of the earth: "You will spread abroad to the right and to the left"

111

(Isa. 54:3). Luke's view of the mission of the disciples was that it should begin in Jerusalem and Judea, proceed to Samaria, and extend to the end of the earth (Acts 1:8). Present-day readers will see here a pattern of the expanding circle of salvation from place to place and group to group in many parts of the earth.

THE NEW SOCIETY: KINSHIP ASSOCIATIONS

The tribal territories were allotted "according to their kinship associations" (RSV "families"). This formula is repeated twice for each tribal grant (see, e.g., Josh. 13:15, 23). It is apparently an ancient formula that reveals an important part of the social structure of ancient Israel.

In the Canaan pattern, the integrity of the extended family, the natural unit of society, was constantly being eroded by debt slavery, sharecropping, and economic hardship. The poor were being marginalized. The Israelite kinship association (Heb. *mishpahah*) grouped a number of extended families (RSV "father's house," Heb. *beth-ab*) together in a way that reintegrated and strengthened them. Since kinship could be acquired by mutual agreement, marginalized families could thus be integrated into the association.

Land Administration

The land granted to the tribes was subdivided according to the number of kinship associations. These associations parcelled the land to the member families, and arranged for redistribution of the parcels periodically, perhaps every seven years, according to changing circumstances.

Protective Functions

The association protected member families from being forced to sell their land outside the association, thus preserving the original titles to the land. The association also made sure that loans to a poor family were interest free, and that the period allowed for debt slavery was limited to seven years. The principle of mutual assistance thus made it possible for families in dire straits to survive.

Military Functions

The kinship association was also responsible for providing a muster of soldiers for tribal defensive action. This muster, numbering from ten to twenty men from a given association, was called an *eleph*. A later meaning of this word during the monarchy was a standardized unit of one thousand fighting men. This double meaning of the same word *eleph* may explain the large numbers in the census figures in Numbers 1 and 26. It is probable that "six hundred three thousand" should be translated "six hundred and three units supplied by kinship associations." This is made probable by the note that the figures were taken "by their kinship associations" (Num. 26:12; RSV "families"). The resulting figure would be about five or six thousand men, depending on the size of the units (N. K. Gottwald, *Tribes of Yahweh*, 270-76).

This method of interpreting the meaning of *eleph* helps make sense of the numbers given for the battle of Ai. The first group to go up was three units (7:4; RSV "three thousand"), which could be forty to fifty men. The ambush consisted of five units (8:12; RSV "five thousand"), or thirty units (8:3; RSV "thirty thousand"), which might number either sixty or three hundred men.

Religious Functions

Although the records are not clear, it seems from 1 Sam. 20:6, 28-29 that the kinship association (RSV "family") also had religious functions. In the case of David, we read of a "yearly sacrifice for the kinship association."

From the above, we can see that this intermediate level of organization between the individual extended families and the tribe served to bind the social groups together, to incorporate the poor into the mainstream of society, and to maintain conditions for peaceful and productive life on the land.

THE NEW SOCIETY: CITIES AND VILLAGES AS LIVING PLACE

City Lists

Prominent in these chapters are the lists of cities with their villages, designating the living place of the extended families and kinship associations. The lists themselves are taken from the court annals of the period of the monarchy. The original lists may have been made at the time of David's census (2 Sam. 24:1-9), though the lists as we now have them are from a later period.

The survey mentioned in Josh. 18:2-4, 8-9 may point to some kind of earlier listing of cities. What stands out in the city lists is the great detail, especially in the cases of Judah (15:20-63) and Benjamin (18:21-28). Scholars who have studied the lists have concluded that those of Judah and Benjamin together are arranged in order of the fiscal districts used for tax collection in the kingdom of Judah. (A convenient map is found in J. M. Miller and G. M. Tucker, *The Book of Joshua*, 126.)

Canaanite and Israelite Cities

In the Canaan pattern of society, walled cities were centers of power, domination, wealth, and privilege. The domination of the cities destroyed the wholeness of village society. Israelite cities in the early period, on the other hand, served only as market-places, administrative centers, and places of refuge in time of danger. They shared juridical and religious functions with the villages.

Villages, the New Focus

Surrounding the cities in the hill country were unwalled villages. Here the basic production unit was the extended family, which shared land, tools, animals, and threshing floor. The main products were grain, wine, olive oil, fruit, and vegetables. Some bovine cattle, sheep, and goats were also raised. People lived in one-room houses constructed of sun-dried bricks or stone.

Important technological innovations just at this time made extensive and intensive agriculture in the hill country possible, and thus facilitated the expansion of the Israelites into unoccupied land. Popular access to iron tools permitted land clearing and cultivation. Rock cisterns could be cut, and lime-lined cisterns allowed holding of water at a distance from springs or streams. Rock-walled terracing made hillsides possible for cultivation.

New self-supporting villages sprang up as a result of these technological changes, and expanded across the hill country. The better-fed population multiplied and prospered with no exploiting urban elite to cream off surplus production. Small-scale but intensive agriculture was well suited to the extended family as a working unit (Gottwald, *Tribes of Yahweh*, 656, 662).

Cities and Villages Today

The relevance of the Israel pattern for many parts of Asia, Africa, and Latin America today is obvious. Rural areas continue to suffer the disintegrating effects of poverty. There is constant migration from the villages to the cities in search of jobs and excitement. At the same time more and more land is passing into the hands of large landholders. Rural areas are being organized for agribusiness by transnational food processors, while villagers are transformed into marginalized wage earners. There is a great need for viable new patterns of society which build on the importance of village life in wholesome interdependence with urban centers.

THE NEW SOCIETY: BOUNDARIES AS LIMITS OF LIVING SPACE

Another component of these chapters is the boundary lists, dating from the time before the monarchy. These delineate the areas belonging to each tribe.

Domain

Boundaries are more than markers of territory. They define areas of responsibility, limits of control, and protection against aggression. Mutually recognized boundaries are necessary for peaceful and creative coexistence, as long as they do not become barriers preventing fruitful social intercourse. Respect for boundaries is one way of summarizing the meaning of the last five of the Ten Commandments. More specifically, the tenth commandment warns explicitly against transgressing the boundaries of the neighbor's house and field and anything within his domain (Deut. 5:21; M. L. Chaney, "You Shall Not Covet Your Neighbor's House," *Pacific Theological Review* 15 [1982]). Such boundaries were frequently violated by the rich and powerful in the days of the monarchy when many aspects of the Canaan pattern of society returned (see above, pp. 58-59).

Inclusive Space

The ancient boundary lists from before the monarchy were available to the Teacher because they had been used and adapted in the days of the monarchy. David and Solomon expanded the

115

territory of Israel to include areas on the Mediterranean coast
and the Plain of Esdraelon which had remained independently
Canaanite during the time of the judges (Gottwald, *Tribes of
Yahweh*, 159). The royal surveyors thus extended the ancient
boundary lines "to the sea" (Josh. 15:4, 11, 13, 46, 47; 16:3, 6,
8, 11; 17:9, 10; 19:29), in order to incorporate the new areas and
peoples into the national administrative system. They were assigned to the nearest tribes.

This kind of inclusive space was a designation of the intention
of the king to include these new elements of the population as
part of the people and the royal purpose. From a theological
point of view, we could say that all those living in this inclusive
space are part of God's purpose because of the presence of God's
people there. In modern times boundaries would not define the
small area occupied by the tiny Christian movement in an Asian
land. These boundaries would refer to the entire nation or the
territory as part of God's plan. The Christian community is a
sign of God's intention for the wider area.

THE DYNAMIC NATURE OF THE NEW SOCIETY

Part III of the Joshua story is portrayed both as a fulfillment and
an unfinished task. The "already" is the settlement on the land.
The "not yet" is suggested by various signs and clues in the story.

The Risk of Failure

The pile of stones at Achor (see above, pp. 56-57) casts its
shadow over the land as a warning that what was given by the
owner may be taken away. It is in the pleasant villages that the
wicked "sits in ambush . . . murders the innocent" (Ps. 10:8).
"Great and goodly cities" (Deut. 6:10) may be laid waste (Lev.
26:31, 33), or burned with fire (Isa. 1:7; 6:11; Jer. 2:15). The
story of the hazardous covenant with Gibeon (see above,
pp. 74-85) reveals in a humorous way the seductive influence of
Canaanite values and ways, in order to underline the risk of
living in that land, or any land. Readers of Joshua would remember that Judean cities had chosen their own gods (Jer. 2:28;
7:17-18), and villages had kept their high places (Jer. 2:20). They
would recall the words of Ps. 106:35, 38:

They mingled with the nations
  and learned to do as they did. . . .

They poured out innocent blood . . .
  of their sons and daughters,
whom they sacrificed to the idols of Canaan;
  and the land was polluted with blood.

The Teacher was fully aware of the grave nature of the risk in the days of King Josiah. Yet the possibility remained open to "cause this people to inherit the land" (Josh. 1:6).

The Unfinished Task

The land distribution narrative with its lists is introduced by the words: "There remains yet very much land to be possessed," i.e., brought into the Israel pattern of life and faith (13:1). The same idea is restated at the beginning of the Shiloh phase (18:3). Specific areas are mentioned: the Philistine coast (13:2-4), the central coast guarded by Gezer (16:10), the coast south of Carmel guarded by Dor (17:11), the coast north of Carmel (13:5-6), the Plain of Esdraelon guarded by the cordon of fortress cities (17:11), northern Transjordan (13:13), and even the city of Jerusalem (15:63; see above, p. 85). These historically accurate notes remind the reader of the dynamic nature of the new society. Despite the risk of failure, there is always the call to bring new areas into the circle of liberation.

Reinterpretation during the Exile

The scope of the unfinished task is radically expanded by Deutero-Isaiah's reinterpretation of Josh. 13:1:

Enlarge the place of your tent,
  and let the curtains of your habitations be stretched out;
hold not back; lengthen your cords
  and strengthen your stakes. (Isa. 54:2)

The prophet in Babylon saw the land (Heb. *erets*) of Israel as a paradigm for the whole earth *(erets)* created by God. The "much land to be possessed" was not to be found only within the ideal borders of Davidic Israel but included the whole earth (Isa. 42:5). The "Creator of the ends of the earth" (Isa. 40:28) will not rest until "all the ends of the earth" (Isa. 45:22) are included in the tent of his living space (Isa. 40:22). For this he has commissioned his servant people as light and covenant to establish justice on the earth (Isa. 42:4, 6).

CHAPTER 12

PARABLES AMONG
THE ARCHIVES
Joshua 13:1 – 19:51

I will tell you a story with a meaning,
I will expound the riddle of things past.   — Psalm 78:2 NEB

The people shall hear, and fear,
and not act presumptuously again.   — Deuteronomy 17:13

The Teacher has inserted a number of brief parable-like episodes
here and there among the archival lists of cities and boundaries
that make up the bulk of these chapters. In so doing, he not only
enlivens the dull prose of the lists, but teaches a number of lessons
for the task of land administration in the 7th cent. B.C. as well
as across the generations down to our own age.

BALAAM IS DEAD: NO MORE
CORRUPT RELIGION! (13:22)

Although the story of Balaam takes up three chapters in the book
of Numbers, and Balaam is referred to seven times in the OT
outside these chapters, this is the only time that he is called a
"soothsayer" (Heb. *qosem*, more commonly translated in the RSV
as "diviner"). It seems likely that the Teacher has added this
descriptive title to the record he borrowed from Num. 31:8. He
may have been relying on Num. 22:7 which refers to "the fees
for divination," and 23:23 which speaks of "divination against
Israel." His purpose was probably to use Balaam as an illustration of the stern warning against divination as one of the "abominable practices" (see above, pp. xix-xx) of Canaanite society
(Deut. 18:10, 14).

118

The Diviner

The diviner, like the prophet in ancient Israel, was supposed to be in contact with the divine sphere. We learn from Isa. 3:2 that he occupied an important position in the Jerusalem court along with the political and military advisers of the king. Good counsel to the king might be called the king's "inspired decision" (*qesem,* Prov. 16:10). He had a role similar to the white-robed Brahman astrologers called *Hone* who are advisers to the king in classical Thai drama. Using a Christian term, we might call him the king's chaplain. In the ancient West Asian world he would daub his face with white powder (Ezek. 22:28), shake a bundle of arrows, attempt to get a response from the teraphim idols by means of dice, and examine a sheep's liver (Ezek. 21:21) in order to get a message from God. He might have visions or dreams. Such practices are typical of shamans in many lands.

An Abominable Practice

The practice of divination was classed as an abomination because diviners eating at the king's table were out of contact with God. They offered cheap advice by telling the people in power just what they wanted to hear (1 Kgs. 22:1-12). An example of this kind of cheap advice is found in Ezekiel 22. While the prophets were reporting "false visions and divining lies" (v. 28), the powerful aristocracy were "destroying lives to get dishonest gain" (v. 27), and the people were robbing the poor and needy as well as the defenseless foreigners (v. 29).

The Deuteronomic Historian had written this about the northern kingdom:

> They burned their sons and their daughters as offerings, and used divination and sorcery, and sold themselves to do evil. . . . Therefore the LORD was very angry with Israel, and removed them out of his sight; none was left *but the tribe of Judah only.* (2 Kgs. 17:17-18)

The last few words of this comment are typical of the Teacher's sense of the importance of reform in Judah while there was yet time. The death of Balaam, chaplain of cheap religion, was a reminder that this kind of "empty consolation" —feeding the people with "nonsense" (Zech. 10:2)—was no substitute for repentance and obedience. As Balaam had been put to death on the

119

other side of the Jordan, so the new society must not return to corrupt religious advisers in the new land.

HEBRON AND JERUSALEM: BACK TO COVENANT FAITHFULNESS! (14:6-15; 15:63)

The Teacher has bracketed the allotment of land to Judah (15:1-62) with anecdotal remarks about two cities: David's first capital, Hebron, and Manasseh's corrupted capital, Jerusalem. In this fashion he calls Josiah back to the beginning of the kingdom.

Hebron, City of Covenant Faithfulness

The introductory words of the Hebron incident are strongly reminiscent of David's kingship.

> Then the people of Judah came to Joshua at Gilgal. (Josh. 14:6)
> The men of Judah came . . . anointed David king [at Hebron]. (2 Sam. 2:4)
> So all the elders of Israel came to the king at Hebron; and King David made a covenant with them at Hebron before the LORD. (2 Sam. 5:3)

The Teacher has picked up the notes about Caleb's faithfulness from Num. 14:24 and Deut. 1:36 and purposely emphasized this by repeating it three times (Josh. 14:8, 9, 14). The Deuteronomic Historian used the same phraseology to describe David, who also "wholly followed the LORD" (1 Kgs. 11:6). Caleb's faithfulness is mentioned three times as the condition of his receiving "an inheritance" (Josh. 14:9, 13, 14). This again mirrors the way in which the kings of Judah are measured by what their "father David had done" (see 1 Kgs. 9:6; 11:4, 6, 33, 34; 14:8; 15:3, 5, 11; 2 Kgs. 14:3; 16:2; 18:3, 5). Finally, the Deuteronomic Historian summarized the reign of Josiah in these words: "he did what was right in the eyes of the LORD, and walked in all the way of David his father, and he did not turn aside to the right hand or to the left" (2 Kgs. 22:2).

Jerusalem, City of Abominable Practices

The reference to Jerusalem, on the other hand, appears to be the Teacher's indirect way of pointing to the corruption of Manasseh as the direct opposite of the faithfulness of David. The "Jebusites" remaining in Jerusalem (Josh. 15:63) symbolize "the nations whom the LORD drove out before the people of Israel" (2 Kgs. 21:2). Not only were the people of Judah unable to remove them from power, but Manasseh, like Achan of the Joshua story (see above, p. 58), caused the people of Judah to sin by imitating the "abominable practices" of these successors to the Jebusites, and did "things more wicked than all that the Amorites did" (v. 11). Because Manasseh, unlike David, had violated the conditions of the inheritance (v. 8), Jerusalem would be destroyed like Samaria (vv. 12-15, where the name "Jerusalem" is repeated three times for emphasis).

The Teacher's sorrowful comment on the rulers and people of Manasseh's time was: "They did not listen" (v. 9). In this he echoed the words of Isaiah (Isa. 6:9-10; 30:15-16). This gives the clue to the mention of Jerusalem at the end of the land grant to Judah. It is an urgent final appeal to Josiah and the people of Judah to "choose life" (Deut. 31:19) by going back to the beginning at Hebron.

Caleb and David

The symbolic identity between David and Caleb is shown in other ways. Caleb appears for the first time at Kadesh-barnea as the representative of the tribe of Judah (David's tribe), among the scouts (Num. 13:6), on the expedition which took them to Hebron (v. 22). In all previous listings, Judah had been represented by Nahshon (Num. 1:7; 2:3; 7:12, 17; 10:14). Nahshon is listed as an ancestor of David in two genealogies (Ruth 4:18; 1 Chr. 2:11). In another genealogy, however, which may be later, Caleb is listed as the great-grandfather of "Bethlehem," the city of David (1 Chr. 2:50-51). Nahshon must have died in the wilderness, according to the tradition. Only Caleb and Joshua survived to enter the Land of Promise. Joshua is identified with Moses. Caleb is close to David.

Hebron, a Calebite City

It seems probable (R. de Vaux, *The Early History of Israel*, 526) that the Calebites entered Canaan from the south, and did not accompany Moses and Joshua on the long march from Kadesh-barnea to the Plains of Moab. God's promise to both Caleb and

Joshua that they alone will enter the land of Canaan (Num. 14:30) is divided into two promises by the Teacher (see Deut. 1:36 and 38). This may reflect a tradition of two entries into the land, one from the south under Caleb, and one from the east under Joshua.

Caleb is, moreover, associated with non-Israelite peoples. His brother was Kenaz (Josh. 15:17), which is also the name of an Edomite chief (1 Chr. 1:53), a descendant of Esau (Gen. 36:15). In the group of peoples associated with Caleb, we find Korah (1 Chr. 2:43) whose name is also borne by an Edomite chief (Gen. 36:16), Rekem a Midianite (Num. 31:8; Josh. 13:21), and Shema a Kenite (1 Chr. 2:55).

Caleb's special place in the Joshua story emphasizes the importance of faithfulness to Yahweh (like David's), rather than blood relationship to Israel. In fact, David himself was not pure Judean (Ruth 4:17; cf. 1 Sam. 22:3). This was a different message from that found in the time of Ezra and Nehemiah, when ethnic purity was emphasized: "The holy race has mixed itself with the peoples of the lands" (Ezra 9:2).

Hebron, an Aaronite City

Hebron's double identity is revealed by an examination of the genealogical lists, which often reflect historical relationships. Hebron appears as the "grandson" of both Caleb (1 Chr. 2:42) and Levi (Exod. 6:18; Num. 3:19; 1 Chr. 6:2; 23:12). In most of these levitical genealogies, Hebron is the "brother" of Amram the father of Moses, Aaron, and Miriam. Another, perhaps older genealogy (F. M. Cross, *Canaanite Myth and Hebrew Epic*, 206-7) mentions two levitical families as descendants of Levi: the Mushites, descended from Moses, and the Hebronites, presumably descendants of Aaron (Num. 26:57-58). Cross has suggested that we have here two great priestly families in early Israel. The Mushites had their centers at Shiloh, Nob, and Dan. Hebron was the main Aaronite shrine, and with it, Bethel (see below, p. 145).

David's choice of Hebron as the place to establish his kingship may have been influenced by the support given him by the Aaronite priests (B. Mazar, "The Cities of the Priests and the Levites," *VTS* 7 [1960]:193-205). Cross suggests that Zadok, one of David's priests, may well have come from Hebron (*Canaanite Myth and Hebrew Epic*, 208).

The Teacher emphasized the Calebite connection of Hebron more than the city's relationship with the Aaronite priests. Therefore he placed this incident at the beginning of the Judah land grant narrative. The Aaronite connection was alluded to in a minor way, along with other cities of refuge and levitical cities (Josh. 20:7; 21:11-13). Again, the emphasis is on covenant faithfulness rather than priestly descent.

ACHSAH'S REQUEST: WATER IS LIFE TO THE LAND! (15:16-19)

The story of Achsah's request is a charming interlude between the boundary and city lists of the tribe of Judah.

Water

It is, appropriately, the story of a woman who is, symbolically, "a garden fountain, a well of living water" (Cant. 4:15). Her story tells the reader that the good land, endowed with "brooks of water, of fountains and springs, flowing forth in valleys and hills" (Deut. 8:7), will remain good and life-supporting only when attention is given to the life-giving water that is part of the inheritance. Land without water, as Achsah says (Josh. 15:19), becomes a wilderness where no crops can grow, no animals graze, and no human can live (cf. Ps. 63:1). Competition over access to water could be a cause of bitter strife (Gen. 26:18-19), and a means by which the strong oppress the weak (Ezek. 34:17-19). Stopping up sources of water was an act of war; it threatened a people's existence (2 Kgs. 3:19, 25; 2 Chr. 32:3) until a nation became like "a garden without water" (Isa. 1:30).

Debir

The story is placed in Debir, probably to be located at Khirbet Rabûd about 12 km. (7.5 mi.) S of Hebron. It was an important city in the Late Bronze Age (1500-1200 B.C.), and was fortified during the reign of David and Solomon. Excavations have revealed rock-cut cisterns and, about 2.2 km. (1.25 mi.) to the north, two wells on which Debir was dependent for water. When Sennacherib conquered Debir in 701 B.C., he undoubtedly stopped up these two wells, known as "the upper and lower springs." The same was true when Nebuchadnezzar's armies destroyed Debir again in the 6th cent. B.C.

Achsah's Request

Achsah's first request was for agricultural land (RSV "a field") around Debir. This was apparently granted by her father as a dowry. Her reaction was one of displeasure because the gift had not included access to the water supply. As the narrative describes it, she clapped her hands in anger (Josh. 15:18; an alternative translation to RSV "alighted"). Without a water supply, the gift would be meaningless. To his credit, Caleb responded to his daughter's request by giving her the two wells that meant the difference between life and death.

Water and Land

The Teacher was appealing for care and proper management of water resources as a means of restoring the land to fertility. The upper and lower springs in the story may have reminded his readers of the old lower pool in Jerusalem (Isa. 22:9-11) and the newer upper pool (Isa. 7:3; 36:2) in which the waters of the Gihon Spring were held. We may relate this passage to the words of Amos, "Let justice roll down like waters" (Amos 5:24). The Hebrew word translated "springs" in the RSV of Josh. 15:19 and Judg. 1:15 is used in this sense only in this story in the Old Testament. It is from the same root as the word translated "roll down" in Amos. This suggests a comparison of justice with the "upper spring" and "righteousness" with the "lower spring," as a reminder that land management must include access to water. Only then can the people "draw water from the wells of salvation" (Isa. 12:3). Only in this way can a righteous king, ruling with justice, be "like streams of water in a dry place" (Isa. 32:2). At this level Achsah, representing the people, asks Caleb, who represents the king, for justice and life. Achsah's request reminds us also of the Samaritan woman's request for the water of life. Jesus' gift is for use on the land, in the places where we live, so that our communities may become like well-watered gardens.

THE DAUGHTERS OF ZELOPHEHAD: PRESERVE OUR INHERITANCE! (17:3-6)

According to the narrative in Numbers 27, the five daughters of Zelophehad took the initiative to preserve their deceased father's inheritance for future generations. They demanded an adjustment in the legal regulations which restricted inheritance to male heirs (Num. 27:2-4). As a result of their intervention, the laws were changed (vv. 7-11) to allow the daughters of a man without male heirs to inherit land apart from their husbands. This action would keep the land within the father's house (extended family), or at least within the kinship association (Num. 36:7). The five women married within their kinship associations (v. 10; see Gottwald, *Tribes*, 265).

The Census of Jeroboam II

The names of two of the daughters, Noah (not the same spelling in Hebrew as of the "Noah" of Gen. 6–8) and Hoglah, along with five of their "brothers" (Josh. 17:2), have been found in the ruins of Samaria. These ostraca of Samaria (earthenware sherds used for records) date from the 8th cent. B.C. On them are written inscriptions concerning the delivery of wine and oil to certain individuals from various districts in Samaria. The seven names represent both clans and districts in ancient Israel, and probably were listed in the population census of Jeroboam II (786-746 B.C.) alluded to in 2 Chr. 5:17. According to Aharoni, the clans of the daughters of Zelophehad are to be located in the region to the north of Samaria (Y. Aharoni, *The Land of the Bible*, 256-369).

Preserving the Inheritance

The function of this brief anecdotal reference to the daughters of Zelophehad in the Joshua story is to emphasize their concern for future generations. It is appropriate, as in the case of Achsah, that this concern for the land given by Yahweh should be shown by women. They will carry the next generation in their wombs. They are symbols of the fertility of the land and its people (Ps. 128:3; Ezek. 19:10; Isa. 5:7).

Readers would contrast the daughters of Zelophehad with the daughters of Zion who, in the words of Isaiah, "are haughty and walk with outstretched necks, glancing wantonly with their eyes," while their husbands "devour the vineyard . . . crushing my people, . . . grinding the face of the poor" (Isa. 3:14-15; cf. Amos 4:1). These women were not concerned about future generations, but only about present pleasure at the expense of the poor. Readers would remember how the daughters of Israel "played the harlot" with the Baals of the land (Hos. 4:13), and would praise the daughters of Zelophehad for their faithful concern in preserving the inheritance for future generations.

Readers today will compare the daughters of Zelophehad with those who intervene to change legal structures because of a concern for future generations. They may be opposed to defoliation of crops in a time of war, the pollution of the earth by industrial wastes, the plunder of underdeveloped lands by foreign corporations, the cheapening of the cultural heritage by the tourism industry, the deforestation of the lands of Southeast Asia by foreign corporations, or the thoughtless destruction of natural resources by the marginalized poor.

THE FORESTS OF GOD: PARTNERS IN CREATION! (17:14-18)

The Teacher concludes phase 1B of the land distribution with an anecdote appealing to the readers to restore the beauty of the woods and cultivated land as a way of participating in the new creation.

Joshua as Arbitrator

This episode may be a genuine recollection of Joshua's important work as arbitrator of tribal territorial claims. It begins with a complaint, whose historical background we are not able to reconstruct. The "one lot" (17:14) must refer to "the allotment of the descendants of Joseph" (16:1), although the description which follows gives only the southern boundary line of Ephraim. The "one lot" seems to be the "hill country of Ephraim" (17:15), between Bethel and Shechem. It appears that the "one lot" was expanded (17:17) to include that of Manasseh (17:1) as a second lot. This included "the land of . . . the Rephaim" (17:15), meaning Bashan and perhaps Gilead (Josh. 12:4; 13:12; Deut. 2:20; 3:11, 13), which was assigned to a branch of the tribe of Manasseh (Josh. 17:1, 5-6). The "land of the Perizzites" refers to the territory north of Bethel (Gen. 13:7), around Shechem (Gen. 34:30), and north of Shechem (Judg. 1:4-5; for the location of Bezek north of Tirzah see Aharoni, *Land of the Bible*, 288, map 20). In other words, this is the entire "hill country" (Josh. 17:18) from Bethel north to the cities guarding the Plain of Jezreel. To the complaint of the tribe of Joseph that they had only "one portion" (17:14), Joshua responds by giving Manasseh "ten portions" west of the Jordan (17:5).

Joshua's response to the complainers is that they should trans- form the forest thickets of the hill country into a forest park fit for habitation as God intended.

Forest Thickets in Canaan

The complaint of the Joseph tribe is that the area allotted to them is inadequate for their great numbers. This can refer only to parts of the hill country already brought under cultivation by the sparsely settled Canaanite society. Before rock terracing or water channels or cisterns for irrigation could be arranged for, there was the difficult task of clearing away the forest thickets that covered the land.

We read of other wild, uninhabited forested land in the area around Aijalon (1 Sam. 14:25) and in Judah (1 Sam. 22:5), the Jordan Valley (2 Kgs. 6:4; cf. Jer. 12:5), the Negeb (Ezek. 20:46-47), Gilead (2 Sam. 18:6, 8, 17), Bashan (Zech. 11:2), Leb- anon (1 Kgs. 7:2), and Egypt (Jer. 46:23). This is important for visitors to the Holy Land today to keep in mind as they see the bare hills and the reforestation projects in Israel.

The forests as obstacles to cultivation, and thus to human life, are best described as "thickets of the forest" (Isa. 9:18; 10:34). This includes thorns and briers as well as scrub growth. This kind of forest thicket is also the home of wild animals such as lions (Jer. 5:6; 12:8), bears (2 Kgs. 2:24), and wild boars (Ps. 80:13) which destroy people and cultivated fields.

The Glory of the Land

As we ponder the meaning of Joshua's command to the tribe of Joseph, it is important to explore in a little more depth the mean- ing of forests in Hebrew thought. Forests are seen as a part of God's good creation. The original forest was a park where trees were both beautiful and useful in supporting human and animal life (Gen. 1:11, 12, 29; 2:9). The royal forest preserves of ancient kings (Neh. 2:8; Eccl. 2:5-6) were probably modelled after this original ideal garden. Visitors to Persepolis in Iran will recall the symbolic representations of cedar and palm trees on the Apadana staircase. The Persian word for garden is *parades*. From it we get the word "paradise," used by the Greek translators of Genesis 2.

It was in this kind of forest-park that kings could learn wisdom (1 Kgs. 4:33), and that lovers could find true love (Cant. 2:3; see in these songs many other instances of tree imagery).

The symbolic nature of the forest is seen in the description of the heights of Lebanon as a forest-park (RSV "densest forest"; the Hebrew uses the word *karmel* along with forest). The Assyrian king claimed to have cut down its trees in defiance of Yahweh (2 Kgs. 19:23=Isa. 37:24). Ezekiel's satirical poem about the Egyptian pharaoh draws on the same mythological tradition. He compares him to "a cedar in Lebanon" among "the trees of the forest. . . . all the trees of Eden" in "the garden of God" (Ezek. 31:3-5, 8-9).

Seen in this light, it is no surprise to find forests described as "the glory" of the land, along with the cultivated fruitful land (*karmel*, Isa. 10:18). When Jeremiah described Canaan as "a plentiful land *(karmel)* with fruit and good things" (Jer. 2:7), he was thinking of "fertile land" (*karmel*, 2 Chr. 26:10) and woodlands together as a park, "the pleasant land," and "a heritage most beauteous of all the nations" (Jer. 3:19).

When the proper relationship between God, people, and land (water, wooded areas, cultivated land) is broken, the "fruitful land" *(karmel)* becomes an uninhabited wilderness (*midbar*, Jer. 4:26). The noble forests, the glory of the land, are burned down (Jer. 21:14). Homes where grapes and figs were cultivated revert to the condition of forest thickets (Hos. 2:12). Cities and their surrounding fields become uninhabited forests (Mic. 3:12=Jer. 26:18). The proud cedars of Lebanon and oaks of Bashan are cut down (Isa. 2:13); these symbols of pride and injustice will be destroyed (Isa. 9:18; 10:18-19, 33-34; Ezek. 20:46-47).

In God's new creation, the wilderness *(midbar)* becomes a fruitful field *(kerem)*, and the fruitful field is part of a forest-park (Isa. 32:15; 41:17-20) whose trees support life and restore the wholeness of the land and people (Ezek. 47:12). Justice and righteousness, peace and security return to the land (Isa. 32:16), which becomes "like Eden . . . the garden of the LORD" once again (51:2). For this reason, poets speak of the rejoicing of the trees of the forest at the coming of Yahweh to set things right (Ps. 96:12=1 Chr. 16:33; Ps. 148:9). This reclamation begins with

Israel (Isa. 44:23). Thus any restoration of the forest as a park, or as part of the beautiful land, is a sign of the new creation for all to see (Isa. 55:12-13).

Participating in the New Creation

Joshua's command to the people of Joseph is to go up to the forest thickets and make them into a park, like the garden of God (Josh. 17:15, 17). The verb translated in the RSV as "clear the ground" is the only instance in the OT where this verb, otherwise reserved for God alone, has a human subject. It is possible that this was originally a now unknown homonym of the Hebrew *bara*. With the same spelling but a different meaning, however, other verbs could have been substituted to clear up what would have been understood by the readers as an ambiguity. The Teacher must have known the background of meaning to the word "forest" as outlined above, and his readers would not have been ignorant of the importance of the verb *bara* when used of Israel.

If we accept this meaning of the verb, then, it can only mean to co-create or participate in God's creative act by transforming the forest thicket into a forest park, i.e., making it habitable, life supporting, and beautiful. Only then would they be able to stretch their boundaries out to the sea or to the plains where the Canaanites ruled (17:18). In the 7th cent. B.C. this would have been a call to co-create the "pleasant land" and the "beauteous heritage" as had been God's intention from the beginning (Jer. 3:19). Readers today should likewise heed the words of Joshua, given to us by the Teacher. These words are a call to join in co-creating the beauty of planet earth. They are especially relevant in a time when the earth is threatened by the destruction of forests and cultivated land, and human selfishness is fueled by technological means to turn the garden land into a desert.

CHAPTER 13

A COMPASSIONATE SOCIETY
Joshua 20:1-9

You shall not defile the land in which you live, in the midst of which I dwell, for I the LORD dwell in the midst of the people of Israel.
—Numbers 35:34

Six cities of refuge were part of the Teacher's plan for the new society. They were expressions of God's will that innocent people should not be killed in the land given to Israel as an inheritance (Deut. 19:10). Their importance is seen from two other descriptions (Num. 35:1-28; Deut. 19:1-10) as well as a simply stated law (Exod. 21:13). The purpose of the cities of refuge was to maintain the health of society by preventing the spread of the poison (pollution) of unchecked violence and bloodshed (see Gen. 6:11; Hos. 4:1-3; Jer. 7:6). With such a purpose, these cities have a contemporary relevance in an age marked by increasing levels of violence with its many victims.

THE LAW OF BLOOD VENGEANCE

The ancient Hebrews believed that the death of an innocent person poisoned the land as well as the society living there (Num. 35:33). Taking the life of an innocent person was not viewed as a private act between the killer and the killed. It was seen to involve the whole society because it violated the *shalom* of covenant society under God. "The voice of your brother's blood is crying to me from the ground," said God to Cain (Gen. 4:10). The ancient view was that the pollution caused by bloodshed could be purged from the land and from covenant society only by the death of the murderer (Num. 35:33). No animal sacrifice could cleanse this guilt caused by the violent death of a human being created in God's image (Gen. 9:6).

130

According to ancient custom, the avenger of blood was the next-of-kin of the murdered person (Num. 35:19). Properly speaking, the avenger of blood was not carrying on a vendetta of private revenge in pursuing the murderer (Deut. 19:6; Josh. 20:5), but performing an act necessary and required by law for the maintenance of the health of society. The law was quite specific in guarding against the kind of unlimited revenge that could destroy entire families or clans. The law of blood vengeance permitted only "life for life" (Deut. 19:21).

Behind this custom, which seems strange in our society today, we should sense a deep respect for the value and dignity of each human being, as well as a feeling of grief and outrage when the gift of life is subject to violence and death. On the other hand, we should be careful in drawing conclusions from this ancient tradition about modern practices of capital punishment. The focus of the cleansing action was on the health of the organism, not the death of the murderer. There may well be other means of maintaining or restoring health in a violent society than recourse to the electric chair, the hangman's noose, or the gas chamber.

TWO LAWS IN CONFLICT

As long as the guilt of the murderer was beyond question, the law of blood vengeance worked to preserve a balance of justice and restore peace. In the case of an accidental death, however, the manslayer was considered both guilty (because an innocent person's blood had been shed) and innocent (because he had not intended to kill). A woodcutter's axehead might fly off the handle and kill someone (Deut. 19:5), or a stone innocently set in motion might crush a fellow worker (Num. 35:22-23).

In such a case, two laws were in conflict with each other. The law of blood vengeance required the avenger of blood to kill the manslayer. The law against the shedding of innocent blood forbade such action. The death of the innocent manslayer would only compound the poison on the land by adding a second innocent person's death to the first. This would set in motion a chain of bloody violence. The one law, if allowed to run its course, would weaken and destroy the whole of society. The other would leave unresolved the matter of the pollution caused by the death of an innocent person, even though it was accidental.

CITIES OF REFUGE

The institution designed to preserve society from this kind of escalation of violence was the city of refuge. The Hebrew wording of Josh. 20:2-3 makes clear that these cities were to be established "for you," i.e., for the health and *shalom* of the covenant society.

An innocent manslayer was allowed to flee from the law of blood vengeance to one of six designated locations conveniently located throughout the land, with easy access maintained at all times (Deut. 19:3). In each of these cities there was a resident community of levitical priests, as we can see from Josh. 21:13, 21, 27, 32, 36, 38 where the six are listed as levitical cities.

The purposes of this temporary exile in the city of refuge were, first, to save the life of the fugitive who was not deserving of death (Deut. 19:6), second, to "purge the guilt of innocent blood [i.e., of the slain man] from your midst" (Deut. 21:9), and third, to prevent the further guilt of bloodshed (i.e., of the innocent manslayer) in the land (Deut. 19:10).

Justice

According to the procedure outlined in Joshua 20, every effort should be made to assure that only the innocent are protected, not the guilty. First there is the manslayer's own statement of his case at the gate, i.e., before the city council in official session (v. 4). Later there is a formal hearing before the assembly (vv. 6, 9), to determine whether the death was in fact accidental, or committed with evil intent (Num. 35:20-21).

The Warm Welcome

Three actions are mandated for the priestly community. First, they shall "take him into the city" (v. 4). The Hebrew verb means "to gather people together" (Josh. 2:18; 24:1), or "to gather a harvest" (Ruth 2:7). During and after the exilic period, it was used to describe the gathering together of a scattered Israel (Isa. 49:5), sometimes called the "outcasts of Israel" (Isa. 56:8). In this context it signifies the gathering or warm acceptance of the fugitive into a caring community. As such, it is an imitation of God, who takes the fugitive "into his care" when even parents will not do so (Ps. 27:10 NEB).

A Place to Live

Second, the holy community is to "give him a place" in which to live. Jewish rabbis emphasize the practical nature of this injunction. Accommodations should be rent-free, and the fugitive should be taught a useful skill so that he could be a contributing member of society. There would be plenty of work to be done in the fields and pasturelands attached to the levitical cities (Josh. 21:9).

There is deep insight here into the problems of the *displaced* person who has had to leave "his own town and his own home" (Josh. 20:6) through no fault of his own. Other communities would not be willing to receive him. The plight of the Jewish exiles after the destruction of Jerusalem comes to mind.

> "Away! Unclean!" men cried at them;
> "Away! Away! Touch not!"
> So they became fugitives and wanderers;
> men said among the nations,
> "They shall stay with us no longer." (Lam. 4:15)

The priestly community was appointed to do what others may have been afraid to do, to give the displaced person a place.

This is again an imitation of God, who "gives the desolate a home to dwell in" (Ps. 68:6). The welcoming Levites would be a proof of the grace of God who is a "hiding place" where the one in trouble can be preserved (Ps. 32:7). They would be a living demonstration of the future and hope which God had in mind for the fugitive (Prov. 23:18).

Protection

The third obligation of the host community would be when the avenger of blood came pounding on the gate demanding that the fugitive be turned over to him on the basis of the law of blood vengeance. The keepers of the city of refuge must "not give up the slayer" to them (Josh. 20:5). They must resist the angry demands of the champions of law and order. They are the champions of another law which guards the innocent from violence, lest the land be polluted.

Protection of the innocent from the destroyer is a participation in the work of God, who does not "deliver into the hand of my enemy" (Ps. 31:8). The city of refuge is God's shield (Pss. 7:10; 119:114), guarding the life of the accused (Ps. 25:20).

Atonement

In order to understand the significance of the manslayer's sojourn in the priestly city, we must look briefly at the procedure to be followed in the case of other unwitting sins of a cultic nature, as found in Leviticus 4–5 and Numbers 15. Even though the offender was not aware of the fact that there had been a violation of the cultic law, he was considered guilty and had to "bear his iniquity" (Lev. 5:17). Thus there had to be a ceremony of atonement to remove the guilt, and restore the relationship with God.

The offending party, whether ruler, ordinary citizen, or representative of the entire community, would lay his hand on the head of a sacrificial animal. By this symbolic action a personal relationship would be established whereby the animal served as a substitute in his death "to make atonement" for the offender (Lev. 1:4). The animal was then slaughtered. Its blood was smeared on the altar and poured out at the base of the altar. The fat portions were burned on the altar as an offering. In this way the priest would "make atonement for [him], and [he] shall be forgiven" (Lev. 4:20).

We find a similar ceremony in the case of a slain man found lying in open country, when the slayer is not known (Deut. 21:1-9). With the aid of levitical priests, an animal is slain, and the elders of the nearest town, having placed their hands on its head, swear that they are innocent of the murder. This was a way of purging "the guilt of innocent blood" from their midst.

There is no hint of any such ceremony being conducted in the city of refuge. There is, however, a mysterious reference to the death of the high priest as marking the end of the sojourn of the manslayer in the city of refuge.

Priestly tradition held that the high priest represented the whole people of Israel before God. The symbol of this representative role was a breastpiece bearing the names of the twelve tribes (Exod. 28:29). He wore this when he made intercession for the people. He was representative in another way as well. He was to bear "any guilt incurred in the holy offering which the people of Israel hallow as their holy gifts . . . that they may be accepted before the LORD" (v. 38). Perhaps the death of the high priest (Josh. 20:6; Num. 35:25) was considered to have the same effect as that of the sacrificial animal in the atonement ceremony for unwitting sin.

If we look again at the act of opening their gates to the manslayer, we can see that the community of priests were accepting a person guilty of unwitting manslaughter into their midst. They were allowing their own holiness to be made unholy, so that in due time the guilt of manslaughter could be purged away, and the manslayer could return home. In this sense, the whole community of the host city bore the guilt together. In his death the high priest represented the priestly community as well as the manslayer.

Deutero-Isaiah was using this circle of ideas when he described an innocent sufferer (Isa. 53:9) who could find no refuge among men (v. 3), but would "bear the iniquities" of the nations, and "make many to be accounted righteous," or innocent (v. 11). Paul gave a similar interpretation of Christ, "who was without sin, but for our sake God made him share our sin in order that in union with him we might share the righteousness of God" (2 Cor. 5:21 TEV).

It is not necessary to assume, as some have done, that the office of "high priest" referred to the postexilic temple hierarchy. The same Hebrew expression designates the priest in charge of the temple in Jerusalem (2 Kgs. 12:10; 22:4; see also 25:18). It is best to assume that the "high priest" was to be the one in charge of the sanctuary in the particular city of refuge sought out by the fugitive (see N. M. Nicolsky, "Das Asylrecht in Israel," *ZAW* 48 [1930]: 146-75).

Equal Access to Refuge

It is important to note that the foreigner who was guilty of unwitting manslaughter was entitled to the same justice, welcome, living place, protection, and atoning grace as the native-born Israelite (Josh. 20:9). The death of an innocent foreigner would pollute the land just as much as the death of a full member of the covenant people. In the context of the Joshua story we can see the meaning of this equal access for the Canaanite family of Rahab, the Hivites in the Gibeonite confederacy, and all the others who lived among the Israelites (Josh. 13:13; 15:63; 16:10; 17:12).

The principle of equal access to the cities of refuge for foreigners stands in tension with the principle of "radical discontinuity" with the "abominable practices" of Canaanite society (see above, pp. 54-55). Without this protection for the foreigner the principle of discontinuity could easily become one of "death to foreigners," or at least a second-class status for them. The "hot anger" of the avenger of blood (Deut. 19:6) could easily become a mob spirit like that encountered in the case of Gibeon (see above, p. 83).

HISTORICAL CONSIDERATIONS

With Mosaic authority transmitted to Joshua by God himself (Josh. 20:1-2), we would expect to find evidence of the actual functioning of these cities of refuge in the history of Israel. Unfortunately there is none. Are we to understand that the six cities mentioned in vv. 7-8 were actually "set apart," "designated" (vv. 7, 9), as tradition has it? If so, when did this happen? We are not told.

Available information allows us to guess that the six cities of refuge may have been functioning in the period of the united monarchy. Before that, the situation was too chaotic for such an established system. Israelite control of the territory east of the Jordan was established only in David's time (see above, p. 11). At least two of the six cities, Ramoth in Gilead and Kedesh in Galilee, were outside territory claimed for Israel in the time of the judges (Y. Aharoni and M. Avi-Yonah, *The Macmillan Bible Atlas*, rev. ed., map 68). The plea of the woman of Tekoa to David that "the avenger of blood slay no more" (2 Sam. 14:1) suggests no city of refuge was yet available, at least in Judah. It seems, then, that the system of six cities of refuge was not in operation even in the time of David.

Following the division of the monarchy, the territory east of the Jordan was frequently disputed and finally lost. Mesha, king of Moab, recorded in an inscription that he had rebuilt the ruined city of Bezer (see Josh. 20:8) after capturing it from Israel about 850 B.C. (R. J. Williams, "Moabite Stone," *IDB* 3:420). Ramoth in Gilead was located on the frontier between Israel and Aram and often changed hands (1 Kgs. 22:3; 2 Kgs. 8:28). Golan, probably to be located near Ashtaroth in Bashan (Aharoni and Avi-Yonah, *The Macmillan Bible Atlas*, map 108), was also vulnerable to Aramean pressure (2 Kgs. 10:32-33). Both Ramoth in Gilead and Golan became part of the Assyrian empire in 733 B.C., and Kedesh in Galilee suffered the same fate the following year. Shechem's turn came in 721 B.C. Thus, by Josiah's time, the only one of the six remaining in Israelite control was Hebron.

We must assume, then, that the system of six cities of refuge belongs to the reign of Solomon rather than to the time of Joshua. However, a similar institution may have existed before the monarchy, as suggested by the law in Exod. 21:13. The 7th-cent. B.C. Teacher included this Mosaic tradition in its Solomonic form in his "condensed view of history" (see above, pp. xiv-xv) as a means of communicating a message to the reforming group (see above, p. xv).

THE CITIES OF REFUGE AS PART OF THE REFORM PROGRAM

It is clear that the arrangement of the six cities on both sides of the Jordan, "like two rows of vines in a vineyard" (A. J. Rosenberg and S. Shulman, *The Book of Joshua*, 136), presupposes the restoration of the kingdom according to its dimensions in the reign of David (see above, pp. 10-11). These cities were part of an ideal projection into the future, which, it was hoped, Josiah would bring into reality. What, then, was the particular message of these cities for King Josiah and other leaders of the reform?

Perhaps we may see the meaning of these cities in relation to the problem of innocent blood on the land. Micah had called Jerusalem a city "built with blood" (3:10). During the long reign of Manasseh, grandfather of Josiah, Jerusalem was "filled from one end to the other with innocent blood" (2 Kgs. 21:16; see above, pp. 59, 120-21). The situation had not changed radically with the death of Manasseh or his son Amon, or even with the accession of Josiah. In the days before the reform, Jeremiah made reference to the stains of "the lifeblood of the guiltless poor" on the clothes of the rich and powerful who proclaimed themselves to be "innocent" (Jer. 2:34-35). After the death of Josiah, Jeremiah called for an end to shedding innocent blood (7:6) and denounced Josiah's son Jehoiakim for the same crime (22:17). The historian's view was that "the LORD would not pardon" this continual pollution of the land by the shedding of innocent blood (2 Kgs. 24:3-4).

Against this background, the cities of refuge would be available for the "guiltless poor" who wished to flee from the "oppression and violence" (Jer. 22:17) of the powerful in case they might be tempted to depart from God's Teaching "which is in charge of the Levitical priests" (Deut. 17:18) and "lift up their hearts against" their brothers and sisters (v. 20).

The heap of stones at Trouble Valley was a reminder of the first sin in the Promised Land (see above, pp. 56-57). The cities of refuge were a divinely appointed means of dealing with the continuing effects of sin in the new society in a way which would preserve the health and *shalom* of that society.

One other incident in the history of Israel may have been in the Teacher's mind as he described the cities of refuge. The reform of Jehu in 842 B.C. was meant to "avenge on Jezebel the blood of . . . the prophets and . . . of all the servants of the LORD" (2 Kgs. 9:7). The historian's description of the event is similar to the rhetoric used in the Joshua story (see above, pp. 89-90). Jehu left "none remaining. . . . spared none. . . . wiped them out" (2 Kgs. 10:11, 14, 17). The historian even commends Jehu for doing "what is right . . . according to all that was in my [the LORD's] heart" (v. 30).

Yet the Teacher must have been aware of God's condemnation of Jehu and his whole dynasty because of the "blood of Jezreel" (Hos. 1:4). In retrospect it was clear that in his reforming zeal, Jehu had killed many innocent people. The avenger of blood had compounded the pollution by spilling more innocent blood.

The cities of refuge would serve as protection not only from the violence and oppression of wicked rulers, but from the exaggerated zeal of the righteous avengers of blood.

THE CITIES OF REFUGE TODAY

It is not difficult to find modern analogies to innocent fugitives and angry pursuers. Prejudice, greed, lust for power, or fear may influence the making or interpretation of laws in a way that justifies cruel acts of vengeance on those who are more sinned against than sinning. Reasons can be found for exploitation, theft of land, unjust imprisonment, and torture of those presumed to be offenders. Domestic violence makes women and children fugitives in need of refuge. Wars, revolutions, natural disasters, and impersonal social changes send refugees wandering over sea and land in search of a place to live. Violence pollutes the earth.

Modern "cities of refuge" are those institutions or communities at the local, regional, or international level that reverse the spread of the pollution caused by violence. They provide welcome, a living place, and protection against the forces of destruction, until the fugitives can take their own place in society again. At times these communities may have a part in the "atonement" process by accepting the "guilt" of the fugitive refugees on themselves.

One side of the prophetic message is to "seek justice, correct oppression; defend the fatherless, plead for the widow" (Isa. 1:17). The cities of refuge represent another side of the same message, i.e., to "give counsel, grant justice; . . . let the outcasts of Moab sojourn among you; be a refuge to them from the destroyer" (Isa. 16:3-4).

Christians have themselves "fled for refuge" to the heavenly sanctuary where Jesus Christ is the welcoming host (Heb. 6:18), and the high priest of the city (v. 20). This high priest purifies their conscience by his death, making them free to return to home and country to serve the living God (9:14) by welcoming strangers and remembering those who are ill treated (13:2-3; cf. Matt. 25:35-36). Those who have found refuge will themselves become a source of refuge for other fugitives.

CHAPTER 14

AN ENLIGHTENED SOCIETY
Joshua 21:1-45

Hearken to me, you who know righteousness,
the people in whose heart is my law [Teaching]. —Isaiah 51:7

For it [this Teaching] is no trifle for you, but it is your life, and
thereby you shall live long in the land. —Deuteronomy 32:47

He will not fail or be discouraged
till he has established justice in the earth;
and the coastlands wait for his law [Teaching]. —Isaiah 42:4

If we place this chapter of Joshua in the context of King Josiah's reformation, the forty-eight levitical cities may be seen as the Teacher's substitute for the idolatrous high places, altars, and shrines, with all their paraphernalia, which were destroyed in the cleansing of the land (2 Kgs. 23:5-20). The Levites were then to replace the idolatrous priests, male cult prostitutes, and other functionaries of the old shrines (vv. 5-8), thus reversing the sin of Jeroboam (1 Kgs. 12:31). The centralization of the cult, which was a part of the reform, was not meant to deprive the people of local instruction in God's Teaching.

The levitical cities might be called Torah Centers, i.e., places where God's Teaching would be studied, interpreted, practiced, and taught. The Levites would put this Teaching in the mouths, hearts, and action of the people (Deut. 30:14; cf. Josh. 1:7-8). Such instruction by story and commandments (see above, pp. 6-7) was the sovereign remedy for the rebellious and stubborn hearts of God's people (Deut. 31:27).

The number 48 (Josh. 21:41) is the product of twelve, signifying the tribes, multiplied by four, a number denoting universality (M. H. Pope, "Number," *IDB* 3:565). The meaning of this number is that the influence of God's Teaching was to permeate all aspects of the life of each tribe.

THE KEY SIGNIFICANCE OF CHAPTER 21

The Teacher's carefully constructed presentation of the Joshua story may be seen by noting his summarizing statements at the various turning points in the narrative. We find such statements at the end of the southern (10:40) and northern (11:16-20) campaigns. The statement in 11:23 comes at the conclusion of the military phase and the beginning of the land distribution phase. The completion of the land allotment is marked by another statement (19:51). A brief summary concludes the narratives of the cities of refuge (20:9) and the levitical cities (21:41-42).

The more comprehensive statement in 21:43-45 is a summary covering the entire Joshua story up to that point. It binds the whole narrative together by its obvious references to the beginning, and hence serves to highlight the importance of ch. 21. This will be made clear by looking at the following phrases in relation to ch. 1.

The LORD gave to Israel all the land which he swore to give to their fathers. (21:43; cf. 1:6)

Having taken possession of it. . . . (21:43; cf. 1:11)

The LORD gave them rest. (21:44; cf. 1:15)

Not one of their enemies had withstood them. (21:44; cf. 1:5)

The LORD had given all their enemies into their hands. (21:44; cf. 2:24)

Concluding summary: All the LORD's promises came to pass. (21:45)

The levitical cities, or Torah Centers, are thus presented by the Teacher as a definite and inseparable part of the entire process of inheriting (see above, p. 5), possessing (pp. 9-10), and finding rest in the land (p. 12). Without this system of Torah Centers, he was saying, the process would not only be incomplete, but would be destined to fail.

THE LEVITES AS TORAH INTERPRETERS

In the Joshua story, the Levites are closely associated with God's Teaching (see above, p. 24). They carry the "ark of the cov-

enant" during the great transition from the wilderness into the
Promised Land (chs. 3 – 4), and with it they march around the
walls of Jericho (ch. 6). They sound the trumpets announcing
the Day of Yahweh in Canaan (see above, pp. 50-51), and stand
beside the ark at the reading of the divine Teaching at Shechem
(8:33-34). At the conclusion of the assembly they bless the people
(v. 33; see above, pp. 71-72).

Although not mentioned by name, we may perhaps assume
the presence of the Levites as the teachers of the new generation
at the time of circumcision, Passover, and the Feast of Unleavened Bread (ch. 5; see above, pp. 33-39). Since casting lots to
determine God's will was a function of the Levites (Deut. 33:8),
they may have been present at the trial of Achan (Josh. 7:16-18).
We may even surmise their role as mediators of God's word to
Joshua when the narrative tells of God speaking directly to him
(6:1-5; 7:1-15, etc.).

After the assembly at Shechem described in 8:30-35, there is
no further mention of the ark in the Joshua story. In its place,
and at the climactic position in ch. 21, are the forty-eight Torah
Centers dispersed "in the midst of the possession of the people
of Israel" (21:41). The ark was suitable for a pilgrim people not
yet settled in the land. Torah Centers were the appropriate mode
for a landed people.

Torah Instruction

As the story develops, it is clear that Rahab and her extended
family (see above, p. 19) would have needed continuous instruction in order to become part of the covenant people. Her confession of faith was only a beginning. The same would have been
true for the members of the Gibeonite league (see above, p. 82),
as well as the debt slaves, tenant farmers, and Habiru bands who
joined the Joshua group (see above, pp. 99-100). These actors in
the Joshua drama would have been like mirror images of the
Canaanites who became Israelites when David extended the
boundaries of the kingdom (see above, pp. 115-16). In the time of
the reform movement in the 7th cent. B.C., the anticipated national expansion under Josiah would have meant the incorporation of new peoples into the new society, all of them in need
of education in the faith. In addition to this, the Israelites them-

selves were in need of day-by-day and year-by-year instruction in God's Teaching.

The Levites were seen by the Teacher as priests (Josh. 3:3; 8:33). We can thus apply to them words spoken elsewhere concerning the teaching function of priests. This instructional role is often overlooked because of the extensive treatment of the priestly liturgical roles in Exodus, Leviticus, and Numbers.

Priests were responsible for "handling," or interpreting, God's Teaching (Jer. 2:8; RSV "law"), and giving this Teaching to the people (Jer. 18:18; RSV "instruction"). They were supposed to "teach" (Mic. 3:11) the people without pay. If the priests did not fulfill their obligations to interpret the Teaching (Ezek. 7:26; RSV "the law perishes from the priest"), there would be "no knowledge of God in the land" (Hos. 4:1). The result would be the destruction of the people "for lack of knowledge" (v. 6). A later historian summarized the condition thus: "Israel was without the true God, and without a teaching priest, and without law [God's Teaching]" (2 Chr. 15:3; RSV "law"). A classical description of the "teaching priest" comes from the book of Malachi:

> True instruction (*torah*) was in his mouth,
>   and no wrong was found in his lips.
> He walked with me [God] in peace and uprightness,
>   and he turned many from iniquity.
> For the lips of a priest should guard knowledge,
>   and men should seek instruction (*torah*) from his mouth,
>   for he is the messenger of the LORD of hosts. (Mal. 2:6-7)

A review of Deuteronomy gives us an outline of the kind of instruction which would take place in the Torah Centers. There would be retelling of historical traditions (Deut. 8:1-10), the teaching of basic principles of attitude and conduct (5:6-21; 6:4), the establishing of a firm self-identity (7:6-11), and applying the Teaching to specific cases (chs. 21 – 23).

Torah Ceremonies

The great assembly at Shechem in the Joshua story could serve as a prototype for the assemblies for all Israel every seven years as commanded by Moses (Deut. 31:9-13). In the Deuteronomic version it is the Levites who read the Teaching (v. 12) in the place of Joshua. The purpose of the reading is that all those present, "men, women, and little ones, and the sojourner within your towns, . . . and . . . their children who have not known it may hear and learn to fear the LORD your God, as long as you live in the land . . ." (vv. 12-13; cf. Josh. 8:33, 35).

The educational value of these assemblies, with their recital of traditions of the past and interpretation of the Teaching for the present, is obvious. The role of the Levites as interpreters of God's Teaching is well summarized in the words of the Chronicler: "The Levites helped the people to understand the Teaching [RSV "law"]. . . .they gave the sense, so that the people understood the reading" (Neh. 8:7-8).

Torah Administration

The seventh year on which the tribal league gathered in assembly was also a "year of release" (Deut. 31:10). At that time Israelite slaves would be freed and debts forgiven (15:1-2, 12-15). It would seem natural that the Levites should have responsibility for seeing that the provisions of this law were carried out in each tribe, and each local town. In addition to this kind of administrative duty, the Levites were to assist the judge in making decisions in legal cases (17:9; 21:5). They would serve as counsellors to the king (17:18), and as health officers (24:8). They would also stir up the zeal of the army in time of impending battle (20:1-4).

National Unity

The Teacher stressed the transtribal character of the Levites by noting five times that they were not tied to any particular location, boundary lines, or tribal group. Their heritage was "the priesthood of the LORD" instead of territory (Josh. 18:7). They were a guild group with a special relationship to God (13:33). As such they were entitled to a part of the sacrificial offerings presented to the LORD (13:14), as well as living quarters with pasturelands contributed by the tribes (14:4; 21:3). This special status enabled them to call the tribes away from their parochial and sectional interests to a common loyalty to Yahweh.

WHO WERE THE LEVITES?

A Tribe

The earliest records indicate that at one time the Levites were one of the twelve tribes. One narrative tells how Levi and Simeon

were involved in a violent offense against the Canaanites in
Shechem, and "brought trouble" on their father Jacob
(Gen. 34:30). On his deathbed, Jacob condemned the two brothers to be "scattered" (Gen. 49:7). For Simeon, this meant being
absorbed into the tribe of Judah. For Levi, it meant being "scattered" among the tribes as a priestly guild. R. G. Boling ("Levitical History and the Role of Joshua," in *The Word of the
Lord Shall Go Forth*, eds. Carol L. Meyers and Michael P.
O'Connor) has suggested that the transition from tribe to guild
may have resulted from a religious conversion while in Egypt.

A Guild with Two Branches

Behind the rather artificial and late genealogies of Levi in
Exod. 6:16-25 and elsewhere, F. M. Cross (*Canaanite Myth and
Hebrew Epic*, 195-205) has identified two major levitical families,
tracing their lineage to Aaron and Moses. The Aaronite Levites
were located in the south of Israel, with sanctuaries in Hebron
and Bethel. The Mosaic or Mushite Levites were located in the
central and northern regions. Their chief sanctuaries were Nob
just north of Jerusalem, Shilo northeast of Bethel, Kedesh in
Naphtali near the southwest shore of the Sea of Galilee, and Dan
north of the Sea of Galilee and due east of Tyre (see above,
p. 122).

The Levites before the Monarchy

In the period before the monarchy, the Levites were the teachers,
theologians, storytellers, counsellors, and inspired preachers of
the new society. They helped to integrate into a coherent body
of tradition the memories and histories of the various groups that
came together as part of Israel. They inspired the people to take
up arms against their Canaanite oppressors. They helped bind
the various elements and generations into "one worshipping,
militant, tradition-building, and law-formulating community"
(N. K. Gottwald, *Tribes of Yahweh*, 320).

During the United Monarchy

The Aaronite Levites of Hebron aided David in his rise to power
(see above, pp. 122-23). When David established his government,
he tried to hold the two priestly houses together by having the
Mushite Abiathar from Nob and the Aaronite Zadok of Hebron

as his priests (2 Sam. 20:25; for Zadok's Aaronite descent, see Cross, *Canaanite Myth and Hebrew Epic*, 214).

Many scholars believe that the list of levitical cities found in Joshua 21 and 1 Chr. 6:54-81 originated in David's time (e.g., Aharoni, *Land of the Bible*, 301-5). David's reasons for establishing these centers, mainly in the border regions or in areas newly brought into the kingdom by military conquest, would have been as follows: (a) They could be loyal to the king, since they were not attached to any particular tribe. (b) They could strengthen the king's authority and promote national solidarity. (c) They could teach Yahwism to the new populations brought into Israel. (d) They could perform administrative functions and serve as a militia if necessary (B. Mazar, "The Cities of the Priests and the Levites," *VTS* 7 [1960]: 193-205; for the administrative functions of the Levites, see 1 Chr. 26:29-32; 2 Chr. 23:1-21; Ezra 8:33).

Solomon banished the Mushite Abiathar, leaving the Aaronite Zadok in the dominant position (1 Kgs. 2:26-27). The decline in Mushite fortunes is further evidenced by Solomon's sale of some of the levitical cities in the territory of Asher to Hiram of Tyre as payment for debts incurred in the royal building program (1 Kgs. 9:10-14; cf. Josh. 21:30-31). Mushite support for the northern revolt after Solomon's death is suggested by the fact that the prophet Ahijah from the Mushite city of Shiloh commissioned Jeroboam as the leader (1 Kgs. 11:29-31).

In the Northern Kingdom

Jeroboam's revolt began at Shechem, the sacred site of the tribal assembly and covenant ceremony, presumably with Mushite support, as pointed out above. Several reasons may be suggested for the later alienation of the Mushite Levites. Jeroboam's change of capital, from Shechem to Penuel across the Jordan, would have lessened Mushite influence. His major shrine was the Aaronite city of Bethel where there was the kind of calf worship associated with Aaron (1 Kgs. 12:28; Exod. 32:4, 21-24). His appointment of "priests who were not Levites" (1 Kgs. 12:31) may imply a rejection of Mushite priests in favor of locally popular priests of the village shrines (cf. 2 Chr. 11:14). This would have deprived the northern Levites of an income from the sacrificial offerings. The system of levitical cities still surviving in the north would have collapsed. This may explain the picture of the Levites as wandering bands of teachers dependent on the generosity of the town dwellers (Deut. 12:12; 14:29).

From the Reign of Hezekiah

After the fall of the northern kingdom in 721 B.C., and by the encouragement of King Hezekiah, northern Levites came to Jerusalem and the towns of Judah. They were able to get some financial support from the Jerusalem temple (Deut. 18:6-8). They gathered Mosaic traditions and levitical teaching together to form the major part of the book of Deuteronomy which inspired the Josianic reform (G. von Rad, *Deuteronomy*, 23-77). If the above sketch is correct, it would follow that the Teacher who wrote the book of Joshua as we now have it would have come from this group of Mushite Levites.

THE LEVITICAL CITIES IN JOSHUA 21

In Relation to the City and Boundary Lines

A comparison of the lists in Joshua 13 – 19 with ch. 21 reveals a rough similarity in outline. Both begin with Judah (ch. 15; 21:13-19), proceed north to Ephraim and Manasseh (16:1 – 17:18; 21:20-27), and extend to Galilee (19:10-48; 21:27-33). The Transjordan region which introduces the first list (13:8-33) concludes the second (21:24-40). The basic order is not disturbed by this difference.

If, as we have suggested (see above, pp. 109-11), a program of land recovery and redistribution lies behind the first list, the second suggests a bringing of the whole land under the direction of God's Teaching.

Reunification of the Levitical Families

Some have detected a bias in favor of the Aaronites in this chapter; they receive the first lot (21:10). The Aaronite city of Hebron receives special emphasis (vv. 11-12). On the other hand, the notice about Caleb's claim to Hebronite land represents a limitation of the Aaronite claim (see above, pp. 121-22). Mention of the Mushite Shechem may be seen to balance the Aaronite Hebron. The absence of important cultic sites such as the Aaronite Bethel, and the Mushite Nob, Shiloh, Kedesh in Naphtali, and

Dan from the list shows an absence of polemic in favor of either house. The list would serve the Teacher's interest in promoting national unity by unifying the Levites as interpreters of God's Teaching in the coming new society. Insistence on the superiority of the Aaronite priesthood over the (Mushite) Levites belongs to another situation and time.

ELEAZAR AND HILKIAH

"Eleazar the priest," the son of Aaron (Deut. 10:6), connects the Joshua story with the priestly tradition. We find his name mentioned thirty-four times in Numbers. He was present at Joshua's commissioning, and was appointed to "inquire for him by the judgment of the Urim before the LORD" (Num. 27:18-23. The Urim were small objects, perhaps in the shape of dice, something like the pair of banana-shaped pieces of wood in Chinese temples. By the way they fell an answer of yes or no could be obtained from God). Eleazar was designated, along with Joshua, to preside over the land distribution (Num. 34:17). In the Joshua story, no liturgical role or any task of interpreting God's Teaching is ever suggested for Eleazar. He never acts alone. In each case he appears with Joshua and the "heads of the fathers' houses of the tribes of Israel" (14:1; 17:4; 19:51; 21:1). The Levites' role is of far greater importance than that of Eleazar.

Some relationship may be discerned between the figure of Eleazar in the Joshua story and his descendant Hilkiah (1 Chr. 6:14) the high priest, who found the book of God's Teaching in the time of Josiah (2 Kgs. 22:8). In the Joshua story it was Eleazar's duty to see that the Levites were installed in their places according to God's will. Hilkiah has a parallel role in the Josiah story. He mediates God's will not by the Urim, but by the book of God's Teaching, whose interpretation was the responsibility of the Levites. In both cases, the priests function to make the Teaching effective in the land. "Knowledge of God" had priority over "burnt offerings" (Hos. 6:6; cf. Matt. 9:13).

SHILOH AND JERUSALEM

Shiloh appears in Josh. 18:1 for the first time in the Old Testament. There is no explanation of how it became the central shrine of the Israelite tribal league. The presence of the "tent of meet-

ing" designates its central importance. In Deuteronomic terminology, Shiloh was for the tribes "the place which the LORD will
choose out of all your tribes" (Deut. 12:5). It could thus be seen
as a mirror image for Jerusalem with its tent (2 Sam. 6:17) and
temple (1 Kgs. 8:4, 6). At the same time Shiloh was remembered
as the place which the LORD had destroyed, probably following
the battle of Aphek (1 Sam. 4:10-11). A Jerusalem psalmist described the reason for God's action as the faithlessness of the
northern kingdom. "When God heard, he was full of wrath, and
he utterly rejected Israel. He forsook his dwelling at Shiloh, the
tent where he dwelt among men" (Ps. 78:59-60). In the days of
Josiah there was no longer any room for complacency in the
southern kingdom. Jeremiah was prophesying the downfall of
Jerusalem: "This is the city which must be punished; there is
nothing but oppression within her" (Jer. 6:6). When the death
of Josiah and the end of the reform made things look even darker,
Yahweh spoke through Jeremiah: "If you will not listen to me,
to walk in my law [Teaching], . . . then I will make this house
like Shiloh, and I will make this city a curse for all the nations
of the earth" (26:4, 6; cf. 7:12-14).

Joshua's act at Shiloh of establishing Torah Centers in all parts
of the land, with the full cooperation of the people and by God's
express command, implies an urgent appeal to king, priest, and
people to do the same in the 7th cent. B.C. while there is yet
time, lest the history of Shiloh be repeated. "Be warned, O Jerusalem, lest I be alienated from you; lest I make you a desolation, an uninhabited land" (Jer. 6:8).

TORAH CENTERS AMONG THE NATIONS

God of Israel, God of All the Earth

According to Jewish legend, God's Teaching was written in seventy languages at Shechem (see above, p. 68). Another legend
tells how God offered the Teaching to all the nations of the world,
but when none would accept it, the Teaching was given to Israel
(G. F. Moore, *Judaism in the First Centuries of the Christian Era* 1:
277). The clear implication is that the Teaching was intended for
the nations from the beginning.

A close look at the Joshua story will reveal a universal context
for the Torah Centers of Joshua 21. The Jordan crossing was

commanded by the "Lord of all the earth" (3:11, 13) in order
that "all the peoples of the earth" might come to a knowledge of
Yahweh's power (4:24; see above, p. 25). The written Teaching
was "planted" in the land for all to read, with the possibility that
when it was no longer confined to the ark, it could be "transplanted" to the lands of the seventy nations (see above, p. 70).
The narrative of the Gibeonites "from a far country," which the
Teacher carefully fitted into the Joshua story immediately following the public reading of God's Teaching, provided an indirect
clue to the interest of the nations in the divine Teaching, as suggested in Deut. 4:6 and elsewhere (see above, pp. 79-80).

Whether the full implications of this universal context of the
work of the Levites was in the mind of the Teacher or not, we
cannot know. There are links with other parts of Scripture, however, which should come into consideration as we ponder the
meaning of the Torah Centers and their function of bringing the
divine Teaching to the people and to the nations.

A Kingdom of Priests

The first of these is the ancient covenantal promise that a faithful
Israel would be or become "a kingdom of priests" in the service
of the Lord of "all peoples" and "all the earth" (Exod. 19:5-6).
When we place this text alongside Joshua 21, a new insight becomes possible. The role of the Levites in interpreting God's
Teaching "in the midst of" the twelve tribes is, in this text, to be
carried out by the whole people of God among the nations.

The same thought is echoed in the postexilic prophecy about
the coming age when "you shall be called the priests of the LORD;
men shall speak of you as the ministers of our God" (Isa. 61:6).
We find it again when Christians are called "a royal priesthood"
(1 Pet. 2:9). Jesus himself was a teacher (Mark 1:27; Acts 1:1,
etc.), and he commanded his disciples to teach all nations to
observe what he had commanded them (Matt. 28:20). The Jews
in Paul's time thought of themselves as "a guide to the blind, a
light to those who are in darkness, a corrector of the foolish, a
teacher of children, having in the law [Teaching] the embodiment
of knowledge and truth" (Rom. 2:19-20). If we keep in mind the
teaching function of priests, it is possible to see here a development of the idea of the "kingdom of priests." Seen in this way,

wherever Jews or Christians find themselves, there would be potential Torah Centers in the midst of the nations.

Some suggestions for the vocation of God's people as priests may be found by rereading the Joshua story with an eye to the role of the Levites.

(1) As the Levites carried the symbol of God's presence and purpose (i.e., the ark and the Teaching) to guide the twelve tribes into a new kind of life in the Promised Land, so the faithful people of God should bear similar symbols to "guide the nations upon earth" (Ps. 67:4) to the life of the kingdom of God on earth.

(2) As the Levites sounded the trumpets at Jericho, so the faithful people of God should announce the coming of God in judgment and grace in the midst of the oppressive forces at work today.

(3) As the Levites interpreted the meaning of God's Teaching to all ages and classes of Israelites, the "royal priesthood" should make the Teaching intelligible in all languages and cultures in terms of everyday ethical decisions.

(4) As the Levites were a teaching association that transcended narrow tribal loyalties, so the "royal priesthood" should transcend the clashing interests of narrow nationalism in the name of a common humanity under one God.

(5) As the Levites offered sacrifices on behalf of the twelve tribes "to maintain and enhance . . . solidarity between God and man" (see above, p. 70), so the priestly people should work for reconciliation between conflicting forces in society and between nations, individuals, and God. Paul spoke of a ministry of reconciliation entrusted to Christians by God in Christ (2 Cor. 5:18) and called on believers to offer themselves to God as living sacrifices (Rom. 12:1).

(6) As the Levites blessed the people (8:33), so the priestly teachers should mediate God's blessing from their Torah Centers in the communities where they are to live among the nations. This would be a fulfillment of the promise to and mission of the descendants of Abraham (Gen. 12:3; see above, pp. 71-72). It would also be related to Jesus' purpose that "abundant life" be made available to all (John 10:10, 16).

(7) As the Levites needed centers in which they could live, study, and gain strength from each other for their mission, so the "kingdom of priests" should have communities in which to do

research and maintain a corporate life of discipline and worship, so that they might be "messengers of God" among the nations.

To Magnify God's Teaching

Another part of Scripture with links to Joshua 21 is the book of Isaiah. In a time when there was "no dawn" in sight, and only "distress and darkness [and] gloom of anguish" in the future (Isa. 8:20-22), when the nation was headed in the wrong direction (8:11), Isaiah gathered a group of disciples (Heb. *limmudim*) who would preserve the Teaching and the testimony (8:16). Both of these terms are associated with the ark and the Levites in the Joshua story (Josh. 4:15; 8:32-33).

This group of disciples would serve as a sign of God's hidden grace and a portent of his imminent judgment (8:18) in a way that reminds us of the trumpets of Jericho. They would also call a confused and apostate people to turn from mediums, wizards, and necromancers (cf. the "abominable practices" of the nations in Canaan) "to the teaching and to the testimony" (8:19-20).

They were a kind of Torah community keeping alive God's Teaching, interpreting it in times of historical crisis, and calling people back to God.

During the deep crisis of the Babylonian exile, a member of the Isaiah community set out to form a new group of disciples (Isa. 50:4; Heb. *limmudim*, RSV "those who are taught"). Twice he made a direct appeal to the exiles with the words "Who among you?" The first was for volunteers who would prepare themselves for "the time to come," i.e., for future service in the time following the fall of Babylon (42:23). The second was a call for those willing to be loyal only to God, not fearing the darkness of pain and suffering (50:10).

These disciples would hold God's Teaching in their hearts (51:7; cf. Josh. 1:7-8; Deut. 30:14) and would learn that this Teaching was meant for all the peoples of the earth (Isa. 51:4). They would understand that the failure of past generations to believe and obey the Teaching had terrible results not only for Israel (42:24) but for the nations as well. They were commissioned to go out from Babylon among the nations with the power of God (42:1). Despite discouragements and setbacks, they would present the message of God's reign so effectively that peoples all over the earth (i.e., "the coastlands") would wait expectantly and with longing for the divine Teaching (RSV "law"), which would mean life and hope for them (42:4; cf. 51:5).

This kind of mission to the nations is more akin to the continuing presence of the Torah Centers than to the transient visit of a pilgrim band or a traveling preacher. The tasks of making justice flow forth (42:1, 3) like "an everflowing stream" (Amos 5:24), and planting justice in the soil of each nation (Isa. 42:4) are not accomplished in a short time. The methods to be employed are not quick and simplistic, or violent like those of the fierce beast in Daniel's vision (Dan. 7:7, 19). The servant community would be gentle, so as not to crush the weak or snuff out the life of the hopeless (Isa. 42:3; cf. Matt. 12:18-21). In fact, it would require silent suffering (42:2) in obedience to the vocation of discipleship (50:5-6), so that God's Teaching would be honored among the nations (42:21; 49:3).

Torah Centers in an Age of Pluralism

In the present day, what we have called Torah Centers may be homes, congregations, denominational headquarters, councils of churches, specialized communities, study centers, monasteries, ashrams, religious publishing houses, and the like. These centers preserve, practice, and interpret the contemporary meaning of God's Teaching in story and commandment as found in the Hebrew Scriptures (OT) and the Apostolic Writings (NT). The key position of the levitical cities in the Joshua story underlines the importance of such centers as these today.

Two Different Situations

The situation in the mind of the Teacher who composed the Joshua story was, however, very different from that contemplated by the prophet of the Exile who wrote approximately a hundred years after the Teacher. The Teacher was reinterpreting the events of the 13th cent. B.C. for the reform movement in the 7th cent. B.C. As he wrote he had in mind the restoration of the kingdom of David under Josiah.

The prophet of the Exile was reinterpreting all the ancient traditions of Israel, including the Joshua story, for the confused and despairing exiles in Babylon. In his mind was not only the restoration of Israel as a servant community, but the misson of Israel as part of God's plan to restore peace and harmony to the society of nations (Isa. 49:6, 8; see E. J. Hamlin, *Comfort My People, A Guide to Isaiah 40 – 66*, 126). The task of the "royal priest-hood" was thus set in the context of a pluralism of histories, cultures, social structures, and religions. This complex situation resembles our own pluralistic age more than it does the picture found in the Joshua story.

No Simple Application

Consider a few examples of the wrong use of the Joshua story in an age of pluralism. It would be a mistake for "Torah Centers" in Thailand to make a simple equation between the Buddha image in a Theravada Buddhist temple and the images of Baal and Asherah which Josiah destroyed in his reformation (1 Kgs. 23:6; cf. Deut. 9:21). There may indeed be similarities, but there are also important dissimilarities. Again, the three-month period spent by young male Buddhists in a monastery for moral and spiritual training is in no way comparable to the ritual sacrifice of Canaanite children (Jer. 7:31). Moreover, there is no way in which the coming of missionaries to a new land could be identified with Joshua's southern campaign (Josh. 10:28-40). Even the principle of "radical discontinuity" (see above, pp. 53-54) must be applied with great caution, lest the "new society" to which a convert is called prove to be a modified version of the old society from which the missionary comes.

Certainly there are practices in all nations and cultures which are "abominable" in God's sight (see above, pp. xviii-xix). The same is true of the "false gods" that debase and destroy human life. But it is not right to identify "abominable practices" and "false gods" with the great religions of the world, as though these religions and not human sinfulness were the cause. The Teaching specifically warns against self-righteous claims to innocence by those who serve God (Deut. 31:16, 27).

A Multilingual Kingdom of Priests

The "royal priesthood" in an age of pluralism must be multi-lingual, like the people of Singapore who speak English, Mandarin Chinese, several Chinese dialects, Bahasa Malaysia, and Tamil. The first language they must know is "Torah language." This language will help them to know God and his plan for the world, the meaning of Israel, Jesus Christ, and their own identity and discipleship. It is only as they have a strong sense of identity ("I have called you by name, you are mine!" Isa. 43:1) that they can speak God's message to the nations ("Turn to me and be saved, all the ends of the earth!" Isa. 45:22). In many parts of the world, such as Indonesia and Africa, the numerical growth of Christian congregations is so rapid that the new converts cannot be taught Torah language due to a lack of trained teachers.

A second language we will call "Dharma language." The term "Dharma" comes from Hinduism and Buddhism, and one translation of the word is "teaching." Here, however, we use it in a representative sense to include Hindu, Buddhist, Taoist, Confucian, Quranic, and primitive religious languages. Learning Dharma language is a way to gain a sympathetic understanding of the traditions, relationships, moral codes, spiritualities, and world views of the great world religions among which the "royal priesthood" is sent to live (in the sense of Jer. 29:7; Isa. 42:6; John 20:21).

A knowledge of Dharma language will of course aid in the proper adaptation of Torah language in order to "help the people understand the law [Teaching]" (Neh. 8:7-8). It will also send the "messenger of God" (Mal. 2:7) back to "search the scriptures" (John 5:39) with new questions and insights from his study of Dharma language. Such knowledge will also stimulate people to consider the possibility that the one true God ("and there is no other," Isa. 45:5) has been at work among those who did not know him (vv. 5-6). They may ponder anew the one river in Eden which divided into four streams to bring life to all the earth (Gen. 2:9). They may also think of God's covenant blessing of life given to all the peoples of the earth (Gen. 9:1, 9, 19).

Besides Torah language and Dharma language, we may mention "market language," again in a representative way, to cover political, military, commercial, advertising, consumerist, scientific, and other languages used by modern people in their everyday activities.

Torah Centers would need specialists in particular languages in order to fulfill their task of interpreting the Teaching, and to bring new questions for use in searching the Scriptures. Thus the Teaching might "revive the soul . . . make wise the simple . . . rejoice the heart . . . enlighten the eyes. . . ," warn the nations, and keep them from "presumptuous sins" (Ps. 19:7-13). In other words, the Teaching would make life possible and abundant for the nations on God's earth.

THE GOOD PROMISES

The Joshua story comes to its concluding chapters on a note of fulfillment. God's good promises, we read, had all come to pass. This fulfillment is called into question in the book of Judges, and the subsequent history of Israel. A faithful Israelite could even say in a time of troubles, "Are his promises at an end for all time?" (Ps. 77:8). Another could affirm, in spite of the oppression of the poor and the exaltation of "vileness on every side," that "the promises of the LORD are promises that are . . . purified seven times" (Ps. 12:6). The Joshua story thus carries a kind of anticipation of a future fulfillment for which faithful disciples may wait in hope (Isa. 8:17).

Christians believe that "all the promises of God find their Yes" in Jesus (2 Cor. 1:20). This "Yes" is both present ("the kingdom of God is at hand," Mark 1:15) and still to come ("until the kingdom of God comes," Luke 22:18). The following words from a Christian "Torah Center," probably in Asia Minor, provide a fitting conclusion to this chapter:

> His divine power has granted to us all things that pertain to life and godliness, through the knowledge of him who called us to his own glory and excellence, by which he has granted to us his precious and very great promises, that through these you may escape the corruption [i.e., "abominations"] that is in the world because of passion, and become partakers of the divine nature. (2 Pet. 1:3-4)

CHAPTER 15

A PEACEMAKING SOCIETY
Joshua 22:1-34

I thought you would call me, My Father,
and would not turn from following me. —Jeremiah 3:19

I will heal their faithlessness;
I will love them freely,
for my anger has turned from them. —Hosea 14:4

God was in Christ reconciling the world to himself, . . . and entrusting
to us the message of reconciliation. —2 Corinthians 5:19

When all the people of the world love one another, the strong will not
overcome the weak, the many will not oppress the few, the rich will
not insult the poor, the honoured will not despise the humble, and the
cunning will not deceive the ignorant. Because of universal love, all
the calamities, usurpations, hatred, and animosity in the world may
be prevented from arising. —Mo Ti, Chinese philosopher,
cited in C. S. Song, *Third Eye Theology*, 93.

The scene depicted in the first part of this chapter (vv. 1-9) completes the symmetry formed by the story of the East Jordan tribes. The element of climax is signalled by three time words. "Then" (v. 1; cf. 8:30; see above, p. 69) indicates a critical turning point in the narrative. "To this day" (v. 3) points to past events leading up to this moment. "And now" (v. 4; cf. 1:2; 5:14; see above, pp. 4, 41) looks to the future which grows out of the past and present. These three time indicators are balanced by the seven references to "this day" or "today" in vv. 16-32 (vv. 16, 17 [RSV "even yet"], 18, 22, 29, 31), which emphasize the momentous importance of the events described in the narrative.

SHALOM FULFILLED

At the beginning of the story, Joshua had laid a charge on the three tribes of Reuben, Gad, and East Manasseh (1:14-15; see

above, pp. 10-11). They were commanded to "help their brethren." Here, at the end of the story, we learn that they had "not
forsaken [their] brethren" (v. 3). The tribes who crossed the Jordan in solidarity with the others (4:12-13) were about to return
with their task well done. Their claim to land tenure in Transjordan had been recorded (12:1-6). Territories assigned to them
had been designated (13:8-22). They were ready to settle in "the
land which belonged to them according to the decree of the LORD
given through Moses" (22:9 NEB). The notice that the Levites
were to receive no inheritance in Transjordan (13:33; 14:3) prepares the way for the designation of three cities of refuge (20:8)
and ten levitical cities (21:27, 36-39) there. As they went on their
way, they carried their share of the spoils of war already mentioned at the close of the story of the conquest (11:14; 22:8). Just
as God had given "rest" to their brethren (21:44; 22:4), they
themselves were to receive their own "place of rest" (1:13). The
beautiful tale of the East Jordan tribes seems complete in every
respect.

SHALOM THREATENED

Part two (vv. 10-34) is the retelling of an ancient tradition about
an altar on the banks of the Jordan River which threatened to
destroy hard-won "rest." It emphasizes the contingent character
of Israel's tenure of the land. It takes up the themes of Achan's
sin (ch. 7) and is related to the altar on Mt. Ebal (8:30-31). The
successful mediation and reconciliation with which the chapter
concludes are also a preparation for the covenant ceremony
which is the climax and conclusion of the story (ch. 24).

The Altar by the Jordan

The returning tribes left Shiloh and proceeded on the route de-
scending to the Jordan Valley at Gilgal in order to cross by the
ford. This was the place where they had crossed with the other
tribes at the beginning (chs. 3–4), where the "second circumcision" took place, and where the Passover and Feast of Unleavened Bread had been celebrated for the first time in the Promised
Land (ch. 5). There they built a memorial altar large enough to
be seen from both sides of the river.

Textual Note on 15:10-11

Modern translations differ as to whether "the region about the Jordan" (RSV) should be Geliloth, a place name (NEB, TEV, NIV), or a descriptive phrase, "circles of stone" (JB). Geliloth appears as a place name in Josh. 18:17 but not at this location. Another version of the same boundary list between Benjamin and Judah calls the same place Gilgal (15:7). It is held by some that the location of the altar was not at Gilgal but north at Adamah (J. N. M. Wijngaards, *The Dramatization of Salvific History in the Deuteronomic Schools*, 5). It seems likely that in its present form a location at Gilgal is intended.

Some hold that the altar was originally erected on the east bank. They believe that the phrase "in the land of Canaan" (v. 10) was not part of the original story (see NEB), but there is no textual support for this conjecture. The word translated "frontier" (v. 11) has been interpreted ambiguously as "border" (NIV) or "facing the land of Canaan" (NEB, NAB), implying a location on the east bank.

The word translated "side" (v. 11) is interpreted as "passage" by the King James Version. The Hebrew word is *'eber*, a noun derived from the verb *'abar*, "to cross" (see above, pp. 22-23). With a slight change of spelling, we could read *'abarah*, which means "ford" as in 2 Sam. 15:28; 17:16. This is the interpretation that seems to fit the story best, since it relates to Josh. 2:7 and chs. 3-4. The importance of the Jordan fords is shown in the stories of Ehud (Judg. 3:28), Saul (1 Sam. 13:7), and David (2 Sam. 15:28; 17:16; 19:18). A monument at the western end of the ford would establish a firm relationship with the tribes in the land of Canaan.

War Fever

The story develops dramatically with unconfirmed reports which are misinterpreted, resulting in the rise of war fever. Deuteronomic law states clearly that any city which is so deluded as "to go and serve other gods" should be utterly destroyed (Deut. 13:13, 15:16). The erection of "another altar" (Josh. 22:19) brought fears of religious apostasy and its attendant "abominable practices." However, the law also requires careful inquiry to determine whether the reports are true (Deut. 13:14). Thus the war fever was held in suspension while a delegation went to hear what the party under suspicion had to say.

Dialogue in Gilead

In what seems like an OT analogue of the Jerusalem council (Acts 15), the two sides met. The delegation from Shiloh openly stated its suspicions about the altar and cited two past examples of rebellion, each with dire consequences for the entire people. The East Jordan tribes stated their case, and called God to witness that their intentions were pure. This was not an altar for worship, but a monument of witness to the unity of the entire tribal league. The delegation was satisfied with this explanation (v. 31), and returned to Shiloh to report that war was not necessary. The unity of Israel was maintained.

THE SEVENTH-CENTURY B.C. SETTING

Early History

The early history of the Transjordan tribes suggests that what we find in this chapter is a condensation and simplification of historical events for teaching purposes. The following reconstruction of the early period has been made on the basis of a careful study of the evidence (de Vaux, *Early History of Israel*, 591-92). According to de Vaux, the tribe of Gad was already living in Gilead, south of the Jabbok River, when the Moses group came on the scene out of Egypt in the 13th cent. B.C. Gad would have joined the Moses group, welcoming their protection from Ammonite and Moabite pressure.

The tribe of Reuben, says de Vaux, was probably part of the Moses group. Some elements of Reuben lived on the western side of the Jordan. "The stone of Bohan the son of Reuben" (Josh. 15:6; 17:17) was on the border between Benjamin and Judah. The crime of Reuben (Gen. 35:21-22) took place at the town of Eder, which is located between Bethlehem and Hebron (*IDB* 2:23). The main group of Reubenites lived on the eastern side of the Jordan. We read that they were attacked by Hagrite nomads in the days of Saul (1 Chr. 5:10). David's census (2 Sam. 24:5) mentions only Gad to the north of the river Arnon, implying that by that time Reuben had been absorbed by Gad. De Vaux concludes that "neither Reuben nor Gad took part in the conquest of Canaan on the western side of the Jordan" (de Vaux, *Early History of Israel*, 592).

As for East Manasseh, de Vaux holds that this branch of the tribe was originally on the western side of the Jordan, known as the clan of Machir (Josh. 17:1; Judg. 5:14). It was only in the latter part of the period of the judges that they migrated eastward and settled in the area between the Jabbok and the Yarmuk rivers.

With this sketch of the early period, it is obvious that the real meaning of Joshua 22 is not to be found in the historical time of Joshua. Rather, we should relate it to the time when the Teacher was retelling the story in the 7th cent. B.C.

Developments in the Seventh Century B.C.

Several scholars believe that Josiah's reform and national renewal movement extended to Transjordan (L. Ginzberg, "Judah and the Transjordan States from 734 to 582 B.C.E.," *Alexander Marx Jubilee Volume,* 347-68; J. Bright, *A History of Israel,* 317; Y. Aharoni, *The Land of the Bible,* 404; D. L. Christensen, *War Oracle,* 96). A psalmist had stated Yahweh's claim to the Jabbok Valley and the whole of Gilead, as well as his coming victory over Moab and Edom (Ps. 60:6-8; see above, p. 11). Zephaniah's oracle of 628 B.C. refers to the "taunts of Moab" and Ammon and their boasts "that they would seize their [i.e., East Jordan tribes'] land" (Zeph. 2:8 TEV). This may well have been a reference to a revival of Moabite power ca. 650-640 B.C. It is also evidence of Israelite claims to Gilead. By Josiah's time, Arab attacks from the east had weakened Moab and made possible his advance across the Jordan. The words of Zephaniah's prophecy that Israelite survivors (East Jordan tribes?) "will plunder them [Moab and Edom] and take their land" (v. 9 TEV) may have been part of what has been called "a theological basis for Josiah's program of political expansion at the expense of Assyria" (Christensen, *War Oracle,* 161).

The earlier preexilic tradition which lies behind the postexilic prophecies found in both Obad. 1-10 and Jer. 49:7-16 may also have formed part of the theological justification for Judah's advance "into the Negeb at the expense of Edom" (Christensen, *War Oracle,* 166).

If these lines of evidence are valid, we must see the hopes for recovery of the Transjordan areas once held by David and Solomon as part of the background for our understanding of

Joshua 22, and with it the special interest in the Transjordan tribes throughout the entire Joshua story.

The Exile of 732 B.C.

According to 2 Kgs. 15:29, the Israelite inhabitants of Gilead, more specifically described in 1 Chr. 5:26 as the three Transjordan tribes, were taken into exile by Tiglath-pileser III of Assyria to northwestern Mesopotamia. The year was 732 B.C. A second group followed in 721 B.C. after the fall of Samaria to Shalmaneser V (2 Kgs. 17:6). The Chronicler states the reason for this exile (1 Chr. 5:25): "They transgressed against the God of their fathers, and played the harlot after the gods of the people of the land [i.e., Transjordan]."

The exile of 732 B.C. was the end result of an anti-Assyrian coup d'etat by Pekah, an army general who murdered the Israelite king Pekahiah. His power base may have been in Gilead (H. B. Maclean, "Pekah," *IDB* 3:708). Fifty Gileadites helped him seize power (2 Kgs. 15:25).

Hosea, speaking in the same period of time as the anti-Assyrian coup in Samaria, called Gilead "a city of evildoers, tracked with blood" (Hos. 6:8). When the priests and people crossed the fords at Adamah, he said that they "transgressed the covenant" (v. 7; see above, p. 23). It was perhaps the "iniquity in Gilead" (12:11) that caused them to "incur guilt through Baal" (13:1), and led to the demise of the northern kingdom and the exile of its population. (Note: Hosea's frequent mention of the corruption of the priests [6:9; cf. 4:4, 6, 9; 5:1; 10:5] supplies some background for the Teacher's plan for the levitical cities.)

Hosea further linked the iniquity of Gilead with the ceremonial sacrifice of bulls on the altars of Gilgal (12:11). It was there, said Hosea, that Yahweh "began to hate them" (9:15), and declared that he would "cast them off" to be "wanderers among the nations" (v. 17).

In the light of this sorry history, it is no surprise that the northern kingdom with its Transjordan components should be called "faithless Israel," Yahweh's "divorced wife" (Jer. 3:6-9). When the Teacher wrote Joshua 22 the East Jordan tribes had been in exile for more than a century.

Any Place for Exiles

This background can help us understand the anxiety implicit in the words of the Gileadites (i.e., the Transjordan exiles) in the dialogue with the delegation from Shiloh. Their fear was that "in time to come your children might say to our children, 'What have you to do with the LORD, the God of Israel? . . . You have no portion in the LORD' " (Josh. 22:24, 25, 27; cf. Neh. 2:20). After their long years in distant lands and burdened as they were with the guilt of the past, would the "older brother" Judah accept them despite their strange dress, language, customs, and culture? Would they be forgiven and welcomed back to the family of the LORD, the God of Israel?

We can place these anxious questions beside the imaginative reconstruction of such a reunion by Deutero-Isaiah, where "Mother Zion" says,

Who has borne me these?
I was bereaved and barren,
    exiled and put away,
    but who has brought up these?
Behold, I was left alone;
    whence then have these come? (Isa. 49:21)

AN EXAMPLE OF BROTHERLY LOVE

Joshua commended the Transjordan tribes with the words "you have not forsaken your brethren" (22:3).

Absence of Love

If we are to believe the prophets, this kind of brotherly love was not characteristic of Israelite society in the later years of the monarchy. Then, there was "no faithfulness or kindness or knowledge of God in the land" (Hos. 4:1). It was "every man for himself" (Isa. 9:19 TEV), a time when "everyone hunts down his fellow countryman" (Mic. 7:2 TEV), and "no one can trust his brother. . . . They do one violent thing after another" (Jer. 9:4, 6 TEV).

The violation of the "covenant of brotherhood" (Amos 1:9) was shown in the stories of Cain and Abel, Jacob and Esau, Joseph and his brothers, and, on a national scale, in the conflicts between Ephraim and Judah (Isa. 9:21). The question of Abner calls out for a new beginning: "Shall the sword devour forever? Do you not know that the end will be bitter? How long will it be before you bid your people turn from the pursuit of their brethren?" (2 Sam. 2:26).

A similar condition of social chaos is described by the Chinese philosopher Mo Ti:

> At present feudal lords know only to love their own states and not those of others. Therefore, they do not hesitate to mobilize their states to attack those of others. Heads of families know only to love their own families and not those of others. Therefore they do not hesitate to mobilize their own families to usurp others. And individuals know only to love their own persons and not those of others. Therefore they do not hesitate to mobilize their own persons to injure others. (C. S. Song, *Third Eye Theology*, 92)

Contemporary readers will think of the shameful way dominant social groups have treated minority brothers and sisters — American blacks and native Americans, depressed castes in India, Koreans in Japan, underclasses in Latin America, and political dissidents in many lands.

A New Model of Brotherly Love

The Teacher was looking beyond the failures and sins of the men of Gilead to what they had been at the beginning and, by God's grace, could be again. They were models of a radically new loyalty to the brother and sister, a self-sacrificial kind of caring in which no sector or segment of society would seek benefit at the expense of the others. It is the kind of faith that can defer partisan benefit until the whole group has attained the goal — as the author of Hebrews put it, "that apart from us they should not be made perfect" (Heb. 11:40). It was the kind of morality indicated by Jesus: "Seek first his kingdom and his righteouness, and all these things shall be yours as well" (Matt. 6:33).

The Circle of Caring

The circle of caring responsibility envisaged by the Teacher did not extend to the Moabite or the Ammonite (Deut. 23:3-6), probably because of historical factors at that time. It did, however, include the hated Edomite, "for he is your brother," and the

Egyptian who had given them a welcome as guests (Deut. 23:7-8). The great prophet of the Exile dared to believe that God was actually forming other non-Jewish nations to be his sons and daughters (Isa. 45:11), thus extending the "covenant of brotherhood" without limitations. A prophet of the postexilic community believed that Yahweh would accept the sacrifices of foreigners. He said that the Jerusalem temple should be "a house of prayer for all peoples" (Isa. 56:7). We read also of a new Assyria as God's own creation, and a new Egypt as God's own people. Along with Israel they would be a "blessing in the midst of the earth" (Isa. 19:24-25).

Jesus expanded the scope of the "covenant of brotherhood" across lines of kinship, race, culture, and nation (Mark 3:35), and taught that being a neighbor meant not forsaking a brother in need (Luke 10:36-37). Paul saw each person as a "brother for whom Christ died" (1 Cor. 8:11).

The Gileadites in this story are the opposite of Cain: We are our brothers' and sisters' keepers. We are not to forsake them.

GOD'S TEACHING FOR EXILES

The summary of God's Teaching which forms part of Joshua's farewell words to the departing tribes (22:5) is the first and only such summary to be found in the Joshua story. The incomplete and fragmentary words found in 23:6, 11 are not a true summary.

There is a strong similarity to many parts of Deuteronomy, especially 10:12– 11:1, which, like the Joshua passage, is introduced by the important words "and now" (10:12). That passage is in the form of "a declaration of basic principles" of the covenant (G. von Rad, *Deuteronomy*, 83). It is part of Moses' farewell instruction to the Israelites before they cross the Jordan River into the land of Canaan. Joshua, on the other hand, is restating basic principles of the covenant for those about to cross over Jordan in the opposite direction *out of* the land of Canaan.

Into Exile

Viewed from the perspective of the 7th cent. B.C., the journey of the tribes across Jordan did not end in Gilead, but went on to exile in Mesopotamia. Joshua's words may thus be understood as an exhortation to those whose descendants would become ex-

iles. These basic principles of the covenant were valid even outside "the LORD's land" in an "unclean land" (Josh. 22:19; Amos
7:17), far away from the central sanctuary. Since the covenant
LORD is "the Lord of all the earth" (Josh. 3:11), covenant faithfulness is not a matter of where one lives, but of how one lives.

From Exile

The words of encouragement to the exiles "among all the nations
where the LORD your God has driven you" (Deut. 30:1-10; cf.
Deut. 4:27-31; 1 Kgs. 8:44-53) are usually considered as referring
to the Babylonian exiles of 597 and 587 B.C. It is also possible
that they originally referred to the exiles of 732 and 721 B.C.,
and that the hopes expressed in these passages for a return were
linked to the reform and national renewal movement under King
Josiah. This adds another dimension to Joshua's exhortation. It
would be supplying a moral and spiritual dimension to the hoped-
for return, when the Jordan would be recrossed (Josh. 22:19),
and land repossessed (Deut. 30:5), and a new circumcision given
(Deut. 10:16; 30:6; cf. Josh. 5:8; see above, p. 35).

TURNING AND RETURNING

Physical Turning

The Hebrew word *shub* appears seven times in ch. 22, with many
overtones of meaning for the sensitive reader. The basic meaning
is "to turn." Thus it describes the physical movement of the
Transjordan tribes back to their own land after the completion
of their task (vv. 8-9), and the journey of the delegation back to
Shiloh (v. 32). We have already mentioned the overtones of exile
in the departure of these tribes from the land of Canaan, the
LORD's land. Hosea described the Exile as a "return to Egypt"
(Hos. 8:13).

Shub can also mean movement in the opposite direction, i.e.,
back to one's land. Jeremiah used the word in this sense when
he sent God's comforting word to the northern exiles: "A great
company . . . shall return . . . from the land of the enemy . . . to
their country . . . [and their] cities" (Jer. 31:8, 16, 17, 21). This
double sense of the word *shub* would give a double meaning to
the journey of the Transjordan tribes. As Jeremiah said, "If one
turns away (*shub*), does he not return?" (*shub*, Jer. 8:4).

166

Turning Away from and Back to God

The word *shub* may also describe the direction of the life of a person or nation. Turning away from God in rebellion means "walking contrary" to God's will and purpose (Lev. 26:40). Turning back to God would mean, in Jeremiah's words,

> Change the way you are living and stop doing the things you are doing. Be fair in your treatment of one another. Stop taking advantage of aliens, orphans, and widows. Stop killing innocent people. . . . Stop worshiping other gods, for that will destroy you. (Jer. 7:5-6 TEV)

It would mean to "leave their way of life and change their way of thinking" (Isa. 55:7 TEV).

Faithless Turning Away

The word translated "faithless" in the third chapter of Jeremiah is formed from the verb *shub*. It means a willful turning away from God. In that chapter Jeremiah tells of God's disappointment: "I thought . . . you . . . would not turn from following me" (Jer. 3:19). The northern kingdom had already turned away (v. 6), but God still had hope. "I thought, 'After she has done all this she will return to me'; but she did not return" (v. 7). The result was the deportations of 732 and 721 B.C., which were symbolically described as a "decree of divorce" (v. 8). During the reign of Manasseh, Judah had imitated the northern kingdom and polluted the land (vv. 8-9). Even when there were outward signs of a return, it was "not . . . with her whole heart, but in pretense" (v. 10).

A Call to Return

In spite of this, Jeremiah continued Hosea's pleading (Hos. 14:1-2). Three times he pressed God's urgent appeal to return to God (Jer. 3:12, 14, 22). He said they should confess their rebellion. God would "heal [their] faithlessness" (v. 22).

A similar appeal for radical change in national and personal direction of life is found in Deuteronomy 30. Only by an inward turning back to God could there be a physical return to the land and a restoration of national life (Deut. 30:3, 5). Jeremiah went even further. He said that a genuine return to God (Jer. 4:1) would mean not only healing for the nation itself, but blessing

for the nations in fulfillment of Abraham's mission (Gen. 12:3):
"Then all nations will ask me [i.e., Yahweh] to bless them, and
they will praise me" (Jer. 4:2 TEV).

Turning Away in Gilead?

In the dialogue about the altar, the word *shub* is used twice to
express the suspicion and alarm of the delegation that the tribes
in Gilead were "turning away from following the LORD" (Josh.
22:16, 18). This is exactly what Jeremiah was saying at the very
time the Teacher was retelling the story.

On their part, the Gileadites twice protest that they had no
intention of turning away from the LORD. They are a model for
a repentant Israel that had indeed returned to Yahweh. This
seems again to be an idealized portrayal of the past which presents possibilities for the future in which there need be no suspicions of apostasy or divisiveness in the new Israelite society.

THE BASIC QUESTION

The question raised by the delegation about the altar has a sharp
relevance to Israelite history.

> What is this treachery which you have committed against
> the God of Israel in turning away this day from following
> the LORD, by building yourselves an altar this day in re-
> bellion against the LORD? (Josh. 22:16; cf. 8:30-35; see above,
> p. 70)

Altars in Israel were, according to Hosea, the source and symbol of corruption in a materially prosperous nation.

> The more altars the people of Israel build for removing sin,
> the more places they have for sinning! . . . The more pros-
> perous they were, the more altars they built. . . . The people
> whose hearts are deceitful must now suffer for their sins.
> God will break down their altars. (Hos. 8:11; 10:1-2 TEV)

The question to the Gileadites might well have been asked
about the altars of Jeroboam (1 Kgs. 12:32; 2 Kgs. 23:15), Ahab
(1 Kgs. 16:32), Ahaz (2 Kgs. 16:10-15), and Manasseh (21:3;
23:12). Jeremiah cried out in indignation that "the people of
Judah have as many gods as they have cities, and the inhabitants

of Jerusalem have set up as many altars . . . as there are streets in the city" (Jer. 11:13 TEV).

The question should prick the consciences of sensitive readers in every generation. Are beautiful buildings, rich liturgies, large congregations, and vast electronic church audiences a cloak for "treachery" and "rebellion" against the LORD (see above, p. 70)? Are not sound teaching (the meaning of the levitical cities) and compassion (the meaning of the cities of refuge) the only guarantee against corruption of worship?

NO OTHER ALTAR

The delegation insisted that there should be no other altar "than the altar of the LORD our God" (22:19). There are two altars in the Joshua story, one at Shechem (8:30-31) and the other at Shiloh (22:29). Both of them were for the worship of Yahweh. In the view of the delegation, the altar by the Jordan was built for the purposes of the builders ("[for] yourselves," v. 16), without reference to Yahweh. The point at issue here, then, is not that there should be only one altar for the nation, but only one kind of altar, namely, an altar of or to Yahweh. The Gileadites insisted that theirs was a "copy" (Heb. *tabnit,* v. 28; cf. 2 Kgs. 16:10, "pattern") of the altar of Yahweh at Shiloh. It was not an altar designed for sacrifice, but a sign or witness to remind all that these Transjordan tribes were a continuing part of the greater Israelite "covenant of brotherhood."

The importance of the principle of "no other altar" is underlined by two examples, both related to the location of this altar in the Jordan Valley. One was "the sin at Peor" (v. 17); the other was "the treachery of Achan" (v. 20 NEB).

The Sin at Peor: Immoral Sacrifice

Peor was the name of a mountain (Num. 23:28) and a town near Mt. Nebo, almost directly to the east of the fords at Gilgal in the highlands of Gilead. "Baal-peor," or "Lord of Fire," was the name of a god brought from what is now Turkey by immigrants to Transjordan. There they joined with the Midianites (G. E. Mendenhall, *The Tenth Generation,* 108-9).

The narrative in Numbers 25 describes an outbreak of bubonic plague among the Midianites while Israel was in nearby Shittim

(v. 1). Hebrew fear of contracting the dread disease prompted them to participate in the ritual designed to halt it. This consisted of sacrifices to the angry spirits of the dead who were believed to have caused the disease (v. 2; cf. Ps. 106:28), a ritual meal establishing a close relationship ("yoke," Num. 25:3; cf. Isa. 65:4) with the spirits in order to influence them, and ritual sexual intercourse in order to please them.

Their "cure," as we know from the modern study of bubonic plague, only brought about the further disastrous spread of the disease, with thousands of Hebrew deaths (Num. 25:9). Physical contact with the infected Midianites communicated the plague bacillus directly into the lungs of the Hebrews, with a one-day incubation period before death. (With an insect bite there is a seven-day incubation period [Mendenhall, *Tenth Generation*, 113].)

A well-meaning Hebrew took what he thought was the most effective step to prevent the epidemic from spreading. He brought a Midianite princess into the "inner room" of his home for ritual intercourse (v. 6). The end of the plague, however, was brought about not by this ritual act but by the death of the pair at the hands of Phinehas the priest (vv. 7-8).

The incident was not remembered for its medical aspects. In the course of time the Israelites developed a detailed sanitary code designed to prevent the outbreak and spread of disease. This code is found in the Pentateuch (R. K. Harrison, "Healing," *IDB* 2:541-48). This incident served rather as a paradigm for the corruption of worship in Israel. It is possible that Israelites from the west crossed the fords at Gilgal to participate with the tribes in Gilead in the cult of the "Lord of Fire."

"The sin at Peor" was to make the wrong sacrifice on the wrong altar, to the wrong God, in a wrong way. It became a famous example of turning away from God (Ps. 106:28-31; 1 Cor. 10:8).

Perhaps we may draw an analogy. The Baal-peor way of solving problems failed because it was without the moral and spiritual guidance of Torah. Modern technology is also a way of manipulating the forces and structures of nature to accomplish its own ends without the moral and spiritual guidance of divine Teaching. Technology may be used to pollute the earth, produce poverty, and maintain power and privilege for some at the expense of others. As in the case of the incident at Baal-peor, the supposed solution may only make things worse. For example, the diversion of disproportionate amounts of technological research into the production of more and more deadly weapons seems like the ancient sacrifices to the "Lord of Fire" which may destroy us. Technology must be guided by Torah if it is to sustain and enhance the quality of life on earth.

The Treachery of Achan: The Immoral Use of Wealth

Achan's breach of faith (Josh. 7) took place at Jericho near Gilgal, just after the crossing into the Promised Land. The lesson is that wealth must also be under the control of Torah. The God who gives "power to get wealth" (Deut. 8:18) requires from his covenant people a strict stewardship in its use. To be careless in the use of wealth is to "forget the LORD your God and go after other gods and serve them and worship them," a path that leads to destruction (vv. 19-20). Here again, we may see modern analogies to Achan's "treachery" in a world where the poor and oppressed cry out for justice.

In the Joshua story, these two paradigms of "rebellion" took place before the reading of the Teaching (Josh. 8:30-35). They anticipate the covenant (ch. 24). The blessings and curses of the covenant are also part of the Teaching. Offerings on the wrong altars are not acceptable to the God who demands that "justice roll down like waters, and righteousness like an ever-flowing stream" (Amos 5:24).

NO OTHER GOD

The response of the tribes accused of rebellion begins with an emotional, twice-repeated appeal to the covenant God of Israel as witness and judge of their intentions and actions. The triple name for God is worth our attention. It is "The Mighty One (*El*), God (*Elohim*), the LORD (*Yahweh*)!" (Josh. 22:22).

El is the general Semitic term for God. We can see this from its variant form Allah, the Muslim name for God. In Canaanite religion, *El* was thought of as the father of all the gods. The Chinese term for *El* would be *Shangti*, the "heavenly Emperor." In Buddhist thought the nearest equivalent would be "Ultimate Truth," and in Thai, *sajja*. *El* is the designation of the mysterious and powerful reality that is above, beyond, and behind all things, the reality sought for by all religious thought.

Elohim is a plural form of *El,* but is almost always used as a singular noun. It expresses "fulness of deity . . . divine plurality in unity" (B. W. Anderson, "Elohim," *IDB* 2:413). In this plurality we may see the dynamic activity of God, expressed in the OT as God's hand, mouth, face, eyes, ear, name, spirit, messenger, zeal, love, purpose, etc. In this name all the functions of divinity are absorbed. *Elohim* is both the "high and lofty one who inhabits eternity" and the one near at hand "to revive the spirit of the humble" (Isa. 57:15).

The appropriate Chinese word for *Elohim* would be *Shen.* It can refer to local spirits or the great *Shen* with all the functions of divinity. In Thai the comparable word would be *Chao.* It also has the double sense of being both near at hand and highly exalted.

Yahweh is the particular name by which Israel knew God (Exod. 3:15; 6:3; Gen. 12:8). This is the name of the *Elohim* of Israel. He is the Savior, Liberator, Chooser, Guide, Covenant-Maker, Landowner, Lover, Judge, Holy One, the God who is always related intimately to his people.

These three names for God appear together in the statement of the general conditions of the covenant referred to above:

For *Yahweh* your *Elohim* is *Elohim* of *Elohim* and Lord of lords, the great, the mighty, and the terrible *El,* who is not partial and takes no bribe. He executes justice for the fatherless and the widow, and loves the sojourner. (Deut. 10:17-18)

Taken by itself, *Yahweh* could come to mean simply a tribal God of Israel. Covenant faith held that *Yahweh* was also *El,* the universal God of all nations and peoples, creator of heaven and earth: "I am *El,* there is no other" (Isa. 46:9). *Yahweh* is also the dynamic *Elohim* whose sphere of action is not limited to Israel. He is actively involved in the affairs of people and nations all over the world to accomplish his divine purpose: "I am *Elohim,* and there is none like me" (v. 9).

The altar's name was a witness to all who would cross the fords of Jordan out of (as to exile) and back into the land of Canaan that "*Yahweh* is *Elohim*" (Josh. 22:34). The altar on the frontier thus expresses the deepest calling of God's people through all the trials and changes of her history: " 'You are my witnesses,' says *Yahweh,* '[and] I am *El'* " (Isa. 43:12).

THE DAY OF RECONCILIATION

The dialogue between the adversaries comes to an end with the realization that Yahweh was "in [their] midst" (22:31). Their awareness of the presence of God was not due to a military victory, or a mystic vision. It was rather because the Gileadites had shown themselves loyal to Yahweh and had preserved the integrity and health of the people of Israel. God had been "in the midst" of the whole process in order to heal divisions and restore the people's "rest" and *shalom.*

As a result, the war fever changed to joy. Plans of war were abandoned. Strategies to "destroy the land where the Reubenites and Gadites were settled" were transformed into a peace agenda. "Happy are those who work for peace; God will call them his children!" (Matt. 5:9 TEV).

PART IV

THE END AND THE BEGINNING

Joshua 23 – 24

CHAPTER 16

FAREWELL
Joshua 23:1-16

*See, I have set before you this day life and good, death and evil.
. . . therefore choose life.* — Deuteronomy 27:9; 30:15, 19

*The Bible is essentially a narrative, a story which we must pass on
by retelling it, and in this way it can come about that the story may
"happen", so to speak, to those who listen to it.*
— K. H. Miskotte, *When the Gods Are Silent*, p. 204

The Joshua story comes to a fitting climax with his farewell address at Shiloh and the covenant ceremony at Shechem just before his death. Looking backward in the biblical narrative, we can see a parallel with Moses' farewell address and covenant which precede his death on Mt. Nebo (Deut. 29–34). It was a fateful time of transition marking the end of one era and the beginning of another. Looking ahead in the narrative, we can see Josiah's covenant which in the condensed account precedes his death (2 Kgs. 23:1-4, 28-30). Looking still further we find the NT "Joshua" following the same pattern: a farewell address (John 14–17), a covenant ritual (Mark 14:22-25), and death (15:1-39). In each case, farewell and covenant indicate the end of an age and the beginning of a new age. A new unity is created which can survive and grow amid the temptations and dangers of life in the Promised Land, whether it be Canaan or any living place for God's people on the earth.

The climactic position of the farewell address and the covenant ceremony in the Joshua story carries a clear message: "possessing," "inheriting," and the security of "rest" can be complete and enduring only when there is personal and corporate commitment to love and serve God. Vows must be made, false gods abandoned, and bonds accepted in order that the living space given by God may become and remain an arena of justice and freedom, instead of terror, oppression, and servitude.

DO CHAPTERS 23 AND 24 BELONG TOGETHER?

At this point it is necessary to divert our attention from the theological significance of these chapters to consider literary and historical problems: Do these two chapters form a unity? When we examine details, several questions emerge.

(1) In ch. 23, Joshua is very old (v. 1), near death (v. 14). Yet in ch. 24 he seems quite vigorous. Did the Shechem assembly (ch. 24) really follow the farewell address (ch. 23) at the end of Joshua's life?

(2) The natural conclusion to 23:16 seems to be 24:28-33. Is 24:1-27 a later addition that didn't belong to the original story?

(3) We find two identical lists of officers (23:2; 24:1), and two very different historical reviews (23:3; 24:2-13). Is this evidence that two independent accounts have been artificially combined?

Rather than deal with these questions individually, we offer the following three suggestions to help the perplexed reader think about these and similar problems in the Joshua story. *First*, we should not think of the biblical text as a simple historical report by an eyewitness. It is rather a carefully constructed narrative with its own inner dynamic. The unity of the two chapters does not come from an eyewitness report but from the author who put them together at the end of the story. The Teacher was an inspired interpreter of the Joshua tradition. The unity of the two chapters may thus be said to come from the divine inspirer as well as the inspired writer. From this angle, we must *discover* the relationship between these two chapters by patient study of the text.

Second, while actual events and situations lie behind the story, the original sequence may have been condensed and even rearranged in order to make the message clear. For example, the covenant ceremony described in ch. 24 may originally have included a reading of the Covenant Teaching by the levitical priests (8:30-35). If so, the Teacher has divided an original ceremony into two segments for his own purposes. In fact, we cannot be sure whether the covenant ceremony took place at the end of Joshua's life, or whether its location at the end of the story was part of the artistry of the Narrator.

Third, it is quite probable that the Teacher had ancient materials in hand when he wrote the Joshua story, and that these were incorporated into the story with some additions for teaching purposes. This covenant ceremony may preserve the actual form used by Joshua, "a recollection of an epochal event, foundational for Israel as a whole" (N. K. Gottwald, *Tribes of Yahweh*, 139). Another possibility is that it is a fragment of an ancient covenant festival celebrated in Canaan every year in the period before the monarchy (F. M. Cross, *Canaanite Myth and Hebrew Epic*, 84, n. 15). On the other hand, it is probable that Joshua's address as we have it in ch. 23 is largely the work of the Teacher himself, as was the case with ch. 1.

THE SHILOH ASSEMBLY: PREPARATION FOR COVENANT

The location of the assembly at which Joshua delivers his farewell address is not expressly stated. Since the assembly in ch. 24 is located at Shechem, we may assume that ch. 23 stands in continuity with chs. 18 – 22, where the action is all centered at Shiloh. It is at this administrative center of the tribal league that the farewell address is given. It is here that the problem of forsaking Yahweh is posed, and the temptations of the gods of the land emphasized. It is at the seat of administration that the ominous warning against covenant-breaking sounds three times like the tolling of a bell: "You shall perish quickly from off the good land which he [the LORD your God] has given you" (23:13, 15, 16).

RIGHTEOUS LEADERS

The farewell address is directed primarily to the assembled civil leaders of Israel, "their elders and heads, their judges and officers." We find the same group at the reading of the Covenant Teaching (8:33), and at the covenant ceremony (24:1). References to these leaders in the prophetic writings of the 8th and 7th cent. B.C. help us to fill in some of the background for this picture of an idealized past. It was the heads and rulers, said Micah, "who hate the good and love the evil, who tear the skin from off my people. . . . who eat the flesh of my people. . . . who abhor justice and pervert all equity, who build Zion with blood" (Mic. 3:1-3, 9-10). It was the elders of Jerusalem, said Isaiah, "who have

devoured the vineyard. The spoil of the poor is in your houses.
. . . crushing my people, by grinding the face of the poor. . . .
who lead this people astray" (Isa. 3:14-15; 9:16). It was the powerful princes and judges who "ask for a bribe. . . . acquit the
guilty . . . and deprive the innocent of his rights!" (Mic. 7:3; Isa.
5:23).

The leaders of the people were under a sentence of doom from
God, said Isaiah.

> For, behold, the Lord . . . is taking away . . .
>   stay and staff . . .
> the mighty man and the soldier,
>   the judge and the prophet,
>   the diviner and the elder,
> the captain of fifty
>   and the man of rank,
> the counselor and the skilful magician,
>   and the expert in charms. (Isa. 3:1-3)

God's promise was to "restore your judges as at the first, and
your counselors as at the beginning," so that Jerusalem would
"be called the city of righteousness, the faithful city" (Isa. 1:26).
The 7th-cent. B.C. Teacher was expressing a similar hope by his
portrayal of an original righteousness at the Shiloh assembly.
Josiah was himself a sign of hope. He "turned to the LORD with
all his heart and with all his soul and with all his might" (2 Kgs.
23:25), and "judged the cause of the poor" (Jer. 22:16).

THE NATIONS: PROBLEM AND OPPORTUNITY

The word "nations" (Heb. *goyim*) appears seven times in Joshua
23, and nowhere else in the entire book. This should alert the
reader to expect an important theological statement on the relationship of Israel to the nations, which is a major concern of
the whole Bible. The sevenfold occurrence of this word corresponds to the two lists of seven "nations" at the beginning (3:10)
and end (24:11) of the Joshua story.

As we have noted (see above, pp. 28, 53, 91), the actual
ethnic groups living in Canaan before the coming of the Hebrews
had been merged with Israel by the time of David's reign. The
lists of nations became code words referring to (1) *the powers* (cf.
"principalities and powers," Eph. 6:12), i.e., the political, eco-

nomic, cultural, and religious influences and structures which surrounded Israel at the time of the establishment of the new society in Canaan, and (2) *the peoples* (cf. the NT expression "Gentiles," Matt. 5:47) who lived under these influences and were a part of the structures.

Joshua speaks in 23:4 of two groups of "nations": (1) those who remain, i.e., whose power was still unbroken (see above, p. 117), and (2) those already overpowered by Yahweh, i.e., the peoples still living under the influence of the gods and the ways of the "nations" even after the structures of power had been broken.

We may identify modern analogies to these powers and peoples in the power structures, the cultural and religious environment ("the kingdoms of the world," Matt. 4:8; Rev. 11:15) in which the Christian community lives — whether as a tiny minority of less than one percent as in Thailand, China, or Japan or as a major segment of the population as in the countries of Europe and North America.

The Teacher has developed his ideas about "the nations" around three themes: disarming the powers, the covenant at risk, and openness to the peoples.

FIRST THEME: DISARMING THE POWERS (23:3, 9)

The twice-repeated assertion that "Yahweh fought (or fights) for you" links this theme with the second part of the Joshua story (chs. 6–12) where the statement also appears twice (10:14, 22). Overpowering, oppressive political and economic powers are part of God's struggle in its two phases: the liberation — formation — land phase, and the creation — new creation phase (see above, pp. 95-97). The struggle had reached a decisive point in the Joshua story, but was to continue into the future as well (23:13). It would eventually lead to a struggle against these very powers within Israel, and the loss of the land itself.

The victories of God over the powers were among the "good things which the LORD your God promised concerning you" (v. 14). These victories in the Promised Land as well as those related to the Exodus from Egypt are the "marvelous things" referred to in Israel's worship (Ps. 98:1), which they "call to mind" and "meditate on" (Ps. 77:11-12). To Israel these victories were proof of Yahweh's greatness. They were done before their eyes (Josh. 23:3; cf. 24:7), and were part of the firsthand experience of Joshua's generation (23:14, "you know in your hearts and souls"). It was after the death of the elders who "had known all the work which the LORD had done for Israel" (24:31) that things began to go wrong (Judg. 2:10). Remembering God's "mighty deeds" in the Promised Land was a way of strengthening their loyalty (Ps. 77:12).

At the same time, as we learned in Josh. 4:24, these deeds were for the sake of the powers and peoples of the earth. "Thou art the God who workest wonders, who has manifested thy might among the peoples" (Ps. 77:14). Israel was a sign in the midst of the peoples that "God . . . the king of all the earth. . . . reigns over the nations" (Ps. 47:7-8). Israel was to "tell among the peoples his deeds" (Ps. 9:11), so that they too might know his saving power, and praise him (Ps. 67:2-3).

SECOND THEME: THE COVENANT AT RISK
(23:6-8, 12-13, 15-16)

The major part of this address to the leaders of Israel consists of warnings against the risks and dangers of living in the Promised Land. The Teacher has already touched on this theme in the story of Achan, which concerned the last five of the Ten Commandments (see above, pp. 58-62). The story of the Gibeonites also carried implied cautions about the dangers hidden in Canaanite culture (see above, pp. 78-84). In this chapter the Teacher focusses on the heart of the problem: the temptations which the gods of the powers ("nations") represent for the leaders and people of Israel. Our attention is here drawn to the first three commandments of the Decalogue.

The root of the disorder in the world is here seen as the alienation of persons and social groups from the Ultimate Reality, through the influence of powers which victimize individuals and destroy societies. Some of these powers have been disarmed, though their influence persists. Others remain strong or become resurgent in times of trouble. They may take the form of ideologies, oppressive structures, mass hysteria ("the spirit of harlotry," Hos. 4:12; 5:4), idolatrous search for security, wealth, or power, perversion of sexuality, etc. These demonic forces exist in every society, even in the Promised Land. The covenant is always in danger of being broken by the influences of these powers in individual lives, families, communities, and governments.

The four temptations mentioned by the Teacher in 23:7 show a progression in terms of the degree of subjection to the powers. There is first the taking of their names on the *lips,* then the making of oaths by raising the *hand.* The *knee* is bent to acknowledge the sovereignty of the powers and commitment to serve them. Finally the *whole body* lies prostrate before them in an attitude of complete surrender.

First Temptation: To Make Mention of the Names of the Powers

This was expressly forbidden (Exod. 23:13) because it meant the beginning of a relationship which could mean walking in their ways (Mic. 4:5). Israelite sanctuaries were places where Yahweh's name was mentioned or remembered (Exod. 20:24; cf. Ps. 16:4). Yahweh delivered Israel so that his name would be known in all the earth (Exod. 9:16; cf. Rom. 9:17). When Israel forgets Yahweh's name (Jer. 23:27), God's purpose in calling Israel is frustrated.

In Isaiah's vision, it is only God who can cleanse the prophet's lips (Isa. 6:7). Hosea believed that God himself would have to remove the names of the Baals from the lips of his people (Hos. 2:17). When this was done, and Israel mentioned only Yahweh's name, then, according to Zephaniah, God would "change the speech of the peoples to a pure speech, that all of them may call on the name of the LORD and serve him with one accord" (Zeph. 3:9).

Second Temptation: To Swear by Other Powers

Swearing, or oath-taking, involved speaking the name of the god who would guarantee the integrity of the person taking the oath. It was performed at shrines (Hos. 4:15), and was an act of social responsibility by which important agreements were sealed. Agreements in covenant society were sworn in Yahweh's name (Deut. 6:13; 10:20). We learn from the prophets that Israelites were breaking the covenant by swearing by the name of other powers (Amos 8:14; Zeph. 1:5; Jer. 5:7). Jeremiah appealed for a return to the integrity of the sworn oath, and told of its effect on the nations: "If you swear, 'As the Lord lives,' in truth, in justice, and in uprightness, then nations shall bless themselves in him [God], and in him shall they glory" (Jer. 4:2; cf. Gen. 12:3). Later in the book of Jeremiah, we read that the peoples of the nations will learn from God's people how to swear in Yahweh's name, and "be built up in the midst of my people" (Jer. 12:16). Continuing this thought, Deutero-Isaiah proclaimed God's will that "every tongue shall swear" by using his name. Each would find righteousness and strength as a member of the wider family of the new Israel (Isa. 45:22-25).

Third Temptation: To Serve Other Powers

The word "serve" describes acts of worship, as in the English term "worship service" (Exod. 3:12; 10:26; Deut. 8:19). More than that, it involves loving, seeking, following after the other powers (Jer. 8:2). It is the acknowledgment of the supremacy of that power and willingness to serve as a loyal vassal. Serving other powers means breaking covenant with Yahweh. "They have gone after other gods to serve them . . . [and] have broken my covenant" (Jer. 11:10). A loyal Israel, bending the knee to Yahweh as sovereign Lord, is a paradigm for all the peoples in the future, when "every knee shall bow" to the Lord of all the earth (Isa. 45:23). Serving other powers destroys the meaning of the paradigm.

Fourth Temptation: To Worship Other Powers

The Hebrew verb translated "worship" means to prostrate the whole body before the deity. It is the final act of alienation from the only true object of worship. The word is often used together with "serve," as in the case of Kings Ahab (1 Kgs. 16:31), Aha-ziah (22:53), Manasseh, and Amon (2 Kgs. 21:21). The northern kingdom came to an end, in the words of the historian, because they "served idols. . . . went after false idols, and became false. . . . followed the nations that were round about. . . . forsook all the commandments of the LORD their God, . . . worshiped all the hosts of heaven, . . . served Baal. . . . [and] sold themselves to do evil" (2 Kgs. 17:12-18). Yet Israel at worship looked forward to the day when the peoples of the whole earth would prostrate themselves before the one true God (Pss. 66:4; 96:9). How could this happen when God's people were prostrating themselves in complete surrender before other powers?

These four temptations are balanced, in Joshua's address, by four dangers (v. 13). The very powers which seem so fascinating and alluring in the Promised Land if they are not resisted will bring ruin to Israel. They will be like a hidden trap or a snare. They will cause trouble like enemy raids at the borders. They will blind the eyes like poisonous thorns.

THIRD THEME: OPENNESS TO THE PEOPLES

The inheritance of Israel, previously described as tenancy rights to *the land* (see above, p. 5), is here at the end of the story expanded to include *the peoples* of the nations. Opposition to the powers of the nations, seen in the first two themes, is here changed to an openness to the peoples of the nations. The rhetoric about annihilation in the struggle for the land (Josh. 6:21; 8:22; 11:20; cf. Deut. 7:2) must be understood in the light of this third theme. We have already mentioned the cases of Rahab and the Gibeonites, who accepted Israel's God and joined her fellowship. The assembly at Mt. Ebal included "sojourners" or resident aliens (8:33, 35). Joshua's challenge to choose whether to serve Yahweh or other gods (24:15) assumes the presence of many individuals and groups who had not yet made up their minds. These were all peoples of the "nations" who would give up their dependence on the powers of the nations and become part of the inheritance of Israel.

This theme of openness to the peoples of the nations is a welcome one to modern readers. Still, in many ways it appears to be too narrow. It seems to be saying that the only way for the peoples of the nations to find true life is to become part of Israel. We must remember the limited horizon and chief concern of the Teacher in the 7th cent. B.C. He had no knowledge of the world outside of West Asia and Northeast Africa. He knew nothing about India or China. He could not know of the accomplishments of the peoples of Central Africa, Southeast Asia, Japan, North and South America, and the islands of the Pacific, many of which were to develop after his time. His primary interest was in the renewal of the people of Israel. Implications of this for the future could be left to the Lord of all the earth. In the meantime, the theme of openness to other peoples was full of future possibilities.

Some of these possibilities were developed during the Exile by Deutero-Isaiah. It is highly possible that he was using the theme of inheriting the nations from Joshua's farewell address in which he said that the new Israel of the future would "possess the nations" (Isa. 54:3, 17; see above, p. 10). He saw individuals like Rahab (44:5), groups of caravan merchants from Africa like the Gibeonite embassy (45:14), and whole peoples like the Hivites of the Gibeonite federation (55:5) all becoming part of Israel.

He said that Yahweh had commissioned the exilic remnant as a "covenant to the people" (Heb. *berith 'am,* 42:6; 49:8). A modern translation has given a valid interpretation of this difficult Hebrew expression: "Through you I will make a covenant with all peoples" (TEV). Like Joshua, the servant people were to bring the divided peoples of the earth into a new unity through a covenant with Yahweh. In this, the prophet was combining the model of the Sinai covenant with that of the covenant with Noah and his descendants (Gen. 9:8-17), who are symbolic of the peoples of all the earth (9:18-19; 10:1-32).

Deutero-Isaiah used other pictures. Israel was the divine harvester's joyful thresher separating out the seed (peoples) from the chaff (powers, Isa. 41:15-16). The seed was for God's new planting of nations after the failure of the old planting (40:24). God was forming new children (nations) in addition to Israel his "first-born son" (Exod. 4:22). These are Yahweh's "sons and daughters" (Isa. 43:6) who join the enlarged covenant family of Zion in the eschatological age (49:12, 20-21). They are prepared for this covenant by the Covenant Teaching brought by the servant people and planted in their midst (42:4; cf. 51:4).

The redemption of Israel for which the Teacher hoped, was understood by Deutero-Isaiah to be the sign of the restoration of the whole earth (44:23; 49:13). By using the model of the covenant with Noah, he was able to see the new nations as being formed in the midst of their own cultures and histories, fulfilling the promise and true accomplishments of their own existence.

THE HEART OF COVENANT TEACHING

Covenant Teaching was the sole reliable guide for successful living in the Promised Land (Josh. 23:6). By this Teaching, Israel and the peoples of the nations who were to be Israel's inheritance could escape the perils of one extreme (selfish gain at the expense of the poor) or the other (subjection to the powers of death and alienation). It is rather surprising to find the whole Teaching summarized in two verbs which are not at all legalistic. The way of avoiding the temptations and dangers that put the covenant at risk is to "cleave to" and "love" Yahweh (vv. 8, 11). By this intimate relationship with the Ultimate Reality the world will be renewed!

Cleaving (Heb. *dabaq*) *to Yahweh* describes the deep personal attachment that creates a new unity (Gen. 2:24). It springs from an awareness of the yearning love in the heart of the divine Other for such a relationship with his people. There is a special Hebrew verb for this yearning love, translated by the RSV as "set the heart" (*hashaq*). "Behold, to the LORD your God belong heaven and the heaven of heavens, the earth with all that is in it; yet the LORD *set his heart in love* upon your fathers and chose their descendants after them, you above all peoples, as at this day" (Deut. 10:14-15; cf. 7:7; K. Aryaprateep, "Studies in the Semantics of the Covenant Relationship in Deuteronomic Teaching," 206-9).

Cleaving to God is an attachment that brings great joy: "Thou hast been my help, and in the shadow of thy wings I sing for joy. My soul clings (*dabaq*) to thee; thy right hand upholds me" (Ps. 63:7-8). A modern philosopher has described this kind of relationship as "being in love with God without limit, qualification, condition, or reservation" (B. Lonergan, *Method in Theology*, 105). Such attachment is exclusive (no other gods), and supersedes all other attachments (cf. Matt. 10:37). In a beautiful figure of speech, Jeremiah said that Israel made God visible to the world because of this special cleaving relationship.

> For as the waistcloth *clings* (*dabaq*) to the loins of a man,
> so I made the whole house of Israel and the whole house
> of Judah *cling* to me, says the LORD, that they might be for
> me a people, a name, a praise, and a glory. (Jer. 13:11)

The problem in the 7th cent. B.C. was that "they would not listen." They had succumbed to the temptations of the other powers in the Promised Land. Joshua's appeal to "cleave to Yahweh" was a call to a corrupted Israel to return to their first love (Josh. 23:8, "as you have to this day"; cf. Jer. 2:2).

Loving Yahweh is presented by Joshua as a conscious act, as we see from the exhortation, "Take good heed to yourselves." It means turning the whole person and the whole people toward God (Deut. 6:4). This turning will involve the "heart" and "soul." The Hebrew word translated "heart" (*leb*) is used to refer to the power of planning, understanding, memory, judgment, and will (H. W. Wolff, *Anthropology of the OT*, 46-55). To love God with these rational faculties means a commitment to devote all of them to the divine cause.

The Hebrew word translated "soul" (*nephesh*) emphasizes the longing, desiring, striving, thirsting, vulnerable, incomplete aspects of personality (Wolff, *Anthropology*, 10-25). Loving God with this emotional, needy side of nature means reaching out for a realization of the true self, the fulfillment for which all seek.

These two sides of human existence may be seen as roughly analogous to the Yin (*nephesh*) and Yang (*leb*) of Chinese thought. It is these two sides of human nature both individual and corporate that are united and kept in balance when they are turned toward God in love.

Present-day readers who heed Joshua's appeal to cleave to and love God with heart and soul will rediscover what we are meant to be.

CHAPTER 17

THE COVENANT BOND
Joshua 24:1-33

The people of Israel were singled out, under a divine providence in-explicable to us and even to them, not to present themselves to the rest of the world as the nation through which God's redeeming love would be mediated, but to be a symbol of how God would deal redemptively with other nations.

— C. S. Song, *"From Israel to Asia," Mission Trends No. 3,* 216

The covenant at Shechem is more than the climactic event of the Joshua story. It is the key to understanding the faith of Israel throughout her history. At the same time it is a difficult idea for people of other faiths to comprehend. "How odd of God to choose the Jews," said Gertrude Stein. Christians share this concept of being a chosen people, and hence share in the disbelief or even ridicule of those who see it as a mark of narrow egocentricism if not arrogance. This concluding event of the Joshua story is thus of great importance for our understanding of the meaning of the covenant in one particular context.

A COVENANT RENEWAL

The covenant described in ch. 24 is not the first to be mentioned in the Joshua story. Achan's sin was a violation of a covenant already in effect (7:11). The warning in Joshua's address implies a covenant already in existence rather than the one about to be made (23:16). The Covenant Teaching read at the assembly on Mt. Ebal was Mosaic. The covenant assumed in all these references is the covenant made at Sinai (Exod. 24:3-8).

We may call this the *discipleship covenant,* because those who entered it became disciples of Yahweh the covenant LORD. The covenant created a community of disciples out of the "mixed multitude" (Exod. 12:38) who had escaped from Egypt. This was the basis of their unity in the wilderness years and all through their history. The effectiveness of this unifying factor was maintained by renewal ceremonies.

The first renewal was at Moab (Deut. 29:1), just before their entry into the Promised Land. A new unity was created by the admission of people from Transjordan following the defeat of the Amorite kings (G. E. Mendenhall, *The Tenth Generation*, 25-26). The second renewal was at Shechem, when newcomers from Canaan were ready to become full members of the covenant community.

OTHER COVENANTS

We cannot understand the discipleship covenant properly until we look backward in the biblical narrative to the *universal covenant* which God made with Noah and his descendants (all the peoples of the earth, Gen. 9:19), and "every living creature of all flesh" (9:9-10, 16). This covenant with its bestowal of blessing on all peoples (v. 1) is a biblical way of explaining the genuine achievements and values of all nations, cultures, and kinship groups in their lands (10:5, 20, 31). It also implies a harmonious relationship between the human and the nonhuman world. It is this covenant to which Hosea refers in connection with a renewal of Yahweh's relationship with Israel, and with "the beasts of the field, the birds of the air, and the creeping things of the ground" (Hos. 2:18).

The *promissory covenant* with Abraham and his descendants follows the breakdown of the unity created by the universal covenant (Gen. 11:1-9). This covenant looks to the future with a promise of land and numerous descendants (12:1-2). It also includes a promise of blessing for Abraham and, through his descendants, for all nations (12:3). According to one version of this promise, the nations will be drawn into a kinship unity as Abraham's family (17:5).

Putting these three covenants together, we can see that the discipleship covenant is the means by which the intent of the promissory covenant will be fulfilled, and the original unity of the universal covenant recreated (cf. Exod. 19:5-6).

The covenants made by David (2 Sam. 5:3), the regent of

Joash (2 Kgs. 11:17), and Josiah (23:2) were primarily renewals of the discipleship covenant. They were meant to restore the unity of the people and their bonds with God (11:17), and to bind them to observe the stipulations of the Covenant Teaching (23:3).

At the same time, these royal covenants should be seen in relation to Yahweh's covenant with David and his dynastic successors (2 Sam. 23:3; Ps. 89:3, 28, 34; cf. 2 Sam. 7:8-16). We may call this the *leadership covenant* because it deals with the function of government leaders. According to this compact, the rulers should serve as God's vice-regents to make the divine will effective in the affairs of the nation and the world (cf. Rom. 13:4). It is assumed at the same time that the ruling power is subject to the discipleship covenant (Deut. 17:18-20). He should "defend the cause of the poor," bring prosperity and peace to his people, and blessing to the nations (Ps. 72:2-7, 12-14, 16-17).

A fifth covenant lies further ahead in the narrative, and late in Israelite history. It is the one with the priestly tribe of Levi (Mal. 2:4-5). We may call this the *pastoral covenant*, as it stresses the importance of a teaching and pastoral order within the community of Israel (see above, pp. 141-44).

All five of these OT covenants contribute to our understanding of the covenant instituted by Jesus (Mark 14:24). They also furnish a background for a better understanding of the covenant at Shechem.

THE BROKEN COVENANT

The Mosaic tradition as interpreted in the latter days of the Judean kingdom anticipated a broken covenant: "For when I have brought them into the land flowing with milk and honey, which I swore to give to their fathers, and they have eaten and are full and grown fat, they will turn to other gods and serve them, and despise me and break my covenant" (Deut. 31:20; cf. v. 16). The historian notes the fulfillment of this prophecy in the days of the judges (Judg. 2:20), Solomon (1 Kgs. 11:11), and Elijah (19:10, 14). The northern kingdom (2 Kgs. 17:15; 18:12; Hos. 8:1) as well as Judah (Jer. 11:10; 31:32) was involved in covenant violation.

Thus, in a time of broken covenant, the Joshua story ends

with an appeal for a return to the center of Israelite faith. In a time when there were as many foreign gods as cities in Judah (Jer. 2:28), the ringing challenge to choose the true God was directly relevant. In a situation in which Judah was the only surviving remnant of the tribal league still on the land (cf. 2 Kgs. 17:6), the recollection of a covenant with "all the tribes of Israel" (Josh. 24:1), and their solemn oath to serve Yahweh together (vv. 16-18, 24) would evoke hopes of a reunited people under Josiah. A similar hope, also associated with a renewed covenant, appears in Jer. 31:31-34 and Ezek. 37:15-28, and is placed in a wider context in Isa. 49:6, 8.

In a time of political confusion, when national policy shifted rapidly between alliances with Assyria and Egypt (Jer. 2:18, 36; cf. Hos. 7:11; 12:1; Ezek. 17:15), the demand to put away the gods of Mesopotamia and Egypt (Josh. 24:14) would carry a theological and political impact. Some in Judah realized that "from our youth the shameful thing [i.e., Baal] has devoured all for which our fathers labored, their flocks and their herds, their sons and their daughters" and that "we have sinned against the LORD our God, we and our fathers, from our youth even to this day . . . and we have not obeyed the voice of the LORD our God" (Jer. 3:24-25; cf. 16:11-13). This realization would draw serious attention to the demand that the gods of Canaan be put away (Josh. 24:15). The thrice-repeated vow, "We will serve the LORD" (vv. 15, 18, 24), would present the central issue in a time of broken covenant.

THE GRACE OF GOD

"This is not your own doing, it is the gift of God . . . lest any man should boast" (Eph. 2:9).

The covenant ceremony begins by introducing the covenant Lord or Suzerain: Yahweh, the God of Israel (v. 2). Readers of the Joshua story already know that Yahweh is "God in heaven above and on earth beneath" (2:11), and "Lord of all the earth" (3:11, 13). The *exclusive* claim of the God of Israel inherent in the discipleship covenant must be placed alongside the *inclusive* scope of the divine purpose and loving concern for "all the peoples of the earth" (4:24), which relates to the universal and promissory covenants.

The content of the title "God of Israel" is developed in two sections. Section one (vv. 2-13) is a review of the grace of God in the history of Israel up to the end of Joshua's life. Section two (vv. 14-28) deals with the corollary of divine grace, the commitment of Israel to serve the covenant LORD.

The historical review is divided into three periods, and is dominated by twenty-one verbs in the first person singular. These verbs describe the actions of the God of Israel on behalf of his people. We find six such verbs in the narrative of the patriarchal period, seven each in the Exodus and settlement periods, and one in the final climax in v. 13.

From Mesopotamia through Canaan to Egypt (24:2-4)

"I took your father Abraham" (24:3). The verb suggests purposeful intervention. We find similar interventions described with the same verb in the lives of David (2 Sam. 7:8; cf. 22:17), Amos (Amos 7:15), Nebuchadrezzar (Jer. 43:10), Israel herself (Deut. 4:20; 30:4; Jer. 3:14), and finally a Davidic messianic king (Ezek. 17:22). By this intervention, individuals and peoples are drawn into the sphere of Yahweh's plans. This is how Israelite history began. Abraham was taken out of the ancient civilization where his people had lived "of old" (Heb. *me'olam*, the same expression used to describe Babylon as an "ancient nation," Jer. 5:15).

Deutero-Isaiah, using a different Hebrew verb, showed the contemporary relevance of this beginning moment for the exiles in Babylon:

But you, Israel, my servant,
  Jacob, whom I have chosen,
  the offspring of Abraham my friend;
you whom I took from the ends of the earth,
  and called from its farthest corners,
  saying to you, "You are my servant. . . ." (Isa. 41:8-9)

The offspring of Abraham will share his special status and participate in God's purpose for "the ends of the earth."

"I . . . led him through all the land of Canaan" (24:3). The literal meaning of the verb form is "I caused him to go. . . ." It is remarkable that this verb refers to Abraham's God-directed

journey through Canaan, instead of its more frequent use to describe divine guidance in the wilderness journey with its terrors
and sufferings (Deut. 8:2; Jer. 2:6; Amos 2:10). Abraham's faithful response to God's leadership is in sharp contrast to the disobedience of Israel, who is accused of forsaking the LORD "your
God, when he *led* you in the way" (i.e., in Canaan; Jer. 2:17).

"I . . . made his offspring many" (24:3). The births of Isaac,
Jacob, and Esau were the result of Yahweh's miraculous intervention, since both Sarah and Rebekah were barren (Gen. 20:17;
25:21). Thus the many offspring promised to Abraham (Gen.
15:5) were gifts of grace. This ancient fulfillment of promise
became a word of hope for the northern exiles: "There is hope
for your future . . . your children shall come back to their own
country" (Jer. 31:17). Deutero-Isaiah encouraged the exiles in
Babylon with the same tradition: "When he was but one I called
him, and I blessed him and made him many" (Isa. 51:2). He
pictured a miraculous multiplication of descendants from among
the nations (49:12, 20-21) that may have been related to the
covenantal promise that Abraham would be the "father of a multitude of nations" (Gen. 17:5). Paul also drew on this tradition,
noting that Abraham "believed against hope that he should become the father of many nations" (Rom. 4:18). Paul also told
believers that "if you are Christ's, then you are Abraham's offspring, heirs according to the promise" (Gal. 3:29).

From Egypt into the Wilderness (24:5-7)

"I sent Moses and Aaron" (24:5). This intervention was more
direct and specific than in the case of Abraham. The importance
of the Egypt experience for Israel may be seen from the role of
Moses, and to a lesser extent, Aaron. Moses' mission was God's
response to the suffering and degradation of the Hebrews. Without this experience, they would not have known the name of God
(Exod. 3:14-15), or seen his power.

"I plagued Egypt . . . I brought you out" (24:5). The power of
the God of Israel was shown by the plagues (Exod. 8:2), the
protecting envelope of darkness (14:20), the surging sea which
engulfed the pursuers (v. 28), and the impossible escape from the

"iron furnace" (Deut. 4:20). Those entering the covenant at Shechem would experience these events by hearing the story retold: "Your eyes saw what I did to Egypt" (Josh. 24:7; cf. Exod. 19:4). The Canaan generation would appropriate this history: "It is the LORD *our* God who brought *us* and our fathers up from the land of Egypt, out of the house of bondage, and who did these signs in *our* sight" (v. 17).

Readers of the Joshua story would place this word about God's powerful grace beside the story of the plague that came not to Egypt but to Israel at Peor (22:17; see above, pp. 169-71). The solemn warning in the second part of the covenant ritual was a constant reminder that the God of Israel could "turn and do you harm, and consume you, after having done you good" (24:20; cf. Lev. 26:21).

The plagues of the earth described in Revelation with their "pestilence and mourning and famine . . . and fire" (Rev. 18:8) are disturbingly realistic in a time of nuclear armaments poised for instant release. The call to "come out of her, my people, lest you take part in her sins, lest you share in her plagues" (v. 4) is appealing. Yet there is no place to hide from this kind of plague, and it is better to "repent and give God glory" while there is yet time by working for a world pleasing to the Lord of heaven and earth.

"You lived in the wilderness a long time" (24:7). This brief notice does not indicate the "deserts and pits . . . drought and deep darkness" of the impassable wilderness (Jer. 2:6). It was there that Yahweh made covenant with Israel and gave her the Covenant Teaching (Deut. 5). It was in the wilderness that she went through the period of discipline and training (Deut. 8:2-6). The wilderness experience was a vital part of Israel's preparation for serving Yahweh in the land of Canaan and in the world.

From the Wilderness to Canaan (24:8-12)

The venture which began in Mesopotamia now enters its final stage with the divinely managed entry into the borders of the Promised Land and the Jordan crossing. The meaning of the verbs in this section is clear. The establishment of Israel in Canaan was "not by [your] sword, . . . nor by your own arm" (cf. Ps. 44:2-3), lest any should boast, like the king of Assyria (Isa.

10:12-14), or rely on the military might of powerful allies with
no concern for "the Holy One of Israel" (31:1), or say "my idol
did them" (48:5). It was Yahweh alone who gave victory, sent
panic among the enemy forces (the probable meaning of "hor-
net"; cf. Exod. 23:28; Deut. 7:20), destroyed their power, and
protected his people from the power of Balaam's black magic (see
above, pp. 118-20).

The Gift of the Land

"I gave Esau the hill country of Seir to possess" (24:4).
Yahweh's gift of the land to Israel is parallel to a similar gift to
Esau the ancestor of the Edomites (Josh. 24:4; Gen. 36:1). This
notice is remarkable in view of the fierce hostility that developed
between Israel and Edom (see Obad. and Isa. 34). This hostility
may have had its origin in the harsh methods used by David's
general Joab in subjugating the Edomites (1 Kgs. 11:15-16). The
positive view of Edom which we find in this covenant recital is
akin to the Deuteronomic admonition not to "abhor an Edomite,
for he is your brother" (Deut. 23:7), and the Job story with its
Edomite hero from Uz (Job 1:1). We have already mentioned
Caleb's Edomite connections (see above, p. 121).

Perhaps we may sense in this reference to Yahweh's gift of
land to Esau a recognition that "the Most High gave to the
nations their inheritance" (Deut. 32:8) as a blessing of the universal covenant with Noah. May we also see here a veiled appeal
for an end to ancient hostilities and a return to brotherly relations
with long-standing enemies?

"I gave you a land . . ." (24:13). Land is living space and
place for humans in society to fulfill the divine purpose of creation. Space is an "arena of freedom" (W. Brueggemann, *The
Land*, 5). This is symbolized not only by the purposeful separation
of the waters of chaos (Gen. 1:7-8), but also by the stretching out
of the heavenly vault "like a tent to dwell in" (Isa. 40:22). Freedom of space is not possible without the solid security of place,
separated from the waters (Gen. 1:9-10), spread out by the Creator (Isa. 44:24) "to be inhabited" (45:18). "The heavens and
the earth" are normally paired together to signify the double
meaning of land as both space for freedom and place for security.

It is this space-place balance that is destroyed when "the heavens
. . . vanish like smoke" (loss of freedom), and "the earth . . .
wear[s] out like a garment" (loss of security; Isa. 51:6). In order
to restore this balance, the Creator is constantly engaged in
"stretching out the heavens and laying the foundations of the
earth" (v. 16).

Those who receive the land are responsible for protecting space
by justice, and organizing place in order to insure prosperity. For
this, God has given wisdom for "foolish men" to find "knowledge
and discretion," "decree what is just," and "govern the earth"
(Prov. 8:5, 12, 15-16).

In the Joshua story, we have found space-place problems such
as food management (p. 39), land management (pp. 109-10),
land distribution (pp. 111-12), kinship groups as means of production and defense (pp. 112-13), cities and villages as sociological structures (pp. 113-15), boundaries (pp. 115-16), management
of water resources (p. 124), inheritance laws (pp. 124-26), and
land conservation (pp. 126-28). We have also met dangers to
space such as greed (pp. 58-59, 171), corrupt worship (pp. 169-70),
murder (pp. 130-31), and "abominable practices" (p. xix). The
means of preserving the space-place balance as shown in Joshua
are the Covenant Teaching (p. 70), the cities of refuge (pp. 130-39),
Torah Centers throughout the land (pp. 140-56), and patient
peacemaking (p. 173). Thus, according to the covenant recital,
it was Israel's experience in Egypt and the wilderness that gave
her a special insight into the problems of living on the land.

Israel's faith is deeply rooted in the sociological, political,
economic, and cultural realities of particular space-place areas.
As Deutero-Isaiah pointed out, the mission of the diaspora in the
post-Babylonian world was to "restore the earth" as a place fit
for meaningful habitation (Isa. 49:8. For a wider interpretation
of the Hebrew word *erets* in this verse, see C. C. Torrey, *The Second
Isaiah*, 384, and E. J. Hamlin, *God and the World of Nations*, 36).

"A land on which you had not labored . . ." (24:13). The reminder to those entering the covenant relationship with Yahweh
and with Israel that the land given to them was cultivated, built
up, planted, and harvested by others was intended in the covenant recital as a warning to Israel not to "forget the LORD, who

brought you out of the land of Egypt, out of the house of bondage" (Deut. 6:12). For contemporary readers, however, this statement poses problems. Why should Yahweh take the land of others
and give it to his people? Does this not mean that the history of
Israel on the land begins with an act of injustice? The question
presses for an answer in the present day when Israeli Jews are
again living in the land which Palestinians claim for themselves.

We have already noted that the coming of the Joshua group
to Canaan in the 13th cent. B.C., far from being an act of injustice, meant liberation of slaves, tenant farmers, artisans, and oppressed villagers. It was the oppressive structure of society in
Canaan that was the enemy. The space-place balance in the land
had been violated by the "abominable practices" of the Canaanite rulers (Deut. 9:4-5), so that the land became uninhabitable
except for the elite few (Lev. 18:24-25; cf. Isa. 5:8; see above,
p. 91). The purpose of Israel in coming to the land was to restore
the space-place balance as a beginning of the restoration of the
earth. The Joshua story must not be interpreted as a simple
struggle for land in which one population was driven out and
another took its place.

Another question remains: Why *this* land? We find no ultimate
answer except in the mystery of God's will. Given this element
of mystery, however, we must grant that this particular land is
where the history of Israel unfolded, and where the Hebrew
Scriptures came into being. The Joshua story is evidence of the
importance of this land in the memories and hopes of Israel.
Today the historical review of the covenant ceremony must be
extended over almost three millennia until the words "I brought
you to the land" take on a contemporary meaning with the found-
ing of the State of Israel in 1948.

Christians cannot be content to make a simple substitution of
the "gift of the kingdom" (Luke 12:32) for the gift of the land.
The kingdom comes or is hoped for in the concrete space-place
arenas of our human existence, and should not be spiritualized
as pure space without place (see above, p. 23).

At the same time, Christians should come to understand the
State of Israel as evidence of God's enduring faithfulness to the
Jewish people to whom "belong the sonship, the glory, the covenants, the giving of the law [teaching], the worship, and the
promises" (Rom. 9:4). Christians should repent of their active or

passive part in the sufferings of the Jews over the centuries. On the other hand, specific political policies and acts of changing Israeli governments are subject to the same judgments of God as are found in Joshua's farewell address.

Israel-on-the-land is of importance to Christians, not only as a place of pilgrimage, or as a place to await the second coming of Christ, but as the place where our Jewish brothers and sisters bear witness to the rootedness of the Covenant Teaching in the space-place nature of the land. This witness is part of our common task of bringing God's *shalom* to the nations in their various lands.

NO OTHER GODS (24:14-28)

The Day of Decision

The Joshua story began with God's "now" (1:2; see above, p. 4) at the moment of crossing the Jordan River into the new area of responsibility in the land. The story comes to a close with Joshua's "now therefore . . ." at the moment of another kind of crossing over (cf. Deut. 29:12; see above, pp. 22-23) into the responsibilities and privileges of the discipleship covenant. The same sense of urgency is present at the end as at the beginning. The decision for Yahweh must be made "this day" (Josh. 24:15). The covenant was made on "that day" (v. 25; cf. Deut. 27:9; 29:10-15). The future of the people on the land depended on this new and ever-renewed crossing over.

From Gods to God

If we place Josh. 24:14-15 beside 23:7-8, we find that the situation at Shechem is different from that described at Shiloh. What was a matter for warning at Shiloh has become a reality at Shechem. Alienation had already taken place. The gods who had captivated some of the people must be put away. There must be a crossing over, out of the sphere of influence of the "other gods" into the circle of Yahweh's discipleship covenant.

Gods and Religions

The OT writers did not speak of religions as such. They spoke of serving gods or idols over against serving the true God. Modern scientific study has presented religion as a system of beliefs, practices, and social organization. Religion is part of every society. It performs important functions in holding society together, giving a sense of meaning and belonging, and controlling human behavior in socially acceptable ways. Religion also provides a link between human society and the transcendent sphere of the divine, ultimate reality, or the ultimate good. Can this idea of religion be related to the OT concept of the gods?

Before Abraham

Genesis 9–11 is a theological description of the world before God's intervention in the life of Abraham. In these chapters we find three important insights. (1) *The continuous active presence of God* extends to every part of the earth. The blessing of the universal covenant (see above, p. 190) was not cancelled when God called Abraham, and has continued to be in effect. As a psalmist said, "The earth is full of the steadfast love of the LORD" (Ps. 33:5). We should expect to find a response to this active presence of God in the religions which have grown up on the earth.

(2) *The seventy nations* (code word for totality or completeness) listed in Genesis 10 show *a great diversity* of lands (geographical environment), languages (culture), families (social organization), and nations (political structures; vv. 5, 21, 31). We should expect a corresponding diversity in religions, representing the richness of blessing.

(3) *The destruction of this harmony-in-diversity* is the subject of the story of the Tower of Babel (11:1-9). There are already anticipations of breakdown in the proto-imperialist Nimrod (10:8-10), and the disruptive Peleg whose name means "division" (v. 25). In the Babel story, the attempt by one group in the land of Shinar to impose a forced unity on the rest of the earth for its own pride ("to make a name for ourselves") and security ("lest we be scattered") brings on the corruption of religion. The tower to reach the heavens represents an attempt to control the transcendent world for national ends. The result is that diversity becomes division, and harmony is replaced by discord. Religions must henceforth develop not in mutually enriching intercourse, but in isolation from one another.

From this theological picture we can see religions as part of man's response to God's grace, and at the same time part of human assertion to achieve fame and security.

The Gods

Some OT writers speak of a provisional positive role for the gods of the nations. According to one tradition, God assigned his servants — the powers of the created world (Ps. 103:20-21), sometimes called "sons of God" (Ps. 29:1; Job 1:6) — to have charge of the nations as deputies of the Most High. Their responsibility was to see that justice was done to the weak (Ps. 82:3-4). They failed to accomplish their assigned task. The afflicted suffered further affliction, and the wicked were rewarded (v. 2). They were unable to control human pride and aggressiveness, and therefore were subject to divine judgments: "You shall die like men" (v. 7).

The "gods" represent part of the good order of creation which has been corrupted. They represent the negative or destructive aspects of religion. Putting away the gods is a way of returning to the harmony-in-diversity of Genesis 9– 10. It means purification and renewal rather than the abandonment of religion.

Three Kinds of Gods

The covenant ritual in Joshua 24 identifies three kinds of gods which must be put away.

The gods of ancient religious tradition inherited from past generations may prevent necessary changes in times of transition, while the religious tradition itself is of enduring value.

The gods of Egypt support the imperialist or colonial ambitions of the powerful nation, and so degrade the oppressed and corrupt the oppressor. At the same time the nation's religion has much that is noble and fine.

The gods of popular religion pervert the inner drives and exploit the weaknesses of human nature by fetishism and sorcery, although there is much true wisdom in the religion of the common people.

When the gods are put away, the values of traditional religion will reappear. The nobility of great and powerful nations will serve the cause of peace. The deep needs of human nature will be fulfilled in life-creating ways.

Conversion

Crossing over from the force-field of the gods into the redemptive power of Yahweh means conversion. We have seen that subjection to the gods is a process (see above, p. 183). Conversion should also be seen as a process in three stages (W. Johnston, *The Inner Eye of Love,* 268).

First, there is *religious conversion.* This is close to the meaning of cleaving or clinging to God in love (see above, p. 187), a joyful new attachment to the true center of meaning which unites the personality and gives a sense of freedom.

Second, there is *moral conversion,* which is a change in values and priorities. This stage may be described as serving the LORD, in the sense of acts of worship and seeking God's rule and righteousness in everything and before all else (Matt. 6:33). It is this aspect of conversion that is strongly emphasized in the covenant ritual. The verb "serve" appears fourteen times in vv. 14-28. Serving the LORD is not a matter of words only. That is the meaning of the words in the ritual, "you cannot serve the LORD" (v. 19). It is a matter of learning by doing, suffering from mistakes, and trying again. That is why covenant renewal is necessary.

Third, there is *intellectual conversion,* a radical change in world view, a new insight into the nature of reality. This means the remaking of the heart as the seat of thought (see above, p. 188). In the covenant ritual, Joshua exhorts the people to "put away the foreign gods which are among you, and incline your heart to the LORD, the God of Israel." Ezekiel saw the problem in a more radical way. Although moral conversion would make a new beginning possible (Ezek. 18:31), only God could produce this kind of intellectual conversion by giving "a new heart and a new spirit" (Ezek. 36:26).

You are Witnesses (24:22)

In the context of the covenant ritual, the meaning of these words is clear: "You are your own witnesses to the fact that you have chosen the LORD" (TEV). From now on they live with the full responsibility of this choice. In time of disaster, as had happened to the northern kingdom, they would remember the covenant warnings (v. 20): "Was it not the LORD, against whom we have sinned?" (Isa. 42:24). Likewise, they could always turn to "the faithful God who keeps covenant" (Deut. 7:9) and find "grace in the wilderness" (Jer. 31:2).

The standing stone (v. 27) was also meant as a reminder of the momentous occasion when they had bound themselves to the

LORD. In times of joy and sorrow they could recall "the words of the LORD which he spoke to us."

In the Joshua story, the people-as-witness should be seen in relation to the altar in the Jordan Valley. It too was a witness that "the LORD is God" in East Jordan as well as in West Jordan (22:34; cf. vv. 27, 28). This theme was later transferred to the Nile Valley where an altar would serve as "a sign and witness to the LORD of hosts in the land of Egypt." It would remind the exiles of the faithfulness of God in a far-off river valley, but also make it possible for the Egyptians to know the LORD and be healed (Isa. 19:19-22).

The words "you are witnesses" appear in only three places in the Old Testament. Aside from a legal use in Ruth 4:9-10, we find the expression again only in Deutero-Isaiah. In a passage apparently inspired by the Joshua story, the exiles are told that they are to witness by their own lives among the nations that "the LORD is God."

"I, I am the LORD,
  and besides me there is no savior.
I declared and saved and proclaimed,
  when there was no strange god among you;
  and you are my witnesses," says the Lord.
"I am God. . . ." (Isa. 43:11; cf. v. 10; 44:8)

THE END, OPEN TO THE FUTURE (24:29-37)

Joshua, the Servant of the Lord

Joshua's bones were laid to rest in the place (24 km. or 15 mi. SW of Shechem) which he had rebuilt (19:50) as a sign of the new age of freedom and peace in the land. His great age of 110 years, while appropriately less than that of his great master Moses (Deut. 34:7), is a symbol of his importance in the history of Israel, even though his name is modestly absent from the covenant recital.

Joshua, as Moses' minister (Josh. 1:1), brings the Exodus — formation — land phase of God's work of salvation (Ps. 74:12) to a fitting conclusion. Having himself received Covenant Teaching as the key to successful living on the land (1:7-8; see above, pp. 6-7), he gave it to the people (24:26), along with applications appropriate to this particular time and place (v. 25). He also established Torah Centers as a means of making the Teaching effective in the day-to-day lives of the people (ch. 21).

In sending the people away, "every man to his inheritance" (24:28), he completed his assigned task to "cause this people to inherit the land" (1:6). The account of Joshua's successful life-work as retold by the Teacher would be an inspiration to Josiah in 7th-cent. B.C. Judah, and also to others who would use the biblical Exodus — formation — land model as a way of interpreting events in their own lands (cf. Amos 9:7).

Joseph, Sign of Blessing for the Nations

The burial of Joseph's bones at Shechem signifies the fulfillment of Joseph's deathbed wish in Egypt (Gen. 50:25), the faithfulness of Moses (Exod. 13:19), and the strong sense of continuity with the patriarchal period. Joseph's role in saving "all the earth" from famine (Gen. 41:57) makes him a symbol of the third element in the promissory covenant: blessing to the nations (see above, p. 190). His grave in Ephraim would point to a mysterious future fulfillment of that promise (cf. Gal. 3:14; Heb. 11:39-40). We are left to wonder whether Joseph's wife Asenath, daughter of the Egyptian priest of On (Gen. 41:45) and mother of Ephraim and Manasseh (vv. 51-52), was buried with him at Shechem. More likely she was buried in Egypt as a sign that Egypt would one day become Yahweh's "people" (Isa. 19:25). In Joseph we make contact with the creation — new creation phase of God's work of salvation.

Eleazar, Sign of Future Continuity

Eleazar was buried not at Aaronite Hebron or Bethel (see above, pp. 122, 145), but in Mushite Ephraim (see above, p. 146; R. G. Boling, *Joshua*, 542, suggests that the location of this grave may be related to Bethel, where Eleazar's son Phinehas served as priest [Judg. 20:26-28]). In the Joshua story, Eleazar's role is always subordinate to that of Joshua (see above, p. 148). Yet in the wider OT context, he represents a continuity which begins with Aaron of the covenant recital (Josh. 24:5) and extends down to the days of Josiah (see above, p. 143), beyond the tragic death of that king and the end of the nation (Jozadak; 1 Chr. 6:13), and into the postexilic reconstruction from Jeshua (Ezra 3:2) to Jaddua (Neh. 12:22; see Cross, "A Reconstruction of the Judean Restoration," *Interpretation* 19 [1975]: 187-203, esp. 203). Eleazar's grave thus marks the end of the age of Joshua but also points to the survival of the nation after the end of the monarchy.

BIBLIOGRAPHY OF WORKS CITED

Books

Aryaprateep, K. "Studies in the Semantics of the Covenant Relationship in Deuteronomic Teaching," unpublished Th.D. dissertation (Chicago: Seabury Western Theological Seminary, 1974).

Aharoni, Y. *The Land of the Bible,* rev. ed. (New York: Macmillan, 1979).

Aharoni, Y. and Yonah, M. Avi-, *The Macmillan Bible Atlas,* rev. ed. (New York: Macmillan, 1968).

Boling, R. G. *Joshua.* Anchor Bible (Garden City: Doubleday, 1982).

Bright, J. *A History of Israel,* 3rd ed. (Philadelphia: Westminster, 1981).

Brueggemann, W. *The Land* (Philadelphia: Fortress, 1977).

Christensen, D. L. *The Transformation of the War Oracle in OT Prophecy* (Missoula: Scholars Press, 1975).

Cross, F. M. *Canaanite Myth and Hebrew Epic* (Cambridge: Harvard University Press, 1973).

de Vaux, R. *Ancient Israel* (New York: McGraw-Hill, 1965).

————. *The Early History of Israel* (Philadelphia: Westminster, 1978).

Ginzberg, L. *The Legends of the Jews,* 6 vols. (Philadelphia: Jewish Publication Society, 1968).

Gottwald, N. K. *The Tribes of Yahweh* (Maryknoll: Orbis, 1979).

Hamlin, E. J. *Comfort My People, A Guide to Isaiah 40 – 66* (Atlanta: John Knox, 1979).

————. *God and the World of Nations* (Singapore: ATSSEA, 1972).

Hertzberg, H. W. *Die Bücher Josua, Richter, Ruth.* Das Alte Testament Deutsch (Göttingen: Vandenhoeck und Ruprecht, 1953).

Heschel, A. J. *God in Search of Man* (Cleveland: World, 1963).

Johnston, W. *The Inner Eye of Love* (London: Fount, 1981).

Koyama, K. *No Handle on the Cross: An Asian Meditation on the Crucified Mind* (London: SCM, 1976).

Lonergan, B. *Method in Theology* (London: Darton, Longman, Todd, 1972).

Mendenhall, G. E. *The Tenth Generation* (Baltimore: Johns Hopkins, 1973).

Miller, J. M. and Tucker, G. M. *The Book of Joshua*. Cambridge Bible Commentary (Cambridge: University Press, 1974).

Miskotte, K. B. *When the Gods Are Silent* (London: Collins, 1967).

Moore, G. F. *Judaism in the First Centuries of the Christian Era*, 3 vols. (Cambridge: Harvard University Press, 1927-30).

Rosenberg, A. J. and Shulman, S. *The Book of Joshua* (New York: Judaica, 1969).

Soggin, J. A. *Joshua*. Old Testament Library (Philadelphia: Westminster, 1972).

Song, C. S. *Third Eye Theology* (Maryknoll: Orbis, 1979).

Torrey, C. C. *The Second Isaiah* (Edinburgh: T. & T. Clark, 1928).

von Rad, G. *Deuteronomy*. Old Testament Library (Philadelphia: Westminster, 1966).

Wijngaards, J. N. M. *The Dramatization of Salvific History in the Deuteronomic Schools* (Leiden: Brill, 1969).

Wolff, H. W. *Anthropology of the OT* (London: SCM, 1974).

Articles

Boling, R. G. "Levitical History and the Role of Joshua," in *The Word of the Lord Shall Go Forth*, eds. Carol L. Meyers and Michael P. O'Connor (Philadelphia: American Schools of Oriental Research, 1983).

Callaway, J. A. "Ai," *Interpreter's Dictionary of the Bible*, Supplement, ed. Keith Crim (Nashville: Abingdon, 1976), 14-16.

————. "New Evidence on the Conquest of Ai," *Journal of Biblical Literature* 87 (1968): 318.

Callaway, J. A. and Cooley, R. E. "A Salvage Expedition at Raddana in Bireh," *Bulletin of the American Schools of Oriental Research* 201 (1971): 9-17.

Campbell, E. F. "Moses and the Foundations of Israel," *Interpretation* 29 (1975): 141-54.

Chaney, M. L. "You Shall Not Covet Your Neighbor's House," *Pacific Theological Review* 15 (1982).

Cross, F. M. "A Reconstruction of the Judean Restoration," *Interpretation* 29 (1975) 187-203.

de Vaux, R. "The Settlement of the Israelites in Southern Palestine and the Origins of the Tribe of Judah," in *Translating and Understanding the OT,* eds. H. T. Frank and W. L. Reed (Nashville: Abingdon, 1970), 108-34.

Freedman, D. N. "An Inscribed Jar Handle from Raddana," *Bulletin of the American Schools of Oriental Research* 201 (1971): 19-22.

Ginzberg, L. "Judah and the Transjordan States from 734 to 582 B.C.E.," *Alexander Marx Jubilee Volume* (New York: Jewish Theological Seminary, 1950), 347-68.

Graesser, C. "Gibeah (of Benjamin)," *Interpreter's Dictionary of the Bible,* Supplement, 363-64.

Hamlin, E. J. "The Meaning of the 'Mountains and Hills' in Isaiah 41:14-16," *Journal of Near Eastern Studies* 13 (1954): 185-90.

Harrison, R. K. "Healing," *Interpreter's Dictionary of the Bible,* ed. G. A. Buttrick (Nashville: Abingdon, 1962) 2:541-48.

Kelso, J. L. "Bethel (Sanctuary)," *Interpreter's Dictionary of the Bible* 1:391-92.

Lochman, J. M. "The Kingdom of God and the Structural Constraints of the Day," *Reformed World* 36 (1980): 99-110.

Mazar, B. "The Cities of the Priests and the Levites," *Supplements to Vetus Testamentum* 7 (1960): 193-205.

Nicolsky, N. M. "Das Asylrecht in Israel," *Zeitschrift für die alttestamentliche Wissenschaft* 48 (1930): 146-75.

Pritchard, J. B. "Gibeon," *Interpreter's Dictionary of the Bible* 2:390-93.

Sanders, J. A. "Hermeneutics," *Interpreter's Dictionary of the Bible,* Supplement, 402-07.

Seitz, O. J. F. "What Do These Stones Mean?" *Journal of Biblical Literature* 60 (1960): 247-54.

Song, C. S. "From Israel to Asia: A Theological Leap," *Mission Trends No. 3,* eds. G. H. Anderson and T. Stransky (Grand Rapids: Eerdmans, 1976).

Williams, R. J. "Moabite Stone," *Interpreter's Dictionary of the Bible* 3:419-20.